WONDER BOY

THE STORY OF CARL SCHEIB

THE YOUNGEST PLAYER IN AMERICAN LEAGUE HISTORY

LAWRENCE KNORR

SUNBURY
P R E S S

Mechanicsburg, PA USA

Published by Sunbury Press, Inc.
105 South Market Street
Mechanicsburg, Pennsylvania 17055

www.sunburypress.com

ISBN: 978-1-62006-413-9 (Hard cover)

Library of Congress Control Number: 2016908747

FIRST SUNBURY PRESS EDITION: May 2016

Product of the United States of America
0 1 1 2 3 5 8 13 21 34 55

Set in Bookman Old Style
Designed by Crystal Devine
Cover by Lawrence Knorr
Edited by Allyson Gard

Continue the Enlightenment!

CONTENTS

INTRODUCTION

The tall white-haired octogenarian strode slowly and confidently to the ticket window with his diminutive companion, his wife, Sandy, at his side. The couple were at Camden Yards in Baltimore, the home of the Orioles. It was a beautiful late spring day – perfect for baseball. The two were heading back to San Antonio from her Long Beach Island, New Jersey home to his in Texas and decided to see a ballgame.

"Two tickets, please," said the gentleman, passing a credit-card-sized gun metal plate to the agent.

The ticket agent took the plate, thinking it was a credit card of some sort.

"That will be . . ." she began

"Is there something wrong?" asked the gentleman.

"I am not sure what this is," she replied, confused and somewhat embarrassed.

"I am Carl Scheib – see my name on the pass?" he said patiently. "This is my lifetime pass for my major league service."

"I am so sorry, Mr. Scheib," she replied, "but I am not familiar with this kind of pass. I've never seen anything like it before!"

"Well, I am supposed to be able to see any game I want," retorted Carl, losing a little patience.

"Excuse me," she said, "I'll need to show this to my manager."

For several minutes, the ticket agent was gone – somewhere in the back – upstairs – downstairs. Who knew. Regardless, a former major leaguer with his lifetime pass, was waiting a little too long to gain access to the game.

Then, there was activity at the window. A middle-aged man had joined the young lady.

"Mr. Scheib?" he asked. "How can I help you?"

"I'd like two tickets to today's game, please."

"Uh, I don't think I can do that," the manager returned. "I can give you one ticket – not two."

"Then what will I do with my wife?" Carl growled.

"You'll have to pay for her," came the response.

"But, in Philadelphia, they always give me four tickets!" growled the old man.

1

"I'm sorry, Mr. Scheib, but you aren't in Philadelphia."

The man handed the pass back through the opening at the bottom of the window. Carl snatched it back, and saying nothing more, returned it to his wallet, where it had been for decades. He stuffed his wallet in his back pants pocket and did not retrieve a credit card or any cash.

"One ticket will be . . ." began the manager, wanting to conclude the transaction.

"You're kidding me, right?" Carl snapped before he could finish.

"Oh, Carl," said Sandy, "Let's just get on the road."

She started to pull the towering man like a Lilliputian trying to topple Gulliver.

"I wanted to see a ballgame," said Carl, "in Baltimore. Hell, I used to play with Brooks Robinson in the Texas League . . ."

Carl paused, while his wife continued to nudge him.

"Mr. Scheib," began the manager.

"What?" snapped Carl.

"Here's two tickets . . . enjoy the game . . ."

1.
Early Life in Gratz

Carl Alvin Scheib was born January 1st, 1927, the third of four children, and the second son of Oliver D. (1896-1953) and Pauline G. (Wolfgang) Scheib (1899-1984), in the small farming community of Gratz, Pennsylvania. Carl had been preceded by a sister, Alfreida, and a brother Paul. Carl's younger sibling was a sister, Edna.

Oliver, a small-time farmer and occasional coal miner, and Pauline, a housekeeper, assembled their family of six just in time for the Great Depression.

The Scheib Hide and Leather Company, run by Oliver's great uncle William, was a successful business in town from the Civil War until 1907. The *Harrisburg Telegraph* of Monday October 28th, 1901, announced the marriage of William's daughter, Elizabeth Louise Scheib, 28, to millionaire Ethan Allen Doty, a 64-year-old widower. Doty, from Brooklyn, had met his bride in Atlantic City, at her boarding house, and swept her off her feet with expensive gifts. Unfortunately, for Oliver's branch of the Scheib family, no such good fortune was in store. Rather, it was a life of long days and hard work.

"My father was very stoic," said Carl. "Before he got married, he walked back and forth to a coal mine each day—ten to twenty miles. Then he'd come home and work on the farm. After he married my mother, he quit the coal mines and bought a ten acre farm.

"We didn't have any electricity and no refrigeration," continued Carl. "We grew a lot of our own food and raised hogs and steers. We'd kill the hogs and beef and cure, salt, smoke or can them. We'd put salt in water until an egg would float, put the meat in it twice to get the blood out and then freeze it in the barn. We had a big smoke house for hams and sausage. If the hams got moldy, we'd just cut off the bad parts.

"We had no water in the house. There was a well outside and we had to bring water in. There was no plumbing in the house, so we used an outhouse. We used kerosene lanterns for light."

Brother Paul Scheib remembered how he and Carl would raid the milk crock that was kept in the basement in order to keep it

3

1930's Draft

cool. "Carl and I would go down to the basement and drink the entire crock. Mother would complain there was no cream to make butter!

"I remember when Carl left home to play ball," continued Paul, "Dad called me and said the food bill was cut in half!"

The lack of "modern" conveniences at this time was actually very common. Before World War Two, many rural communities functioned as they had since they were settled, touched by only hints of technology,

In *Memories Volume 5*, published by the Gratz Historical Society, Charles Schoffstall, the current caretaker of the Society's museum and longtime Gratz resident, fondly recalled his childhood during the same time period:

Kerosene lamps provided lighting in our home during my early childhood because electricity only started to be added to homes in the late 1920s. When I was born, the Great Depression was in effect and as a family, we would have been classified as quite poor. We did have minimum electricity in one home in the late 1930s. As a child, I never felt deprived of anything, never went to bed hungry. I have wonderful memories growing up in this small town of Gratz.

Phone service was first installed in the area around 1910. Few residents in town had a telephone. In fact, the only ones I can remember having phones were Shimmel's General Store, and other places of business. These phones, battery magneto types, were mounted in a wooden box on the wall. To make a call, one would ring the operator by turning a crank, and then give her the number you desired. The telephone company gave each customer a specific number of rings with their number and these rings identified incoming calls. A line could have as many as fifteen customers on it and anyone could pick up the phone and listen to your conversation.

Most shopping was done at Rebucks (Shimmels), S. O. Smeltz or Miller's general stores. Payment for groceries was usually made by charge (tick). Purchases were recorded in a book provided for this purpose and payment was to be made every two weeks on payday . . .

A kitchen coal stove and a heatrolla in the living room (parlor) heated our home. To heat the upstairs, metal grates (registers) were mounted in the ceiling to allow the warm air to reach the upper floor. Most everyone wore long johns during the winter months, so sleeping in a very cold room with thick comforters and blankets kept you warm and healthy. Our bed mattress was filled with straw.

As kids, we all had chores to do. One of my chores was to keep the coal buckets filled with coal from a shed (coalhouse) in the rear of our lot. Water was obtained from a deep well next to the house and had to be hand-drawn. A bucket was lowered from a rope on a wench that turned by hand to lift the bucket to the surface. So, water had to be drawn for cooking, laundry and bathing. On wash day, my brother, Blair, and I would fill the large black kettle at an outdoor fireplace with water from the well. We would then start a fire and boil the water for my mother to wash the clothes in a hand-turned-wringer washer. She had two rinse tubs that we also filled with water. After the laundry was done, we emptied the washer and tub and carried the water to the garden area. Bathing was usually done in a large tub set up in the kitchen on a Saturday night—only one bath a week whether you needed it or not! The water was drawn from the well, heated on the kitchen coal stove, poured into the tub, and then taken to the garden after the bathing.

We never had indoor plumbing in our home when I was growing up. All homes had outhouses (privies) that were usually two seats with a half moon cut in the door. These facilities were used into the early 1950s when indoor plumbing started to be the fashion in Gratz.

There was no mail delivery in town. You had to pick up your mail at the post office. You had to ask the postmaster for your mail if you could see something through the glass by your number . . .

Doctors made house calls. They dispensed needed medicine, so trips to the pharmacy were almost nil . . .

To get a haircut, my father cut our hair with a hand clipper that would often not cut properly and pull your hair, which, as a kid, I didn't care for much. Later, in my teen years, the barber across the street, Gloppy Buffington, cut my hair. The cost of a haircut was twenty-five cents and no tips.

Starting school at age 6 (in 1936), I learned my ABCs, reading, writing and arithmetic in first grade-no kindergarten or prior home-schooling. The school consisted

SCHOOL

of two buildings two stories high (one wood and one brick). My wooden double desk was always shared with another pupil. To attend school, all kids had to walk every step of the way, as there was no bus transportation like today. Some students had to walk a few miles and bring their lunch. I only had about three town blocks and could easily run home at noontime.

Heat for the building, on each classroom level, was provided by a large potbelly stove, which used coal. It was the teacher's responsibility to be his or her own janitor. There was no plumbing in the buildings. Outhouses bordered the back of the school property. As boys, we always welcomed the chance to fill the coal buckets and clap the erasers to remove chalk dust. The buildings did have town water supplying a faucet and sink only. A well and hand pump was used in earlier years.

For recreation, during recess (one in the morning and one in the afternoon), and also during the lunch hour, the boys played baseball, tag ball over the coalhouse, and similar games. Marbles was always a popular game most anywhere. A circle was drawn on the ground or floor after which each player placed a predetermined number of small marbles into the ring. Each player would have one large marble called a knuckler. Each player would use this knuckler and shoot with his thumb at the smaller marbles. When all the marbles were knocked out of the circle, the player who knocked out the most would be declared the champion and would win all the marbles that were knocked out by him. The girls also played marbles, jump rope, jacks, tag, cats in the cradle (a string game) and hopscotch.

During winter months, when snow was on the ground, boys and girls would bring sleighs to school to enjoy sledding along with snowball fights. Some of the kids would bring their bicycles to school if the weather permitted it. There were no school closings due to bad weather. It was a rare occasion not to have school. The holiday celebrations were always a lot of fun. During Halloween, we always dressed for the occasion and each classmate tried to identify each other. The teacher always had many games to keep us busy, like bobbing for apples, making arts and crafts items or pumpkins, cats, and witches to decorate the school. After school, we would dress in costumes for (Halloween) and go door to door for trick or treat. However, after getting the treats and under cover of darkness, we would begin our mischievous escapades. This included putting a button on a string or a thread spool with notched edges, twisting it tightly and rapping it on a window. We would also throw corn at windows. Using a piece of string with a thumbtack on one end and rubbing it with rosin was also a fun way to make screeching sounds. Most homes had wooden fences in front of their properties, and we would remove the gates and place them on the grass plot area in town. One year, we carried old tires over to the school flagpole, pulled them up, and flipped them down over the pole. After Halloween, we had the job of trying to get the tires off the flagpole . . . Another fun time was when we put Shank Motter's hunting dog in his neighbor's barn, which had pigs (his son helped us). The following morning, which was the first day of small game hunting season, Shank called his dog and found only an empty chain. He then heard his dog barking and went over to his neighbor's barn and opened the door—out came the pigs and dog! The pigs were running around town for a few days. We had a nice big old town dog, Rex, that belonged to no one, but everyone loved and fed. During Halloween, we would open the front door of someone's house and put Rex into the house. Shortly thereafter, he would come sailing out the door. This we did until a home had children that would not put him out . . .

I was very fortunate to work for the local farmers at a very early age. My brother, Blair, and I would pick rocks off the fields into a wagon drawn by two horses and then fill in the dirt roads where needed. I learned how to mow and rake hay. I remember feeling like an adult when I could throw the harness over the farm horses and hitch them up to the wagons. The corn required cultivation, cutting, shocking, husking, and hauling to the corn crib. The wheat required binding into sheaves, shocking, hauling to be thrashed for grain, and later using the baler for the straw. Oats required the same work as for wheat. It was always fun to fill the silo with corn, soybeans, etc., because it smelled so good. The newly mowed hay also had a wonderful smell as well as the newly plowed ground. After working for the farmers for a few years, I could select whom I wished to work for, because the pay rate (fifty cents

1930's
Gratz

an hour) was the same. The farmer's wife helped me to make the decision. If she was a good cook, that is where I worked. Working ten hours a day with at least one meal thrown in was important to me. They normally fed me a morning and afternoon break of tea and cookies, and always a big dinner/lunch and sometimes supper. Then one farmer who I worked for most of the time had a large peach orchard plus other fruit trees. When picking peaches, I usually ate one of the perfectly ripe peaches on each tree. There was always work to be had around this town all year long—from picking strawberries, tomatoes, potatoes, cleaning chicken houses, removing old tree stumps, mowing lawns, trimming hedges, shoveling snow, hauling ashes, delivering newspapers, etc. During the winter months, it was profitable to trap for skunk and muskrat. We would get from $2 to $3.50 for a skunk pelt and $3 to $4 for a muskrat pelt. After I bought a Marlin .22 rifle, it became much easier to trap skunks. No more problems being sent home from school when the teacher detected skunk odor. I also had an interesting job for a few years taking care of the Simeon's Lutheran and Reformed Cemetery. A gasoline eighteen inch reel-type hand mower was used to cut the grass, and hand clippers for trimming. The graves were dug by hand. I was paid $25 a grave, which was good money if you could dig it in two days . . .

We always had hunting dogs in our family. Many days were spent hiking to the top of Short Mountain with dogs, 22 rifle, and other boys my age. A favorite spot on top of the mountain was the fire tower and a place called Addis Rock, where the Indians were supposed to have carved the saucer-like dish for sending smoke signals. My dad made sure we boys knew how to handle a gun after age twelve, which allowed us to hunt rabbits, grouse, squirrels, pheasants and deer. When hunting season arrived, I could hardly wait to start . . . the valley around Gratz was prime small game hunting. The normal results of a day of hunting was four rabbits and two ringed-neck pheasants each. There was no posted land. Game was abundant because the farming techniques at the time supplied plenty of food. Now, with spray, and new farming methods, the days of small game hunting are almost gone.

Carl recalled doing many similar things in his youth, including digging graves for $20 to $25 and septic tanks.

"There was an old bachelor in town, Lewis Hess," said Carl. "He was welcome anywhere. No one locked their doors. Lewis would come for a visit and give my mother a box of candy. We would dig graves together. Sometimes we would dynamite septics in the winter. Everyone had dynamite back then. On one occasion, we tried using tires to muffle the sound and blew the tires onto the roof!"

Carl also enjoyed trapping and recalled getting $3 for skunks and muskrats and fifty cents for weasels from the justice of the peace.

"One of my chores around the house was to keep the stoves and lanterns ready—with corn cobs, coal and kerosene. I remember one day, when I was little, the snow was so deep my dad carried me to school on his back!

"In the summer, we didn't wear shoes much," remembered Carl. "My feet were so tough. One time I stepped on a rusty nail and soaked my foot in coal oil."

Like Schoffstall, Carl was also in demand as a farm hand from a young age. For thirty cents an hour, he would walk two miles to a neighboring farm at 4 AM. He'd start with the cows and would then have breakfast, after which he worked in the fields until dark. He'd return home in the evening and get a bath.

Sisters Edna and Alfreida worked in nearby factories. Carl washed dishes to help out. Mother Pauline made most of their clothes and knitted quilts. She had over forty quilts when she died.

The family made money in other ways, including selling eggs from their chickens. Oliver was a night watchman at a tool shed, at a fork in the road. At one point, he got a job helping to build the barracks at Fort Indiantown Gap. He'd be gone for up to four days at a time, leaving Pauline at home alone with the four children.

"When the WPA started up," said Carl, "my father and I would shovel snow from the country roads for fifty cents an hour. We used to say WPA stood for 'We Poke Along.'

"We heard about the troubles in the cities, regarding the Depression, but we didn't really feel it much, except that flour, sugar and salt were scarce."

Like the Schoffstalls, the Scheibs also raised dogs. Oliver had a number of beagles that he would take to field trials and use for hunting. On many Sundays, the Scheib men would go to church,

1930's Gratz

eat lunch, and then head to the mountains to train the dogs. Once in a while, the preacher would come to dinner, and the boys would be sure to be back and washed-up.

Allen "Spirty" Shade recalled a childhood encounter with Carl in the Gratz Historical Society's *Memories Volume 6*:

> Carl lived on a small farm on the outskirts of town. Every summer, a bunch of us kids went over there. We made paddles out of old shingles (at that time there were always some laying around). Way up in the corner of the barn roof, hornets and yellow jackets made nests. We gathered in a bunch down below and threw stones up at the nests. It made the bees mad, and they came flying down after us. Then we'd all run as fast as we could around the barn. Everybody ran inside the barn and slammed the barn door shut. If you were a slow runner, you were penned out, and had to contend with the bees. That's why you had the paddle.

While quite a bit of his time was spent in school or working, there was time for play. Carl fondly recalled when the "Shadow Ball" troupe came to the area. Called the Ethiopian Clowns, this group of barnstorming ballplayers would perform all over the country, pretending to play baseball, pantomiming a game with unusual tricks and stunts. This group has been referred to by some as "The Harlem Globetrotters of Baseball." They were in the area in 1939 when Carl was 12.

Another baseball-related activity that entertained the town folk was donkey ball. Usually done for charity, the players would attempt to "run" the bases while riding on a donkey or mule. This led to many hilarious situations as the animals would generally do whatever they wished, including relieving themselves in the midst of play.

Of course, there was always the Gratz Fair to distract the locals once every year, held continuously since 1873 at the fairgrounds east of town. Besides the various agricultural and culinary competitions, vaudeville entertainment and music groups would appear.

"I remember high wire walks and acrobats," said Carl of the fair. "I really enjoyed the fair as a kid. There were horse races and Les Brown's Band of Renown would play. When I was six or seven, Edgar Bergen (the ventriloquist) and Charlie McCarthy (his dummy) were there. I also remember the cowboy Tom Mix performing on the ball field."

But, the small town of Gratz and its environs didn't seem to be enough for the strapping young lad. Tall, and strong, Carl was a man among boys, maturing quickly. This made him a target, so he and Paul learned to box in their barn.

"For entertainment," recalled Carl, "there would be fights at the bars and auctions on Friday nights. There was a roller skating rink in the town limits. One night this guy challenged me to a fight at the rink. We went outside, and crossed the street to be outside of town. Someone went to get boxing gloves, but the guy backed out.

"I remember going to Millersburg and fighting in front of car headlights. One night a truck driver challenged me. 'I'll take the guy from Gratz,' he said, 'No rough and tumble shit, just boxing.'"

During the fight, Carl was wearing his brother's sweatshirt, which became torn up. A man pulled him from the brawl. "Can't you go anywhere without fighting?" he yelled at the lad.

Carl headed home in the torn-up shirt. His mother realized the predicament Carl was in and hid the shirt from his brother in a flour chest to protect him.

Carl would roam far from home. He would often walk to Lykens and to the fire tower. One night he got lost and walked to Loyalton and then had to cross the gap to Gratz. Other times, he would walk to Shamokin or Dalmatia or follow the railroad tracks to Selinsgrove to watch girly shows.

"Some of my fondest memories," said Carl, "were the winter nights when it was clear and not too cold. I would take the dogs out for a walk. I remember stopping and laying on a hillside and looking up at the stars. I would dream about doing something other than farming and coal mining."

Town League in the Lykens Valley

2.
BOOBY, BUDDY, GUMMY, OZZIE, & LEFTY

"BUBBY"

Of course, there was baseball. As boys, Carl, known around town as "Booby," pronounced "bubby" in the Pennsylvania Dutch vernacular, and Paul, aka "Buddy," would play one-on-one using a broom stick and a rubber ball. They'd also play tag with the rubber ball. Carl liked to throw rocks on the farm, too. "I had a glove and my brother had a catcher's mitt that our parents got us for Christmas presents. The gloves and a baseball were all my father could afford. When the chores were done, my brother and I would get out in our big front yard, and we'd throw and throw and throw. I would pitch and Paul would catch."

"Before Little League," remembered Carl, "we played in grammar schools. Our high school barely had nine guys. Grades six, seven, and eight were downstairs, nine, ten, and eleven upstairs. The twelfth graders went somewhere else!"

"Gratz was backward," said Paul. "High school only went to the eleventh grade. I went to Elizabethville for twelfth grade and was the only one in the family to graduate from high school."

Carl recalled playing on an American Legion team in the Lykens Valley when he was 14 or 15. He also played on his high school team from eighth through tenth grade.

Paul played in high school and on the Gratz town team as its catcher.

"Saturday afternoons, the town teams would play," said Carl. "There was a town league organized in the valley with teams in Lykens, Gratz, Williamstown, Halifax, Hegins, Tower City, Millersburg, and Loyalton. All of the farmers would play, from high school age on up."

"One year I went out for the town team," said Paul. "They made me the catcher, but I had never caught before! I didn't know how to wear the equipment."

Regarding nicknames, according to *A Comprehensive History of the Town of Gratz, Pennsylvania,* just about everybody in the area had one. Often they "stuck" so well that most people had

12

forgotten their given names. One person lost a local write-in election because the voters did not know his actual name. Another person was unable to receive important long distance phone calls because the caller could not tell the operator the name of the recipient. Following are some of the nicknames of the ballplayers on the baseball teams in the early 40s:

Ralph "Lefty" Knohr
Vincent "Monk" Koppenhaver
Cyril "Zero" or "Shadee" Shade
Elwood "Dix" or "Witty" Witmer
Warren "Mopey" Hepler
Harry "Bus" Hepler
Robert "Austie" or "Ozzie" Coleman
Warren "Hassy" Hassinger
Robert "Gummy" Rothermel
Paul "Buddy" Scheib
Carl "Booby" Scheib

Robert "Ozzie" Coleman recalled similar baseball memories in the Gratz Historical Society's *Memories Volume 5*:

. . . In 1939, no one had a baseball uniform and very few players had baseball shoes. As I recall, I was the only left-hander on the team, and the only glove I had was my brother Mark's very old right-handed glove which had already seen it's good, better, and best days. Worst would be more accurate.
. . . Something great happened to me between the ninth and tenth grades. I grew six inches, and while working on the "thrashing circuit" during the summer, I earned enough money to buy a first-baseman's glove and a pair of baseball shoes.
. . . Something else happened—the big Gratz baseball team got new uniforms. In late winter, each one of the Gratz high school players went out to one of the Gratz town players and got a uniform. I got one from Guy Miller, which fit very well except the pants were all torn. My Mom, being a very good seamstress, put new fronts in the pants to the extent they looked like new. To my knowledge, this is the first time the Gratz high school baseball team had uniforms.

1941 8th grader Carl Scheib pitches for Gratz HS.

The new ninth grade class arriving upstairs had mostly all male students. They were Jacob Sitlinger, Vincent Koppenhaver, Elwood Witmer, Eddie Hartman, Lee Riegle, Harry Hepler, John Bingaman, Cyril Shade, and Ralph Knohr. We needed a pitcher, so the school teachers allowed Carl Scheib who was in eighth grade, to play on the team. For transportation, Arthur Hess had a long bed one-ton truck—no roof—just sideboards—no seats—we used our baseball gloves. It was much better than walking.

The eleventh grade players had several positions sewed up such as Paul Scheib, Carl's brother, was the catcher, George Hartman first base, and Sam Stroup second base. We younger players managed to have our share of playing time. Between tenth and eleventh grades, I grew another two inches and, as the left-hander who had a first base glove, got the first base position.

The lineup for the 1941 team was: catcher Harry "Bus" Hepler, pitchers Carl "Booby" Scheib and Ralph "Lefty" Knohr, first base Robert "Ozzie" Coleman, second base Warren "Mope" Hepler, shortstop Cyril "Shadee" Shade, third base Elwood "Dix" Witmer, outfielders John Bingaman, Vincent "Monk" Koppenhaver, Eddie Hartman, Lee Riegle, Warren "Hass" Hassinger, Ralph "Lefty" Knohr, and Clair "Bosty" Hartman.

In the three years, 1939, 1940, and 1941, the old saying 'it's not whether you win or lose, but how you play the game,' would be more appropriate. I don't remember how many games the Gratz High School baseball team won, but we did our best. No one taught us how to do anything. Our coach, Mr. Bellis, made the line-up and kept the scorecard and did the best he could with the knowledge he had. The score card was the lid of a twenty-four bar candy box.

The Gratz Cardinals won their league-opener on May 5th, 1941, behind a six-hit shutout hurled by their young 14-year-old ace, Carl Scheib. The team beat Valley View 2 to 0.

On June 12th, Carl took a 4 to 0 shutout into the bottom of the 9th against Hegins, but yielded four runs. The two teams quit the game due to darkness an inning later, tied at 4.

On August 11th, 1941, Gratz wrapped up the pennant for the Twin County League. Carl lost a pitchers' duel with Loyalton's Bill Byerly 2 to 0. Gratz then followed up with a 7 to 6 win over Hegins to clinch.

During the playoffs against Berrysburg a week later, the teams split a doubleheader. Carl dropped the first game 3 to 0, but pitched well. Gratz then evened the series with a 7 to 6 victory.

On September 15th, Gratz beat Loyalton for the Twin County title.

A week later, the Cardinals were in the Upper District championship round against Dauphin. They fell 6 to 3, with Carl on the mound. They lost the series the following week.

Coleman continued:

The same team, in 1942 won all their games except the two games they played with Hegins Township High School, in which Robert Coleman (who had come to Hegins from Gratz for twelfth grade) pitched the first game for Hegins and the second game was played at Gratz with Carl Scheib pitching for Gratz and Johnny Miller pitching for Hegins. The score of the game at Hegins was 4 to 2. The score of the second game at Gratz was 6 to 2. Ralph Knohr pitched for Gratz at Hegins.

Ralph "Lefty" Knohr recalled his baseball interactions with Carl Scheib in the Gratz Historical Society's *Memories Volume 5*:

In 1942, World War II was in full swing, and I was a student at Gratz High School. I graduated as a junior since Gratz, oddly enough, had only a three-year high school. In the spring of the year, we fielded a baseball team barely having enough players. We didn't need many players since we had Carl Scheib—a real piece of work. I played first base and pitched in a few games, and probably would have been as good as Carl, except I suffered from a severe lack of talent. So, in 1942, I had the distinct pleasure of playing with Carl.

On Monday, May 18th, 1942, Carl lost for the first time of the season to Lykens as the opposing hurler, Hal Williams, stole home to tie the game. Lykens went on to a narrow 3 to 2 victory, and the Cardinals fell to 7-2, still in first place.

The team went on to clinch the Upper Dauphin County Scholastic League on June 1st, when Carl hurled a four-hit shutout over Millersburg. The 15-year-old ace also batted fourth in the lineup.

8/14/42 Carl pitches BP at Connie Mack Stadium

On Sunday August 1st, pitching for Dalmatia in the West Branch League, "newcomer" Carl defeated Selinsgrove 5 to 3. He gave up only six hits and struck out 13. This League was a town league for adult players. Back in April, they had agreed to allow teenagers from the high school to join the rosters, probably due to the war draft.

The *Sunbury Daily Item*, on Tuesday August 4th, reported the following:

West Branch hurler, 15, to toss for Phils

Carl Scheib, 15-year-old Gratz high school hurler, who has been pitching a smart brand of ball with Dalmatia in Low Circuit action of the West Branch League, will hurl the pill against the Phillies next Friday, according to reports from the lower end of the county. To be sure it won't be in league competition, but there is good evidence that the Phils have their eyes open for some talent of the future.

Scheib, son of Mr. and Mrs. Oliver Scheib of Gratz, RD, will pitch some balls during the Philadelphia club's batting practice giving the lad the chance to try his stuff against big timers and allowing the city big wigs the opportunity to look him over carefully.

Scheib hurled superb ball in high school baseball this spring, leading his team to victory. In fact, he was the team . . . or so they say down Gratz way, where they're plenty proud of the young athlete who shows considerable promise. In West Branch play with Dalmatia, he hurled a two-hitter against the New Berlin Tigers, and added another victory to his list over the weekend snaring one of the two defeats handed Selinsgrove.

Dalmatia improved to 13-5 on August 5th, when they defeated Selinsgrove 9 to 1. Carl played second base.

In the August 6th *Shamokin Dispatch*, it was announced Carl would "toss batting practice against the Phils this week."

The *Evening News* of Harrisburg, Pennsylvania, on the following night, August 7th, reported Carl was in Philadelphia for a tryout with the Phillies. Of course, the tryout was for the A's, and it was scheduled for Friday the 14th.

In his last action before the try-out, Carl was really warmed-up. He threw a one-hitter on August 12th, winning 15 to 0. Only three men reached base on a single, error, and walk.

In a June 30th, 1948 article in *The Sporting News*, reporter Clifford Kachline recounted the story of Carl's discovery. Kachline credited Hannah Clark, a clerk at Smeltz's Grocery in Gratz, with turning on Al Grossman, a traveling salesman, to the high school phenom.

Grossman watched a game and was impressed. He then penned a letter to Connie Mack about the fifteen-year-old Gratz schoolboy.

According to Kachline, Mack received the letter, and remembering how Walter Johnson was discovered by a traveling cigar salesman, looked into the matter. He sent an invitation off to Carl to come to Philadelphia for a try-out.

On Friday, August 14th, it was raining in southeastern Pennsylvania, but Carl and his buddy Robert "Gummy" Rothermel, an older pitcher on the Dalmatia team who had a good car, headed off to Shibe Park.

Said Carl in the article, "I could hardly sleep the night before," he said. "Mother and dad and my brother were all excited, too. I think even the chickens knew what was up, because the rooster crowed early that morning and the hens seemed to do more than their share of cackling.

"My heart almost sank to my shoe tops when it looked like rain-and as we started, a few drops fell, but we kept going. It was drizzling when we reached Shibe Park and the 'Game Off' sign was hanging outside. I almost cried; but we went in. Mr. Mack talked to us and then sent me down to the clubhouse with Dave Keefe.

"My hands were nervous as I dressed and it seemed like it took an hour for me to tie my shoes. But when I got out on the field, Mr. Mack was waiting for me. He watched me pitch for about ten minutes, then put his arm around my shoulder, said he liked my stuff very much, but that I should go back to high school another year.

What was not mentioned in the article is the fact that Hannah Clark's mother was Emma Jane Scheib, the 1st cousin of Carl's father, Oliver Scheib. Carl and Hannah were therefore second cousins. Both were great grandchildren of Joshua Scheib (1831-1891) of Gratz.

Recalled Carl many years later, "I was so innocent in those years. I had never followed big league baseball, and didn't have a television or a radio. I didn't even know what a bullpen was. When I was there for the tryout, they told me to go get dressed. I didn't have spikes. I didn't have a glove. I didn't have a uniform. I didn't bring any equipment with me. They went from locker to locker to outfit me.

Following the try-out, Carl played right field and second base in a play-off victory against Middleburg on the 19th, but he was hit hard in a 6 to 5 loss the following weekend. The two teams did not play the rubber game, preventing Dalmatia from advancing further in the play-offs.

Middleburg went on to defeat New Berlin in the next round. Dalmatia protested, and no champion was declared.

The following snippet appeared in the September 1st edition of the *Mount Carmel Item*:

> Carl Scheib, Gratz schoolboy pitcher, must have made an impression in a recent tryout with the Philadelphia Athletics, judging by word received here by Al Grossman, who, during his daily travels, became interested in the kid and arranged for the trial.
>
> "There is just one thing against the boy and that's his age," Connie Mack himself was quoted as having declared when speaking about young Scheib, only 15 as we recall. "However, bring him down next year as soon as school closes. I'll get a room for him, and Earl Brucker (A's coach) will take care of him. In the meantime, don't let Carl pitch too much."

Knohr continued:

> A year later, in 1943, as a senior, I pitched on the Hegins Township High School team and—can you believe— against the Gratz team with Carl Scheib pitching. Guess who won? If memory serves me correctly, I struck out every time except the last at bat, when I made an out hitting a little dribbler to the infield.
>
> Several weeks later, he was pitching in the Major Leagues for the Philadelphia Athletics. At age 16, he was the youngest player to have ever played in the Major Leagues—both National and American—however, Joe Nuxhall, then of the Cincinnati Reds, now holds that record, being slightly younger than Carl when he broke in, but Carl still holds the American League record. This is unreal!

So, to have played against Carl for a moment in time, when fate treated me rather kindly, I have remembered this slice of life on this dear old planet for a lifetime.

3.
I'M READY!

The 1942 Athletics had finished in last place at 55-99, 48 games behind the pennant-winning New York Yankees. As the United States ramped up its war effort, many players were called to military service, including star center fielder Sam Chapman of the A's, who missed the 1942 season. Without Chapman, Philadelphia was led by Bob Johnson in home runs with only 13. Phil Marchildon led the pitching staff with 17 wins.

During the off-season, Connie Mack tried to improve the team. He plucked Eddie Mayo from the Cubs and Johnny Welaj from the Tigers in the Rule V draft on November 2nd. On December 5th, the team released second baseman Bill Knickerbocker, center fielder Mike Kreevich, and back-up shortstop Eric McNair, and traded for Jo Jo White. Two days later, utility infielder Larry Eschen was released. Kreevich had replaced Sam Chapman in the lineup and hit .255 with one home run in 444 at bats.

Late in spring training, the A's traded left fielder Bob Johnson to the Washington Senators for Bobby Estalella and Jimmy Pofahl.

After school was out in late June, 1943, Carl reported back to Connie Mack and the Athletics at the urging of his father.

"You ain't worth a damn in school," said his father, "so you might as well play."

Carl quit high school and signed on as a batting practice pitcher on June 26th. The team was impressed with his fastball and curve and his good control.

At first, the young pitcher stayed in Philadelphia while the team traveled. He had never been to the city and was staying in a rented room.

Recalling his early years with the A's, Carl said, "When I first went to Philadelphia, I was a shy, bashful kid. I had never been away from home. I had never eaten in a restaurant. My parents drove me down and dropped me off in the big city of Philadelphia, and, hey, it was rough! Most of the players had rooms in Philadelphia, and I had one by myself, too. I missed a lot of meals, living by myself. I had to find a restaurant to eat. I didn't even

I DID NOT know how to read a menu. I had never been 50 miles from home when I left. The Great Depression was just getting over, and our family never had the money to go anywhere or do anything."

At first, Carl was afraid to go anywhere. Then, he began walking the twelve blocks from the ballpark to Broad Street to see movies or buy sandwiches and pie in vending machines at the Horn and Hardart Automat.

In time, he began riding the subway for six or seven stops on the Broad Street Line. He soon learned he could transfer to a trolley and go elsewhere in the city.

Around this time, according to Carl, Pennsylvania native Nellie Fox was invited to hang out with the Athletics. He became fast friends with Carl. In fact, Mack had the two teens room together for a time.

NELLIe FOX

On July 13th, the All-Star game was held at Shibe Park. It was the first time the game was played at night. Carl was on hand to watch as Joe McCarthy's American Leaguers defeated Bill Southworth's Nationals 5 to 3. Dutch Leonard picked up the victory. Bobby Doerr had two hits and three RBIs. First baseman Dick Siebert was the only Athletic on the squad. He went 0-1 before being replaced by Rudy York. The hometown Philadelphia Phillies were also represented by their first baseman, Babe Dahlgren.

The team began taking Carl along on road trips. Carl recalled the train rides: "We'd be on sleeper cars and would sleep overnight on the train. Whether you had an upper or lower berth was listed in the clubhouse when we left. We had the two cars on the back of the train. The guys would walk around undressed and play poker late into the night. Mr. Mack had a separate room and stayed away from the players."

In late August, Carl pitched in the second game of an exhibition doubleheader against the League Island Marines, who were stationed at the Philadelphia Navy Yard. Young Carl worked the final four innings, yielding no hits and striking out seven.

After this outing, Connie Mack approached Carl and said, "Don't you think it's about time?"

Carl replied excitedly, "I'm ready!"

"Have your father come down here and we'll sign a contract," offered the Tall Tactician.

9/6/43
Carl signs an
MLB contract
at 16½ years

A few days later, on Labor Day, Monday September 6th, 1943, Carl, with his father Oliver co-signing, put his signature to a major league contract. Carl was to be paid $300 for the rest of the season. Mack also gave him a $500 signing bonus and handed $1000 to father Oliver for his trouble.

"Now you go down to the clubhouse and get a uniform with a number so you can be identified," Mack instructed the newly-signed rookie.

That very same day, the New York Yankees were in town to face the Philadelphia A's at Shibe Park, as they had done for decades. Usually, the Bronx Bombers came out on top. But today, the two American League teams competed in a twin bill, the first of which the A's won 11-2 to improve to 44-83, 35½ games back of the league-leading Yanks. Roger Wolff was the beneficiary of the double-digit offensive outburst, garnering his 10th victory. First baseman Dick Siebert was the star, knocking in four with three hits, including a key triple. Wolff went the distance, scattering eight hits and allowing only one earned run, dropping his ERA to 2.95, a solid season for the 32-year-old veteran. Wolff had toiled in the minors for eleven seasons before Connie Mack finally opened the door at age 30 in 1941.

Game two pitted Bill Zuber (6-3) for the Yanks versus Don Black (6-11) for the Athletics. Zuber, at the time, was a 30-year-old spot starter and long man, acquired from the Washington Senators after the 1942 season. Black was a 26-year-old rookie who had been a star at Petersburg in the Virginia League, going 18-11 in 1942. Things did not go well for young Black. Though the A's jumped out to a 2-0 lead in the first on Bobby Estalella's RBI single and Irv Hall's sacrifice fly, the Bronx Bombers came roaring back, knocking Don for five runs before the 5th inning.

Johnny Welaj pinch-hit for Black in the bottom of the 8th, and career minor leaguer Orie Arntzen was summoned to pitch the 9th to try to keep it close, with the A's down only 5 to 4. Arntzen, nicknamed "Old Folks," was a 33-year-old journeyman when Connie Mack signed him following a sold season at Williamsport in the Eastern League. Old Folks would struggle, though, as he had most of the season, finishing 4-13 in his only big league action. Though Orie would go on to star for many more years in the minors, the Yankees were onto him late that Labor Day afternoon. A one run deficit soon became a three-run gap as rookie third baseman Billy Johnson singled in two followed by Charlie Keller's bases-clearing triple, plating two more.

SEPT. 6, 1943

With only one out and Keller on third, the Yankees now led by five, 9-4. Bullpen coach Earle Brucker had asked young Carl to begin warming up following the signal from bench coach Earle Mack, who had rapped the dugout wall with his knuckles after the trouble with Arntzen began to mount.

"Warm up, Scheib!" barked Brucker to the young hurler.

Moments later, as Nick Etten, the Yankee first baseman, approached the plate from the on-deck circle, Earle Mack emerged from the dugout and signaled for Carl to enter the game.

As he trotted in, passing third-base on his way from the bullpen, Carl became the youngest major league baseball player in the modern era, at sixteen years, eight months, and six days. Twenty-nine-year-old Etten was having one of his best seasons, on his way to 107 RBI, batting fifth for the league-leading Yankees. Young Carl, who threw two pitches at that point, a fastball and a curve, toed the rubber. Bob Swift, the back-up catcher, took his position behind the plate, signaling for a fastball. Hal Weafer, the home plate umpire, looked on. Etten, at 6'2", was a tall left-handed hitter. He stepped in against the teen, while Keller danced off of third.

Whack! Etten nailed a fastball to the gap in right center. The lanky first-sacker rounded the bases and pulled into third. Keller had scored easily. It was now 10-4, and there was still only one out.

Having gotten his first batter out of the way, Carl settled in. Joe Gordon, the Yankees' right-handed hitting second baseman stepped up next. Carl enticed him to ground to shortstop Irv Hall, who threw over to Siebert for the second out. Etten scored on the play, making it 11-4. The run was charged to Carl. But only one more out was needed. While catcher Rollie Hemsley followed with a single, shortstop Frank Crosetti flied out to left field to end the threat.

Carl returned to the dugout and watched Marius Russo mow down the heart of the A's order – Ripple, Estalella, and Siebert – to close out the win. In two-thirds of an inning, he had yielded two hits and a run, but he had also debuted against the best team in the league.

Unfortunately, the news of the young teen taking the hill was drowned out by the terrible report of a train wreck on the Frankford Line in Philadelphia, killing 79 and injuring 117. Fortunately for the Yankees, this was not their train back to New York.

9/12/43
Carl pitches against Senators

The following (Sunday, September 12th), the Washington Senators were in town for a doubleheader. Ossie Bluege's boys were in second place, 11½ back of the Yankees. The Athletics were now 40 back in last place. In the first game, the A's took an early lead against Dutch Leonard, but let it slip away late, losing 5-4.

Game two was a battle of rookie hurlers. Mickey Haefner, for the Senators, was a thirty-year-old left-hander enjoying his first major league experience, following five successful minor league campaigns. Don Black, now 6-12 for the A's, took the hill for Philadelphia.

In the bottom of the 7th, with the A's trailing 7-4, Black was lifted for a pinch hitter, Frank Skaff. Meanwhile, Carl warmed in the bullpen. He entered the game in the top of the 8th.

Second baseman Jerry Priddy stepped in to face Carl. At 23, Priddy was enjoying his first season as a full-time player, contributing a steady performance. He rolled a ball to his counterpart at second, Don Heffner, who threw wildly to first. Priddy ended up on second on the error. Weak-hitting shortstop John Sullivan followed with a grounder to third that forced Pete Suder to charge, allowing Priddy to third. Sullivan was safe at first.

Carl now found himself with men on first and third and no one out. Pitcher Mickey Haefner stepped into the box for the Senators. He dropped a bunt towards Suder at third. Priddy held while Sullivan moved up one base and Haefner was retired. The Senators had traded an out to put two in scoring position.

All-Star outfielder George Case was next up. Case was in the midst of leading the American League in steals for the fifth consecutive season. He had hit .320 in 1942 and was a hair under .300 in 1943. He popped a ball to center fielder Johnny Welaj, who made the catch, but then threw errantly, allowing Priddy to score and Sullivan to advance to third. Center fielder Stan Spence then fouled out down the right field line, ending the threat.

Carl returned to the dugout having surrendered an unearned run. He appeared to have good stuff, but was not backed by the defense.

In the 9th, down 8-4, Carl continued to show some dominance, getting veteran right fielder Gene Moore to pop out to catcher Bob Swift.

All-Star "Indian Bob" Johnson was next up. He had been a star for the Philadelphia A's over the prior decade, peaking at 30 home runs in 1938. He had been traded in the off-season from Philadelphia to Washington. At 37, he still had some baseball left in him, evidenced by two more solid seasons through 1945. Indian Bob was a tough right-handed bat, facing the young hurler. Carl, able to pitch from the wind-up, likely tricked Johnson with a curve, inducing him to ground back to the pitcher. Carl turned and threw to first, retiring Indian Bob. There were now two outs. Suddenly, pitching in the big leagues didn't seem so tough!

Rookie third basemen Sherry Robertson was next. He had yet to show much of a bat, now in his third stint in the majors. That is, until today. Sherry had three hits off of Don Black, including a triple. As he stepped in against Carl, he was having the game of his career. The lefty-batting Robertson was seeing the ball well. He launched a pitch deep to right, and into the stands for a home run. He finished the day four for five with three RBI. The score was now 9 to 4, and Carl had yielded his first big league home run.

All-Star catcher Jake Early was next in the lineup. It's not known if he made a remark to young Carl, or if Carl was a bit rattled, but Carl promptly plunked him with a pitch, putting him on first base.

Jerry Priddy was next, facing Carl for the second time. The young second-sacker worked Carl for a walk, putting men on first and second. However, this time, rather than giving up a hit to Sullivan, Carl got him to ground to third baseman Suder, who threw to second for the force. Carl had retired the side. His line for his second game was two innings pitched, two hits, one walk, and one earned-run, on the home run by Robertson.

Three days later, on Wednesday, September 15th, the Athletics were back in Yankee Stadium. The last place A's were fodder for the league-leading Bronx Bombers, who sent Hank Borowy to the hill. At 13-9, Hank was in his second season with the Yanks. Orie Arntzen, 4-12, opposed him for the A's.

While the A's couldn't mount a threat against Borowy, Arntzen picked up where he left off the prior week against the Yanks. He coughed up three in the first, and then a double to Crosetti in the 2nd. Carl, who had been warming since the start of the second inning, was summoned to pick up the pieces, now down 3 to 0.

Pitcher Borowy was the first to face Carl. He dropped a sacrifice bunt that moved Crosetti to third. Lead-off hitter, center fielder Roy Weatherly then stepped in. He had singled against

16 + pitching Yankee Stadium Yankee Stadium

SEPT. 15, 1943 – YANKEE STADIUM

Arntzen to lead off the first. Weatherly, grounded out to the right side, scoring Crosetti. The A's were now down 4-0, but two were out and the bases were empty. Rookie Bud Metheny followed with a single, but Billy Johnson flew out to end the inning. Sixteen-year-old Carl had thwarted the Yankee attack in Yankee Stadium.

In the top of the 3rd, Carl stepped to the plate for his first major league at bat. "I remember being in awe of Yankee Stadium," said Carl many years later, recalling the moment.

Hank Borowy had been mowing down the Philadelphia lineup so far, having yielded only a triple to Jo Jo White in the first. Carl, known for his bat as well as his arm back in Gratz, faced off against the pitcher who would soon win a game in the World Series against the Cardinals. Outmatched, he struck out.

The bottom of the 4th was an interesting one for Carl. All-Star left fielder Charlie Keller was in his prime, just before he would be sent off to the merchant marine. He was leading the league in walks, and was on his way to totaling 31 home runs for the pennant winners. He was first up against the teen phenom. Carl got him to ground out.

Next up was Nick Etten. Carl had faced him in his debut. In fact, Etten was the first batter Carl had faced in the majors. Etten had tripled off of him on Labor Day. This time, Nick lined out to center field.

Last up was future Hall of Fame catcher Bill Dickey. Dickey, now 36, was still an All-Star, but was on the downside of a great career. He must have mused at the youth of the hurler on the hill. No matter, he grounded out to second to end the frame.

Borowy stymied the A's again in the 4th. Carl took the mound in the bottom of the inning, and made quick work of Gordon, Crosetti, and Borowy, the latter grounding into a double play.

In the top of the 5th, following ground outs by Swift and Mayo, Carl came to the plate for a second time. Rather than striking out, like he did in his first chance, the young batsmen drove a ball to right, into the waiting glove of Bud Metheny.

The bottom of the 5th was a rough one for Carl. After Weatherly flied to right, Metheny homered, making the score 5 to 0. Billy Johnson and Charlie Keller each singled, putting men on first and third with only one out. No one was warming in the bullpen, as Nick Etten strode to the plate again. He hit a fly to the outfield, deep enough for Johnson to score the 6th run. There were now two outs with Bill Dickey coming to the plate. Once again, Carl got him to ground out to end the inning.

26

The A's were held scoreless again as Joe Gordon stepped up to face Carl in the bottom of the 6th. The All-Star second baseman packed some pop, having hit over 140 home runs in his first six seasons. He was to add another, increasing the Yanks' lead by one. Carl settled down, though, retiring Crosetti, Borowy, and Weatherly to end the inning.

The 7th inning passed quickly for both sides. Siebert, Hall, and Swift went down against Borowy. Metheny, Johnson, and Keller went swiftly for the Bombers. It was the end of Carl's day as Hal Wagner pinch-hit for him in the 8th. In his first lengthy stint in the majors, Carl had performed respectably well against the best team in the American League, facing 23 batters over six innings, yielding five hits and three runs, two on homers. It would be Carl's longest outing of his first season.

It would be eleven more days until Carl took the bump again. On Sunday, September 26th, the St. Louis Browns were in town. The A's and the Browns had been second-division teams for the balance of 1943. Bob Muncrief (12-11) faced off against Lum Harris (7-19). Both pitched very well, but as the A's entered the bottom of the 8th trailing 3 to 1, Jo Jo White was called to hit for Harris. Meanwhile, Carl loosened up in the bullpen.

In the top of the 9th, Muncrief was the first batter faced and became Carl's first major league strikeout victim. He then ended the frame, despite some knocks from Milt Byrnes and former All-Star George McQuinn, by retiring All-Star Chet Laabs on a fly out. It was the first outing for Carl in which he did not yield a run, stranding two hits.

Three days later, on Wednesday the 29th, the A's were in the second game of a doubleheader against the Detroit Tigers. The A's had won the first game 8 to 2 behind a solid performance on the mound by Mexican hurler Jesse Flores. The Philadelphians benefited from 11 hits, including four by rookie outfielders Bill Burgo and George Staller. Game two was not to be as easy. Tiger ace Dizzy Trout was on his way to his first twenty-win season. He took the hill against Don Black.

The Tigers jumped to a 5-0 lead by the end of the top of the 4th. Carl was summoned to pitch the 5th. Except for a shaky 8th exacerbated by an error by first baseman Hal Wagner, it was a strong outing for Carl. In five innings, he scattered 8 hits and yielded no earned runs, though four did cross, including a home

Sept 1943
Carl pitches 18 2/3 innings

run by league-leader Rudy York. The A's dropped their 101st game, but Carl's ERA was now down to 3.07

For the last game of the season, Lou Boudreau's Cleveland Indians were in town on Sunday October 3rd. Veteran Mel Harder (8-7) picked up the ball against A's rookie Norm Brown, making his big league debut.

Norm was over from Boston, having gone 16-11 for Louisville in the American Association. He was traded for Eddie Mayo and Johnny Welaj. While Welaj was done in the majors, Mayo would go on for several more productive seasons in the Detroit outfield, after he was plucked from Boston. Unfortunately for the A's, Brown would never win a major league game, finishing 0-1 in a brief career interrupted by the war. He would win 20 or more games twice in the minors in subsequent seasons but no more opportunities arose for him above AAA.

Brown left the game in the top of the 8th with the score tied 4 to 4. Carl first faced lead-off hitter Oris Hockett. The left fielder, now 33, was in only his 2nd season in the big leagues, given a chance by the war. He had played briefly for Brooklyn in the late 30s, but couldn't stick despite lofty batting averages. Hockett flied out to Burgo in left.

First-baseman Mickey Rocco was next. A star in the International League at Buffalo, Rocco was a 27-year-old rookie in 1943. He popped up to catcher Hal Wagner.

After right fielder Roy Cullenbine walked, All-Star third baseman Ken Keltner stepped in. A perennial participant in the mid-season classic, Keltner was a solid performer for many seasons in Cleveland. This time, though, he drove Carl's pitch to center field, where rookie Woody Wheaton pulled it in. Wheaton was up for a cup of tea after hitting .325 at Lancaster, Pennsylvania, in the Interstate League. Carl had entered a tie game and held the opposition scoreless.

In the bottom of the 8th, Carl had a chance to take the lead. Frank Skaff had reached on an error. Rookie second baseman Joe Rullo then advanced him to second with a sacrifice bunt. Pete Suder failed to improve the situation, instead grounding out to short for the 2nd out. Joe Heving then walked Hal Wagner to put men on first and second with two outs. It was Carl's turn. He was at the plate with the go-ahead run on second. Clearly the Macks wanted to see what Carl could do, in the last game of a 100+ loss season. Carl stepped to the plate against the 42-year-old Heving. Despite his advanced age, Heving had been tough out of the pen in '43. At the time, he was the oldest player in the American League, now facing the youngest. Unfortunately, he became one of Joe's two strikeout victims that day, ending the threat.

The 9th and the 10th passed quickly. Neither team scored. Among the outs was future Hall of Famer Lou Boudreau, the Cleveland shortstop and manager. Against Carl, in the 9th, Lou flied out to center.

OCTOBER 3, 1943

Unfortunately for Carl and the A's, it all fell apart in the 11th. It's hard to believe a sixteen-year-old would have a tired arm. It's more likely the Indians had figured something out.

Rocco slashed a triple to right. Cullenbine then ripped a single to center, scoring Rocco. Keltner sacrificed Cullenbine to second. Hank Edwards, a good-hitting center fielder, plated Cullenbine with a single, taking second on the throw to the plate. The Indians were now up by two with Lou Boudreau stepping in.

Unlike last time, Lou doubled to right, increasing the lead to three as Edwards touched the dish. Light-hitting second-baseman Ray Mack popped to left. With two outs, catcher Buddy Rosar stepped to the plate.

In a crazy ending to an improbable season for Carl, All-Star Rosar ripped a hit to the gap in right, scoring Boudreau. The stocky catcher thought he'd test the rookie Staller and head to third, but was nailed by the throw to Suder. Staller had been plucked from Cleveland's AA team in Baltimore. The assist from right field was nice revenge.

Old Joe Heving promptly shut down the A's in the bottom of the 11th, notching his only win of the season. Carl took his first loss, throwing four innings, and giving up five hits and four earned runs, all in the final frame.

As the A's packed up to head home, Carl's tally for the month of September, his first in the big leagues, was a loss in 18 2/3 innings. His ERA finished at 4.34.

The A's finished 49-105, again in last place in the American League. Bobby Estalella led the team with only 11 home runs. He was also the top hitter at only .259.

On the mound, Jesse Flores finished 12-14, and Roger Wolff was 10-15, but Lum Harris lost 21 games against only 7 victories. The team really missed Phil Marchildon who was off to war.

Nearing the end of the season, the A's had made some helpful moves. George Kell was purchased from Lancaster of the Interstate League. They traded Eddie Mayo and Johnny Welaj to

1944
spring training
Frederick, Md.

the Red Sox for Norm Brown and Orie Arntzen to Toronto of the International League for Luke Hamlin.

On October 11th, Don Heffner and Bob Swift were sent to the Tigers for Rip Radcliff.

On December 1st, Joe Berry was purchased from the Chicago Cubs.

On December 13th, starting pitcher Roger Wolff was sent to the Washington Senators for starting pitcher Bobo Newsom.

4.
ROOKIE SEASON

The year started with the acquisition of future Hall of Famer Nellie Fox as an amateur free agent. Young Fox was only 16.

During spring training in chilly Frederick, Maryland, Mack made another key deal. He sent Sam Zoldak and Barney Lutz to the Browns for veteran catcher Frankie Hayes.

"George Kell and I both had our first spring training together," recalled Carl of the Frederick camp.

Carl's first win came when he hurled an exhibition against the local Curtis Bay Coast Guard team on March 25th.

On April 15th, the A's signed future Hall of Famer Al Simmons to function as a bench coach and occasional pinch hitter.

Thursday April 20th, 1944, in front of only 1500 fans at Griffith Stadium in Washington, D.C., the Philadelphia Athletics faced the Washington Senators in the second game of the season.

Future Hall of Famer Early Wynn took the hill for the Nats, his first start in what would be a tough-luck 8-17 season. Opposing him was Russ Christopher, just off a 5-8 record in his second season. This would arguably be Christopher's best season, ending up 14-14 with a 2.97 ERA.

The two hurlers traded zeros for four innings. In the bottom of the 5th, the Senators got to Christopher, chasing him with only one out. Carl was summoned from the bullpen and pitched the rest of the 5th, as well as the 6th and 7th, allowing three hits and one earned run.

George Case led the Nats with four hits, as they notched a 5-0 victory, Wynn credited with a two-hit shutout. Future Hall of Famer Rick Ferrell caught the game for Wynn, and faced Carl for the first time.

Eight days later, on April 28th the A's were in Boston, playing the Red Sox at Fenway. Philadelphia won this one in sixteen innings, seven to five, to improve their record to 4-2, 2nd in the American League. Carl replaced an ineffective Bobo Newsom, who had allowed three runs in four innings. Carl faced six batters, walking two and giving up one hit and one run. Luke Hamlin

Joe Nuxhall pitched only 1 game as a teenager.

followed with eight innings of three-hit ball, to keep the Sox in check. Joe Berry pitched the last three innings to earn his second victory of the season.

While Ted Williams was off to war, and not in the lineup for Boston, future Hall of Famer Bobby Doerr was. Catcher Frankie Hayes was the star for the victors, hitting two home runs en route to his first All-Star season since 1941.

On May 4th, the St. Louis Browns announced they would end segregation that restricted Negro fans in the bleachers.

Thinking about his handling of Carl, Connie Mack said, "I have seen too many young pitchers spoiled by working them in the majors too quickly. I wasn't going to take any chance with this boy. His muscles were not fully developed and he was still growing fast. I was looking toward the future."

Young Carl sat on the pine for three weeks before his next appearance on May 19th at Shibe Park against the Indians. Carl mopped up the last four innings in a 9-1 loss that dropped the A's to 13-13. Al Smith scattered nine hits for the victors, allowing only the one run to earn his first victory after his 17-7 All-Star campaign the prior season.

Thirty-nine-year-old Luke Hamlin had gotten the start for Philadelphia, but allowed four runs in an inning and a third. Russ Christopher allowed four more runs in three and two-thirds. Lou Boudreau's squad were racking up 17 hits, including four by Oris Hockett.

From the 6th through the 9th, Carl allowed only three hits and one run while striking out three. He also doubled off of Al Smith, and scored a run. This was his first hit in the majors.

One June 3rd, three days before D-Day, the A's were in St. Louis, visiting the Browns at Sportsman's Park. Jesse Flores faced the Browns' Nels Potter, who was in the midst of his best season, on his way to a 19-7 record.

The A's quickly fell behind 8 to 1 by the end of the 3rd, chasing Flores. Potter couldn't get out of the 5th, as the A's rallied for five runs, pulling to 8 to 6. Rookie third baseman George Kell was on fire for the A's, tallying four hits. He would go on to a Hall of Fame career, after he was traded to Detroit in 1946 for Barney McCosky. He had Potter's number, and was showing his potential this day. *(JUNE 3, 1944)*

Carl was summoned to pitch the last three innings, with the score 11 to 6. Carl didn't help matters, permitting five more runs

Joe Nuxhall pitched one game in 1944 at age 15, then disappeared into the minor leagues until 1952, when he returned at 23.

in the 6th and single runs in the 7th and 8th. The game ended 16 to 8. Catcher Frank Mancuso knocked in six for the victors.

On Tuesday June 6th, all major league baseball games were canceled as word came across the air about the D-Day invasion in Normandy.

On Saturday June 10th, the St. Louis Cardinals routed the Cincinnati Reds 18 to 0. With the Cards up 13 to 0 entering the 9th, the Reds summoned fifteen-year-old Joe Nuxhall to take the mound. He yielded five runs on two hits and five walks, becoming the youngest player in modern major league history, supplanting Carl. Nuxhall then disappeared from the majors, pitching in the minors until 1952. Nuxhall would go on to a successful career with 135 wins in sixteen seasons. However, Carl maintained his mantle as the youngest American Leaguer.

Wednesday June 14th, the A's were back in Fenway to play the Red Sox. Pinky Woods hurled a five-hit shutout for the Sox, while Russ Christopher struggled, yielding five runs in five innings. Carl pitched the 6th, allowing only one hit and no runs. Bobby Doerr led the attack with a home run.

The Indians were back in town on June 29th. Allie Reynolds twirled a three-hit shutout for Cleveland en route to a 6 to 0 win. Veteran center fielder Myril Hoag led the attack with three hits. Christopher and Hamlin were responsible for the six runs by the time Carl pitched the 9th. Carl got into some trouble in his inning, giving up one of Hoag's hits, who advanced to 2nd on an error by Jo Jo White in center. Hockett then sacrificed Hoag to third. With one out, Carl plunked Lou Boudreau, putting him on first. He escaped the scoreless inning by inducing Cullenbine and Keltner to fly out.

Nearly a month passed until Carl appeared again. On July 25th, at Sportsman's Park in St. Louis, the Browns won 9 to 1, and increased their lead in the American League to 3½ games over the Yankees. Bob Muncrief went the distance, yielding only one run on eight hits. Lum Harris had struggled to get past the 2nd, giving up seven hits and three runs. Woody Wheaton followed and threw six more runs on the pile. Carl then mopped up. Well-rested, he pitched the final three innings, yielding two hits and no runs. The A's were now 39-52, in last place.

1944 Carl meets Babe Ruth

Five days later, on July 30th, the A's were in Chicago to face Jimmy Dykes' White Sox. Lum Harris struggled again, giving up six runs in four innings. Joe Berry followed with two shutout innings for the A's, while Bill Dietrich tossed a complete game for the Sox, riding a 6 to 2 lead. Left fielder Eddie Carnett led the offensive attack with three hits and three RBIs, raising his batting average to .313. Carl entered the game in the 7th, throwing two shutout innings, allowing only one hit. Carl also batted against Dietrich, striking out.

Wednesday August 2nd, still at Comiskey Park in Chicago, the A's split a doubleheader with the White Sox. Lum Harris won the first game, besting Eddie Lopat 9 to 3. Bobby Estalella led the A's with three RBIs. The second game saw Don Black struggle to get through the 1st, giving up three runs on three hits and two walks. Carl was summoned to pitch the 2nd and lasted into the 6th. He pitched 4 2/3 innings, surrendering three runs on five hits. Veteran second baseman Tony Cuccinello led the attack with four hits. Dick Siebert tallied three hits for the A's, but Carl had two hits, including a double. The Sox won 7 to 3.

The A's were back in Philadelphia for a very special occasion *1944* on August 4th. The club honored Connie Mack's fifty years as a Major League manager. Mack had first managed for the Pittsburgh Pirates August 4th, 1894. On this sweltering summer night, the fans packed Shibe Park despite the restrictions created by World War II and the disruptions caused by a city-wide transit strike.

Art Morrow of *The Philadelphia Inquirer* wrote about the event, "And it remained for fandom to pay the greatest tribute. No greater regard have fans than this, that he should sacrifice his dwindling gasoline, wear out his rationed shoes with no chance for street car or subway; that he should do this to pay tribute to a friend. And 29,166 fans came early and stayed late at Shibe Park last night, with no thoughts of the long trudge home. It was worth it."

Bud Abbott and Lou Costello took batting practice. Abbott wore an A's uniform while Costello dressed as a Yankee. Both singled into the outfield to the cheers of the crowd. Later, they performed their classic baseball skit, "Who's on First?"

As the evening wound down, Connie Mack announced his all-time, All-Star team of living players, personally introducing them as they exited the dugout and lined up near home plate. Mack's choices:

MACK'S ALLTIME TEAM

1B: George Sisler
2B: Eddie Collins
3B: Frank "Home Run" Baker
SS: Honus Wagner
C: Bill Dickey and Mickey Cochrane
LHP: Lefty Grove
RHP: Walter Johnson
OF: Tris Speaker, Ty Cobb, Al Simmons, and Babe Ruth.

Only two of the men were unable to appear. Cochrane, was serving in the US Navy while Cobb was not available.

At some point during the day, Carl sat with Babe Ruth in the dugout and spoke with the icon, exchanging pleasantries.

The A's lost the game to the Yankees 1 to 0 despite a gem hurled by Bobo Newsom.

The homestand with the Yankees continued on Sunday August 6th. The Yanks built a 5 to 1 lead by the 6th, tagging Lum Harris and Don Black. Carl was called to pitch the last two innings. He gave up one run on two hits as New York won 6 to 1. Hersh Martin, Russ Derry, Johnny Lindell, and Nick Etten had two hits each for the Bombers. Frankie Hayes drove in the only run for the A's.

A week later, on the 13th, the Tigers were at Shibe Park for a doubleheader. The A's won the first game 6 to 1 behind Don Black, who gave up only three hits and one run in a complete game, besting future Hall of Famer Hal Newhouser. Irv Hall and Frankie Hayes provided the lumber for the victory.

In the 2nd game, Dizzy Trout was hard to hit, scattering 7 hits in a shutout that ran his record to 19-7. He would throw 352 innings in 1944, winning 27 games. Jesse Flores and Woody Wheaton yielded six runs. Carl pitched a scoreless 9th, walking one.

On Thursday, August 17th, the St. Louis Browns were back in town. A fifteen-hit attack led by Floyd Baker, Vern Stephens, Milt Byrnes, Al Zarilla, Mark Christman, and pitcher Nels Potter produced ten runs. Jesse Flores was chased after five, trailing five to one. Carl pitched a scoreless 6th, but ran into trouble in the 7th.

He was knocked around for four hits and four runs, including a homer by Stephens. Vern was an All-Star shortstop for the Browns, knocking in 109 in 1944.

Shortstop Ed Busch had three hits for the A's, but it was not enough, as they fell 10 to 5.

Ten days later, on August 27th, Boston was at Shibe Park. The Sox got out to a 7 to 1 lead by the end of the 4th, pounding Don Black for 10 hits and 7 runs. Joe Berry got the final two outs in the 4th before handing the ball to Carl for the 5th. Carl pitched four scoreless innings, giving up only one hit and one walk. Though the A's rallied, they fell short 8 to 5. Pete Fox knocked in three for the Sox.

Three weeks later, on September 19th, the White Sox hosted the A's at Comiskey Park. Johnny Humphries tossed a complete game for the Sox, gaining his 7th win. Jesse Flores lasted five, giving up six runs on eleven hits. First baseman Hal Trosky led the way with three hits and two RBIs for the victors. Carl pitched the final three innings for the A's, striking out three and giving up two hits and no runs. In his only at bat, Carl made an out, dropping his batting average to .375.

Carl's last appearance of the season occurred on September 26th, at Briggs Stadium in Detroit. Luke Hamlin allowed 11 hits and six runs to the league-leading Tigers over four innings. Meanwhile, Dizzy Trout tossed a six-hit shutout, winning his 27th game and dropping his ERA to 1.94. Carl pitched the final four innings for the A's, holding the Tigers scoreless on only two hits. He also went 0 for 2 at the plate, dropping his batting average to exactly .300.

Homers by Rudy York and Dick Wakefield proved too much for the A's, who were unable to mount an attack against Trout.

As the season ended, Carl had pitched 36 1/3 innings over 15 outings. He had no record, and a solid 4.21 ERA in mostly mop-up duty.

The A's were much better in 1944, finishing 72-82, tied for 5th place. The St. Louis Browns won the pennant, but fell to the St. Louis Cardinals in six games in what became known as the "Streetcar Series."

Catcher Frankie Hayes led the team with 13 home runs and 78 RBI. First baseman Dick Siebert led the team with a .306 batting average.

On the mound, Russ Christopher led in wins with his 14-14 record. Bobo Newsom was 13-15 with a 2.82 ERA. Joe Berry led the team with 12 saves and a stellar 1.94 ERA.

On November 25th, baseball's first commissioner, Kennesaw Mountain Landis, passed away. He had been commissioner since 1920, when he was appointed to deal with the Chicago "Black Sox" Scandal. He had just be re-elected to a new seven-year term. Landis was installed in the Hall of Fame a month later.

5.

DRAFTED!

Carl celebrated his 18th birthday on January 1st, 1945. Unfortunately, this also meant he was eligible for the draft and would likely have his season interrupted by military service.

The A's announced the signing of Joe Astroth who one day would be the starting catcher on the team.

1945 The A's again trained at Frederick, Maryland. Star pitcher Russ Christopher was the team's biggest holdout, but all of the Mackmen were in the fold when April arrived.

Carl hurled four scoreless innings in a 2-1 win over Toronto of the International League at nearby Hagerstown. Three days later, in a 12-4 loss to the Curtis Bay Coast Guard, he gave up one hit over the final two innings.

Opening day, April 17th, 1945, found the Senators in town to face the A's. Bobo Newsom, who was 13-15 in 1944, took the hill for Philadelphia. He was opposed by All-Star pitcher Dutch Leonard.

The Nats jumped out to a three-run lead in the 1st. Joe Kuhel had his first of four hits on the day, and the first of five RBIs.

Carl remembered Connie Mack sending his son, Earle, out to the mound to pull Newsom from the game. The younger Mack returned to the dugout unsuccessful.

"He won't do it," said Earle to Connie.

"Well, then, I guess he stays in," retorted the elder.

Trailing 4 to 0 in the bottom of the 3rd, Connie Mack pinch-hit for Bob Newsom. Bobby Estalella hit a two-run homer, to pull the A's closer at 4 to 2.

Carl took the hill for the 4th. Unfortunately, he didn't fare much better than Newsom, giving up two runs on three hits and two walks in one inning. In the end, the Senators took the first game of the season 14 to 8.

On April 24th, Albert Benjamin "Happy" Chandler was appointed the second Commissioner of Baseball.

Four days later, on April 28th, the Boston Red Sox were at Shibe Park. They were winless at 0-8, facing the 6-2 A's. Don Black took the hill for the Mackmen, opposing Rex Cecil for the Sox.

The teams were scoreless through three, and then exchanged a run each in the 4th. Black then had trouble in the 6th, knocked from the game after allowing two runs. Lou Knerr entered and got the last two outs.

Joe Berry began the 7th but could not retire a batter, yielding five unearned runs. Carl entered and closed out the game with three scoreless no-hit innings, a big improvement from his first appearance. The A's could not rally, falling short 8 to 4.

May 2nd, the A's were at Yankee Stadium. Russ Christopher was assigned the task to topple the first-place Bronx Bombers. Rookie Al Gettel took the mound for the Yanks.

The Yankees pulled out to a 6 to 1 lead by the 4th inning, chasing Christopher. Johnny Lindell led the attack with three RBIs.

Trailing 6 to 4, Carl was brought in to pitch the 8th. He put the Yanks down in order, but the A's could not close the gap against Gettel, who won his first major league game.

May 5th would be Carl's last appearance in the big leagues for a while. He had been drafted into the Army and would be reporting for duty.

The Athletics were at Griffith Stadium in Washington, D.C., to face the Senators. Roger Wolff got the call to face Bob Newsom.

The Senators took a 4 to 2 lead by the 5th, when Bobo took the mound. After getting an out and giving up a couple hits and a run, Carl was summoned from the pen for his last appearance of the year.

Carl was solid, hurling the rest of the game, giving up only one earned run in 3 2/3 innings. The final score was Senators 7, A's 3.

Six days later, Carl reported for duty and was inducted into the Army. He was sent to Camp Wheeler in Georgia. Later, thanks to having major league experience, he pitched for the base team. By the end of the service season, Carl had won ten games, one of which was a no-hitter. He also helped the Seventh Battalion team win the camp's championship.

5/11/45
Carl reports
for Army duty

Despite all of the fun and games, Carl was preparing to go to war. Germany had surrendered, so the men were preparing to go on a boat for either China, Burma, or India. Four thousand men would have been on the boat, but Japan surrendered. So, plans changed again, and the men were to be sent to be an occupation force in Germany.

On December 1st, Carl was shipped to Camp Danks in New York and then hustled to Camp Shanks for overseas embarkation.

The ride over was nerve-wracking. "We went across the English Channel," recalled Carl. "We had to be guided through the mines. We would shoot at them after we passed. Then we hit fog. It was really tough to navigate."

6.

ARMY CHAMPION

In January, 1946, Carl accompanied his unit to southern Germany for a month or two and then to Nuremberg as a member of the Railroad Transportation Division.

"I was there when the Nuremberg Trials were held," said Carl years later. "We were in charge of the railroad yard and tracked freight movements. We stayed in confiscated houses and worked the late shifts. We lived independently and ate in a beer hall or restaurant. We had everything we needed and skimmed from the shipments that came through. We also made sure the owners of the houses received assistance, but every night, we slept with our rifles by our beds. The German people were breaking into the yard for food. At first Polish guards would shoot at them, and later our M.P.s were sent in. One night dynamite was stolen, and it was thought it was to be used to break out Goering and the others who were on trial. The courthouse was surrounded by machine guns and tanks, but I did not go to see that."

"One day, the owner of the Fort Worth ballclub was calling around Germany trying to organize a ballclub," said Carl. A second lieutenant came into the room and ordered him to answer the phone. He obeyed the order, and was asked to pitch for the 3rd Army. He was transferred to the 60th Infantry of the Ninth Division.

In the summer of 1946, Carl helped the 60th Regiment compile a 30-5 record and win the championship of the American League of service teams. He won 16 and lost one during the season and averaged 16 strikeouts a game.

"We got a case of beer per man per game," remembered Carl. "I remember facing Joe Dobson, and beating him."

Matched against the 508th Regiment, winners of the National League with a 38-4 mark, Carl's pitching and hitting played a big part in his team winning the G.I. World Series of occupied Germany in Frankfurt. He won two games in the playoffs, and Dan Horn, from Pinconning, Michigan, won the title game. The good-hitting Gratz athlete played outfield when he didn't pitch, and his bat contributed to the team's victories.

Nov 1946 discharged from Army

"Germany was all bombed-out," described Carl. "We had to walk down the middle of the streets with our guns until things settled down. We'd trade cartons of cigarettes for vegetables. I was so lucky to have missed the fighting!"

Carl returned from Europe on a British liberty ship. "The ride home was long and rough," winced Carl. "The guys on the bottom deck were always dealing with water, and we went through a bad storm. Men would slide in the slop and run to the garbage cans to throw up from the motion sickness. Between two to four thousand men were sick on that ship, and had to sleep on rope beds that rocked back and forth."

He was discharged in November, 1946. Around the same time, the A's drafted Ferris Fain from San Francisco of the Pacific Coast League in the Rule V Draft.

The next month, on December 16th, the A's signed Lou Brissie as an amateur free agent despite his war injuries.

Carl misses 1945 and 1946 baseball seasons due to Army duty in Germany.

7.

PHILLY PHENOM

Carl returned to the Athletics for spring training in 1947. He recalled working hard to get back into major league condition for the regular season. Sam Chapman had also returned from the military the prior September and would be on hand for a full season.

The team had signed free agents Bill Dietrich, Alex Kellner, and Fred Hahn.

On March 24th, the Athletics traded a player to be named later, Vern Benson, Jake Caulfield and Russ Derry to the St. Louis Cardinals for Eddie Joost. The Philadelphia Athletics sent $30,000 to the Cardinals to complete the trade.

On April 9th, the A's purchased Chet Laabs from the St. Louis Browns.

"We lived on trains in spring training," recalled Carl many years later. "It seemed like we stopped in every town east of the Mississippi. After the game, we'd go to the hotel to shower, change, and dress, and then we'd catch the train. I remember stopping in Birmingham and Atlanta. The train schedule would always be in the clubhouse. It was up to us to make the train on time.

"I talked a lot to Chief Bender around this time. He was in his sixties and would pitch batting practice for us. One time, when I was hitting, I nailed him with a line drive."

On April 15th, Jackie Robinson broke the color barrier when he played for the Brooklyn Dodgers against the Boston Braves at Ebbets Field.

Carl's first appearance in 1947 did not happen until April 25th. The A's were in Boston at Fenway Park. Phil Marchildon started for the Athletics but could not get an out. While this would end up his best season at 19-9, the Red Sox were red hot out of the gate.

Sam Mele and Johnny Pesky hit back-to-back triples to start the 1st. With Dom Dimaggio at the plate, Phil threw a wild pitch, scoring Pesky. Dimaggio then walked, bringing up Ted Williams. Marchildon walked him too.

1947
Carl faces
Ted Williams
at Fenway

The Macks had seen enough, and called for Carl in the pen. Bobby Doerr was next up. He slapped a single into left field, scoring Dimaggio. Carl then got Rudy York to ground into a double play, advancing Williams to third. Carl stranded the Splinter there, getting Rip Russell to fly out.

The A's got one back in the second when Ferris Fain hit into a double play with Buddy Rosar on third. The score was now 3 to 1.

The 2nd was a breeze for Carl. Frankie Hayes, Mel Parnell, and San Mele were retired in order.

Carl led off the top of the 3rd but grounded out to short. Eddie Joost and Austin Knickerbocker followed with outs.

The 3rd inning started well for Carl as he retired Johnny Pesky on a fly to center. He then pitched around Dimaggio and Williams, walking them both. Bobby Doerr followed and struck out. There were now two outs and two on when Rudy York came to the plate. The first baseman was in the midst of his seventh All-Star season. He had led the league in homers and RBI in 1943, while with the Tigers. This afternoon, he turned on a Scheib offering and sent it over the green monster for a three-run round-tripper. Carl retired Rip Russell on a fly to left to end the inning. The Red Sox were now up 6 to 1.

The A's rallied for three runs in the 4th on three hits and a walk. Carl came up with two outs, and ended the rally, grounding out to second.

Carl faced the bottom of the order in the bottom of the 4th. After Frankie Hayes singled, Mel Parnell attempted to bunt him to second, but first baseman Ferris Fain fielded the ball and threw to shortstop Eddie Joost at second, nabbing Hayes. Sam Mele then flied out to right, and Pesky grounded to short. Joost flipped to second baseman Pete Suder, forcing Parnell to end the inning.

Carl watched the A's get another run in the 5th but was replaced by Bill Dietrich, down 6 to 5. The A's would rally for six more runs over the final three innings to win 11 to 7.

On April 27th, the Senators were in New York to play the Yankees on what was promoted as Babe Ruth Day. The Bambino, who had been diagnosed with throat cancer, gave a farewell speech to over 58,000 fans who were on hand.

A month later, on May 28th, the Red Sox were visiting Shibe Park. Joe Cronin's men got out to a 9 to 1 start by the 5th inning, Rudy York blasting another three-run homer, this time off of starter Jesse Flores.

Flores was down 2 to 1 as he took the mound in the 5th. He did not retire a batter, as pitcher Dave "Boo" Ferriss, Wally Moses, and Johnny Pesky all singled, and Dom Dimaggio doubled in two. Flores intentionally walked Ted Williams to load the bases, and was pulled in favor of Bill McCahan.

McCahan, a rookie, was feeling the pressure. He walked Rudy York, forcing in Pesky. The bases were still loaded.

Bobby Doerr then ripped a single to left, scoring Williams and Dimaggio. The rookie did induce Rip Russell to hit into a double play, moving York to third, but instead of getting out of the inning, catcher Birdie Tebbetts singled in York. It was now 8-1.

Tebbetts had a total of two stolen bases in 1947. Half of them came on the next play as he successfully swiped second off of the rattled rookie.

Boo Ferriss was up next. He had won 25 games the prior season, earning an All-Star berth. A good-hitting pitcher, Ferriss drew a walk. With men on first and second, Wally Moses doubled to right, scoring Tebbetts. It was now 9 to 1 with two outs and two more in scoring position.

Well-rested, Carl entered the fray and promptly got Johnny Pesky to pop out to short.

Carl led off the bottom of the 5th, lining a single off of Boo Ferris. He was later retired when Hank Majeski hit into a double play to end the threat.

The meat of the Red Sox order was due in the 6th: Dimaggio, Williams, and York. Carl retired them in order, including a strikeout of York.

The teams exchanged a couple more zeros. Carl retired Russell, Tebbetts, and Ferriss in order following Doerr's single.

Carl batted again in the 7th, ending the inning on a fly out. Back on the mound in the 8th, he retired Moses before Johnny Pesky slapped a single. He then struck out Dom Dimaggio and induced Ted Williams to ground out to first.

Dick Adams, who had replaced Ferris Fain in the 6th, nailed a homer in the 8th to pull the A's a run closer at 9 to 2. Carl then held the Sox again, retiring York, Doerr, and Russell, 1-2-3.

The A's tried to rally in the 9th as Mike Guerra tripled and Eddie Joost walked. With two outs, Carl was allowed to hit, and ended the game with an out.

His line that day was 4 2/3 innings of two-hit shut-out ball against a very tough lineup.

Four days later, on June 1st, the A's were in St. Louis to face the Browns. Phil Marchildon was facing Jack Kramer. Though the Browns' hurler was tripped for two in the 1st on Elmer Valo's two-run homer, he shut down the A's the rest of the way.

Marchildon, meanwhile, gave up four in the 3rd and was struggling in the 5th, giving up three more before he was pulled trailing 7 to 2.

Carl was summoned from the pen with two outs and Wally Judnich on first. With catcher Jake Early at the plate, Carl balked Judnich to second. He then pitched around Early, putting him on in order to face the pitcher, Kramer. Carl got his counterpart to pop out to first to end the inning.

Carl went the rest of the way, giving up only one hit and two walks in 3 1/3 innings. In his only at bat, he hit into a double play.

Two days later, on June 3rd, the A's were in Chicago to face the White Sox. Joe Coleman and Frank Papish traded goose eggs the first three innings. In the bottom of the 4th, Coleman coughed up three runs to the Sox on four singles and a walk.

Chet Laabs hit for Coleman in the 5th to no avail. In the bottom of the inning, Carl retired Thurman Tucker, Luke Appling, and Dave Philley in order. Future Hall of Famer Appling was forty years old this season. He had been playing since 1930. A perennial .300 hitter, this season was no exception as he faced a kid half his age.

Papish retired the A's in order in the 6th. Carl matched him in the bottom of the inning, retiring Jake Jones, Bob Kennedy, and Cass Michaels in order.

Papish continued his dominance in the 7th. Carl gave up a single to Floyd Baker, but then got Mike Tresh to fly out, and Papish to ground into a double play.

In the 8th, Carl stayed in and batted against Papish. He made an out, as did Joost and Valo. Once again, Carl retired Tucker, Appling, and Philley in order.

Frank Papish then quickly finished off the last three Athletics, completing a brilliant three-hit shutout.

Carl had thrown four innings of one-hit ball, dropping his ERA to a measly 1.72.

On Friday June 6th, the third anniversary of D-Day, the A's had evened their record to 21-21. They were in Cleveland to face the Indians at Municipal Stadium. Veteran Mel Harder was on the hill for the Indians. He had been a twenty-game-winner in 1934 and 1935, and had tallied over 200 wins in his career. He was opposed by Bob Savage.

Savage struggled early, tagged for six runs in 2 1/3. Jim Hegan and Dale Mitchell had both hit home runs by the time Carl entered with one out in the 3rd and the bases loaded.

First up was Ken Keltner. He hit a pop fly to first. Ferris Fain ran it down in foul territory, but Metkovich was able to score from third. It was now 6 to 0. Jim Hegan hit a grounder to third to end the inning.

In the top of the 5th, the A's scored twice, once on a Hank Majeski home run. Carl batted in the inning, but grounded out.

George Metkovich greeted Carl with a double to lead off the 5th. Shortstop, player-manager, and future Hall-of-Farmer Lou Boudreau followed with a grounder to first for an out. Eddie Robinson then touched Carl for a single, scoring Metkovich. Joe Gordon, recently of the Yankees, flied out to center. After Keltner singled to put runners at the corners, Hegan fouled out to end the inning.

The teams exchanged zeros in the 6th. Carl retired Harder, Peck, and Mitchell in sequence.

Carl led off the 7th, tapping back to the mound for the first out. Harder then retired the side after Joost walked. Back on the bump, Carl got two quick outs as Metkovich and Boudreau posed no threat. Robinson knocked another single into right. With Gordon at the plate, Robinson advanced to second on a wild pitch. Carl pitched around Gordon, walking him, but he then walked Keltner to load the bases. Fortunately, he got Hegan to fly out to right to end the inning.

In the 8th, Sam Chapman hit a two-run home run to chase Harder. But the A's could pull no closer than 7 to 4. In the bottom of the inning Carl got Klieman, Peck, and Mitchell to ground out in order.

The Athletics posed no threat in the 9th, dropping their record to below .500. Carl had yielded one run in 5 1/3 innings. Connie Mack must have seen enough. The young hurler had shown some moxie in back-to-back extended outings. Feeling he was stretched out, and on a roll, Mack named him the starter to face the first-place Tigers in Detroit on June 11th for the second game of the doubleheader.

Carl's mound opponent was Hal White. The two exchanged zeros for the first six innings. The A's then broke through in the 6th, scoring four—two on a double by Sam Chapman.

47

6/11/47
Carl's a first
start is a shutout
against first place Tigers

It was more than enough for Carl, who was wildly effective, scattering seven hits and seven walks in a complete-game shutout. It was his first major league win) The A's were now 25-24, in 4th place.

Back in Philadelphia on June 17th, Carl took his turn—once again against the Tigers. This time, he faced Al Benton.

Through the first six innings, Carl yielded only two hits, retiring both runners on double plays. Benton matched him frame by frame until the bottom of the 6th. Elmer Valo singled to center. Adams then sacrificed Valo to 2nd. Chapman flied out to right, advancing Valo to 3rd. Buddy Rosar then grounded to third baseman George Kell, who threw across the diamond to first baseman Roy Cullenbine, who dropped the ball. This allowed Valo to score the only run of the game. Pete Suder hit a fly to right to end the inning.

After getting Hoot Evers to fly out to left, Carl faced Vic Wertz. The rookie left fielder was from Reading, Pennsylvania, not far from Carl's hometown of Gratz. Wertz had earlier singled off of Carl. This time up, he put a charge into one, sending it to the deepest reaches of center field where Sam Chapman ran it down. Perhaps a bit rattled, Carl walked Pat Mullin and then gave up a single to George Kell. The runners moved up on the throw from right, putting men on second and third with two outs. Cullenbine then stepped to the dish. Catcher Buddy Rosar let a Carl offering get past him, allowing Mullin to score and Kell to move to 3rd. Cullenbine then hit a ball that tested Pete Suder's range, allowing Kell to score, but Roy was caught in a rundown and retired at 2nd. The A's now trailed the Tigers 2 to 1.

The Athletics got them right back in the bottom of the inning. The team added four runs on two two-run doubles by Valo and Chapman. Carl scored one of the runs after getting a free pass.

Carl settled down to retire Swift, pinch hitter Doc Cramer, and Lake, preserving his 5 to 2 lead. Despite a couple singles in the bottom of the frame against Dizzy Trout, the A's were held scoreless.

Carl then took the hill for the 9th. He walked Mayo, but got Evers to hit into a double play. Vic Wertz stepped in again, and ripped a double to right. Carl then walked Mullin and faced future Hall of Famer George Kell with two men on and two out. Kell was the tying run at the plate. He had been traded from the Athletics the prior season for Barney McCosky. The right-handed Kell launched a bomb to deep left field. McCosky gave chase. The 24,000+ fans in the stands gasped as Barney reeled it in for the final out. Carl was now 2-0. He had pitched another complete game, this one a five-hitter, giving up only two runs.

The White Sox were in town as Carl took his next turn on Sunday June 22nd. It was the second game of a doubleheader. Chicago had won the first game 1 to 0 behind Bob Gillespie. A fine outing by Jessie Flores was wasted by the A's. In game two, Carl faced Joe Haynes.

Neither team scored in the first three innings. Carl added another zero in the 4th. Haynes was replaced by Earl Harrist. He was doing fine until Sam Chapman knocked a double with two out. With Buddy Rosar at the plate, Harrist uncorked a wild pitch, and Chapman rushed home for a 1-0 lead.

The teams exchanged zeros for the 5th and the 6th. Carl also retired the Sox in order in the 7th, including Rudy York who had been traded from the Red Sox the prior week.

The A's added two more runs in the bottom of the 7th thanks to some sloppy play and a double by Hank Majeski. Carl now had a 3 to 0 cushion. It would be all he needed. Despite manager Ted Lyons' pinch hitting maneuvers, Carl mowed them down in order, including getting Luke Appling for the last out.

Carl had just tossed a four-hit shutout for his third consecutive complete-game win. He was now 3-0 and his ERA had plummeted to 1.12. People were talking about twenty-year-old Carl Scheib in Philadelphia:

Work of Scheib Is Current Talk Of Major Loops

PHILADELPHIA (AP) — Young Carl Scheib won't reach voting age in 1947, but he currently is the owner of a pitching record that if continued, will make him a top candidate for "rookie of the year."

The 20-year-old pitching wonder of Connie Mack's Philadelphia Athletics made his debut as a starter two weeks ago. As of now, he owns three victories, no defeats, has given up a mere 22 hits in 43 innings and has yielded only two runs—both unearned.

Scheib worked his third straight complete game Sunday against the Chicago White Sox, and made it his third consecutive victory, of which two were shutouts. He allowed only four hits and no runs In achieving a 3-0 victory against the Pale Hose.

49

6/27/47
Carl faces
Joe D + 38,000 fans

Never in the Minors

The big right-hander never pitched in the minors. Some five years ago, he came down to Philadelphia from his home in Gratz, in the heart of the Pennsylvania Dutch section, and became a batting-practice pitcher for the Mackmen, later seeing a little relief duty.

That kept him busy until 1945 when he went into the Army. He won 11 of the New Cumberland Army Base's 12 games, and might have won the other If he hadn't been scrubbing floors in a barracks.

Next up for Carl was the Yankees who were in town on Friday afternoon, June 27th. The park was packed with over 38,000 fans to see young Carl face the first place Bronx Bombers and former MVP hurler Spurgeon "Spud" Chandler. Now 39, old Spud had gone 20-4 in 1943 with a 1.64 ERA, including 20 complete games and 5 shut outs. He nearly repeated this feat in 1946, going 20-8, 2.10. He entered the game 7-4, versus Carl's 3-0.

In the top of the 1st, the Philly Phenom rolled through the first three batters, retiring Snuffy Stirnweiss, Tommy Henrich, and Johnny Lindell.

Eddie Joost led off the A's 1st with a single off of Chandler. Anticipating a low-scoring game, Barney McCosky bunted Joost to second. Elmer Valo then hit a ball to deep short, reaching first on a single. Men were now on first and third for Ferris Fain. The rookie first baseman was no match for the crafty old Spud. Fain tapped a ball to Stirnweiss at second, who flipped to Phil Rizzuto, who tossed to George McQuinn for the 4-6-3 double play.

The Yankee Clipper, Joe DiMaggio was first up for New York. At age 32, the center fielder was in the midst of his third MVP season. He had missed three seasons to the war, but was back in 1946, as good as ever. He was even better in 1947.

Perhaps thinking a little too much about the man in the box, Carl walked DiMaggio. George McQuinn followed. While Carl concentrated on the batter, DiMaggio took off for second, arriving safely. It was one of only three stolen bases he would tally that season. Carl then got McQuinn to pop up to first.

Third baseman Billy Johnson stepped up to the plate. He was enjoying his only All-Star season. He singled to right field, advancing DiMaggio to third.

Catcher Aaron Robinson, also in the midst of his only All-Star season, batted next. The veteran drove a ball to deep center field, which was hauled in by Sam Chapman. The Yankee Clipper tagged up and sailed home for the first run of the game.

Next up was Phil Rizzuto. Known as "The Scooter," Rizzuto had given up three of his first six seasons to war duty. The future Hall of Famer slashed a double to left-center off of Carl, plating Johnson with the second run. Pitcher Spud Chandler was next. He ended the inning with a ground-out to shortstop.

Chapman, Rosar, and Suder failed against Chandler in the bottom of the 2nd. In the top of the 3rd, Carl gave up a double to Stirnweiss, but he followed it by retiring Henrich, Lindell, and DiMaggio on flies—though Joe's was to deep left.

Chandler and Carl exchanged zeros through the 5th inning. In the top of the 6th, Carl was greeted by a long home run off the bat of Tommy Henrich. After Johnny Lindell popped out to first, Joe DiMaggio followed with a triple to left-center. He wasn't on the bag long, as George McQuinn hit a fly to left. Again, Joe tagged up and scored. The Yankees were now up 4 to 0. Billy Johnson was retired for the final out.

In the bottom of the 6th, Carl helped his own cause with a lead-off single, but Joost, McCosky, and Valo failed to reach base, ending the inning.

Carl started the 7th by getting Aaron Robinson to fly out to left. The Scooter then singled to left. Chandler came up and bunted Rizzuto over to second. With two outs, Rizzuto was in scoring position. Snuffy Stirnweiss stepped in, but Carl balked Rizzuto to third. Snuffy drew a walk, putting men on first and third. Tommy Henrich followed with a double, scoring Rizzuto, and moving Stirnweiss to third. Johnny Lindell ended the inning with a ground-out, but the Yanks now led 5 to 0.

Fain, Chapman, and Rosar went 1-2-3 against Chandler in the 7th. Carl then faced DiMaggio to start the 8th. DiMaggio singled to left. McQuinn then singled to right. Fortunately for the A's, Johnson grounded into a double play and Robinson grounded to first to end the threat.

Trailing 5 to 0 in the bottom of the 8th, Mack sent George Binks up to hit for Carl. While they managed a run, the Yankees added two in the 9th to close out the victory 7 to 1. The A's fell to 31-30, in third place, while the Yankees increased their lead in the American League.

It was Carl's first loss of the season. He had pitched eight innings, giving up five runs on nine hits and two walks. Spud Chandler scattered eight hits for his eighth win.

1947

WONDER BOY

Fenway Park, filled with nearly 33,000 fans, greeted Carl and the A's on Wednesday, July 2nd at 2:23 PM. Carl was slated to pitch against veteran Denny Galehouse who was pitching much better since being acquired from the Browns back on June 20th.

The A's jumped out to a 1 to 0 lead in the top of the 1st against Denny. Carl then took his turn, but after retiring Wally Moses, he walked Johnny Pesky. Ted Williams stepped in against the rookie hurler. The Splendid Splinter, at age 28, was on his way to hitting .343 for the season. He would also lead the American League in home runs and RBI, taking his second triple crown. He had lost three seasons to the war, missing 1943 through 1945, but he returned in his prime and did not seem to be missing a beat. Suffice to say, Ted Williams could hit! Today was no exception. The Splinter ripped a ball out of Fenway for a two-run homer.

Bobby Doerr followed Williams. The second baseman was an All-Star in his own right, packing some pop for a middle infielder. He would also go on to the Hall of Fame. Doerr wasn't fooled by Carl's offerings and launched another ball into the seats. The Sox had hit back-to-back home runs, and led by three in the 1st.

The A's tied the game in the 2nd, and Carl held the Sox scoreless for the next three innings.

In the bottom of the 5th, Boston posted a run to take the lead, but the Athletics countered with three in the top of the 6th. Carl yielded single runs in the 6th and 7th, allowing the Sox to tie things up again, 6 to 6.

With two outs in the 8th, Wally Moses tripled. Mack summoned Bob Savage to take his place, the game tied at six. Savage got out of trouble, and in the 9th, Sam Chapman singled in Barney McCosky to give Philadelphia the win.

Carl got a no-decision that day, giving up six runs in 7 2/3 innings. Had he been able to get one more out, he would have been credited with the victory, despite allowing fifteen base runners. This was the second rocky start in a row, following a fantastic month. Something was amiss.

Larry Doby made his debut for the Cleveland Indians on July 5th, becoming the first black player to play in the American League, fully integrating Major League Baseball.

The Yankees were up next for Carl. He was slated to make his first start in the House that Ruth Built in the first game of a doubleheader on Sunday July 6th. Randy Gumpert, a veteran long

52

man and spot starter for the Yanks, was handed the ball by manager Bucky Harris.

Gumpert was a little wild to start the affair, walking Joost and McCosky, but he retired the meat of the A's lineup in order.

Carl then strode to the mound. A couple weeks ago, he had started the game by retiring the Yanks in order. Today, this was not to be.

Snuffy Stirnweiss was leading off for the Yankees. The second-sacker was an All-Star in 1946. This followed two incredible seasons in 1944 and 1945 when he led the league in hits, triples, runs, and stolen bases and nabbed the batting title in 1945 to boot. While he never hit close to .300 again after the war years, Snuffy was still a dangerous hitter. The speedy Stirnweiss ripped a triple to right.

Tommy Henrich followed with an infield single, holding Stirnweiss on third. Carl then settled down to strike out Johnny Lindell. But the Yankee Clipper, Joe DiMaggio was next up. He blasted a ball out of the stadium for a three-run homer. George McQuinn then singled, and Billy Johnson doubled, putting men on second and third. There was still only one out.

Up to the plate stepped catcher Lawrence "Yogi" Berra, a 22-year-old rookie, who was platooning with Aaron Robinson. The following season, Berra would begin his stretch of fifteen consecutive All-Star appearances, including three MVPs. Berra added fuel to the fire, pulling a single into right field, scoring McQuinn and Johnson. It was now 5 to 0.

"Berra was a great hitter," said Carl years later. "He was so well-balanced. He could hit low or high pitches for power."

Phil Rizzuto followed Berra by flying to center. Pitcher Gumpert then finished the inning with a ground out. The Yankees had batted around on Carl in the 1st, plating five. It was like batting practice.

Randy Gumpert made quick work of the A's in the 2nd, barely giving Carl time to recover from the 1st inning debacle. In the bottom of the 2nd, Stirnweiss led off again, this time grounding out. Henrich and Lindell followed with singles, setting up two men for DiMaggio to hammer another. This time, however, Joe didn't hit it sweet, instead flying out to center. George McQuinn followed with a single up the middle, scoring Henrich, but Johnson ended the inning on a fly.

While improved, Carl was still down 6 to 0, and had given up three hits in the inning. Carl struck out at the plate to begin the top of the 3rd. Again, the Athletics couldn't solve Gumpert.

1947
Carl is "tipping" his pitches

Yogi was first up for the Yanks in the 3rd. He turned on a ball and sent it into the left field bleachers for a homer. After getting the eight and nine hitters, Rizzuto and Gumpert, Carl yielded a single to Stirnweiss. Tommy Henrich then followed with a double to right, driving in Snuffy for the eighth run. Johnny Lindell was out on a fly ball to end the inning.

The A's plated a couple runs in the 4th, but Carl was done for the day. It was an ugly line: 3 innings, 12 hits, including 3 home runs, and 8 runs allowed. The A's would lose this one 8 to 2, Carl being pegged with his second loss, his ERA doubling to 3.36 with just two bad starts.

How did the young phenom from Philadelphia suddenly go from unhittable to what looked like a batting practice pitcher? Carl did not have a sore arm at this time, and his stuff was as good as ever. It's almost like the hitters knew what was coming.

The following season, in the June 30th issue of *The Sporting News*, columnist Cliff Kachline reported that the Yankees were onto Carl's pitches at that time. According to Kachline, "it was learned that Charlie Dressen, clever signal stealing coach of the Yanks, had 'called' every pitch made by the youngster-fast ball or curve-by the manner in which he held the ball."

From the looks of things, the Yankees weren't the only ones who had figured Carl out. Ted Williams and the Red Sox had likely done the same the prior week as well.

Carl wasn't called again until the following Sunday, July 13th. He was to start in Detroit against Virgil Trucks for the second game of the doubleheader. Carl was effectively wild this day, walking six, and surrendering nine hits and four runs, three earned. Trucks was better, holding the A's to only two runs on five hits. It was Carl's third loss, but he was not hit as hard.

The following Sunday, Carl was again tapped to take the mound, this time against the White Sox and Frank Papish.

The A's jumped on Papish, batting around and scoring four in the 1st. Carl held the Sox scoreless until the bottom of the 3rd, when Appling drove in Baker with a single.

The Athletics added two in the 4th, Carl singling and scoring one of the runs. He then shut down the White Sox for another inning.

Struggling with his control, the White Sox got to Carl in the 5th. After a double by Kolloway, Carl walked two to load the bases, with only one out. Cass Michaels hit the next one to Eddie Joost, who let the ball go past for an error. Two runs scored on the play. With men now on first and third, Taffy Wright singled, driving in another. It would be Carl's last pitch for the day. He was pulled for Bob Savage, leading 6 to 4. The A's added one in the 9th to finish a 7 to 4 victory. Savage was credited with the win because Carl did not make it through the 5th, albeit due to the fielding error by the shortstop.

On July 26th, Virgil Trucks and the Tigers were back in town to face the A's. Jesse Flores got the start for the A's. Trucks and Flores exchanged goose eggs for three innings. In the top of the 4th, Detroit rallied for four runs, chasing Flores. Carl was summoned for the 5th, and it seemed like batting practice had begun. The Tigers sent eight men to the plate, tallying five singles, a double, and four runs. If George Kell had not been thrown out at home by center fielder Sam Chapman, the inning may have continued a while longer, and the score would have been worse.

Carl was really wild in the 6th. He gave up a double while walking two to load the bases. Then he hit Kell with a pitch, scoring a run. A double by Cramer cleared the bases, making it 11 to 0. Mack had seen enough. Carl's line was 1 1/3 innings, eight hits, two walks, and seven earned runs. His ERA exploded to 4.24.

Carl was back in the bullpen now, until he could figure things out. On August 4th, Philadelphia was at Yankee Stadium for a well-attended Monday afternoon game.

The A's jumped on starter Randy Gumpert for three runs in the 1st. The Yanks then chipped away at starter Bill Dietrich, scoring one in the 1st, and another in the 2nd before he was pulled with men on second and third and one out.

Carl was summoned from the bullpen to replace Dietrich. First up was left fielder Yogi Berra, who reached on an error by first baseman McQuinn, scoring a run. Carl was then able to get catcher Aaron Robinson to ground into a double play to end the inning.

The Yanks got another run off of Carl in the 3rd. Billy Johnson singled to right with one out. Johnny Lindell then stepped to the plate. Lindell, a former All-Star in 1943, was a steady center fielder for the team. He ripped a double, scoring Johnson. Carl then got two ground outs to end the inning.

The Athletics got hot in the 5th, scoring five runs off of two New York hurlers, while batting around. Carl now had an 8 to 4 cushion. He went the rest of the way, yielding only one more run on a Berra sacrifice fly. The A's added an insurance run as Carl drove in one on a ground out.

The Athletics won 9 to 5, and Carl earned the win pitching the final 7 2/3 innings. He scattered seven hits, walked two, and gave up two earned runs. His record was now 4-3, with his ERA dropping to 4.08.

While Joe Dimaggio was not in the lineup this day, it did appear Carl was through with tipping his pitches—at least against the Yankees.

Nine days later, Philadelphia was back in New York. Carl was back in the rotation, tapped to face Vic Raschi, a rising young pitcher who was 5-0. Raschi would go on to win 20 games three seasons in a row for the Yanks, from 1949 through 1951.

The A's went down in the 1st without scoring. Then the Yankee batting practice began. Carl walked Stirnweiss and Rizzuto before Berra tripled them both in. Allie Clark then grounded out, scoring Berra. Carl escaped the inning, but gave up three runs.

In the 2nd, three of the first four batters got hits, scoring a run and leaving men on first and second with one out. Mack pulled Carl in favor of Russ Christopher.

The Yanks got three more hits off of Christopher, increasing their lead to 7 to 0.

The final score was 8 to 2 in favor of New York. Raschi was credited with his sixth win. Carl fell to 4-4, his ERA soaring to 4.62 after bleeding six runs in an inning and a third.

As the A's arrived at Brigg's Stadium in Detroit to face the Tigers in a doubleheader on Sunday afternoon, August 24th, the two teams were tied for 3rd place. A 6 to 2 win by Virgil Trucks over Joe Coleman broke the tie for the Tigers. Looking to pull even in the 2nd game, the Athletics sent Carl to the hill against future Hall of Famer Hal Newhouser. Prince Hal, as he was known, had won back-to-back MVPs in 1944 and 1945 with 29-9 and 25-9 records, respectively. He followed that up with a 26-9 season in 1946. This season, he was battling to get back to .500 and seemed a little easier to hit than in past seasons.

The two dueled into the early evening. The A's took a 2 to 0 lead in the 2nd, only to be tied in the bottom of the 3rd. By the bottom of the 8th, the A's were back on top by two, 4 to 2.

In that inning Carl walked Roy Cullenbine. Vic Wertz followed, lining a two-run homer into the right field stands to tie the game.

The A's failed to score in the top of the 9th, and Mack allowed Carl to pitch the bottom of the inning. He quickly got two outs, and it appeared the game might go into extra innings. At that point, Eddie Lake doubled, and Cullenbine walked, bringing up Wertz again. Mack ordered Carl to walk Wertz, loading the bases. Vic had three hits in the game, and was crushing Carl's pitches. Pat Mullin then ended the game with a single to first base on which Fain could not make a play.

It was a tough loss for Carl but an interesting duel with Hal Newhouser. His record fell to 4-5, but his ERA inched up to only 4.67.

On Sunday August 31st, the Athletics were back in Boston for an afternoon game against the Red Sox. Joe Dobson was on the hill for the Sox, in the midst of his finest 18-win season. Carl was handed the ball for the Mackmen.

The A's couldn't get it going against Dobson, who had his way with everybody but Pete Suder (3 for 3) and Carl (2 for 2). The Sox chipped away at Carl, scoring one in the 1st, two in the 5th, and two in the 6th, before he was pulled with no one out. Doerr and Pellagrini had doubled. Johnny Pesky had tripled, and Ted Williams hit his 27th home run of the season.

The loss dropped Carl to 4-6 and pushed his ERA to 4.88.

Ten days later, on September 10th, the last place Browns were in town to face the A's. Fred Sanford was on the mound for the visitors, facing Dick Fowler.

The two battled to a 2 to 2 deadlock through six innings. In the top of the 7th, the Browns broke through.

Ray Coleman led off with a triple. Les Moss singled him in. Sanford grounded into what was looking like a double play until Eddie Joost's throw sailed wide, allowing Sanford to scamper to second. Bob Dillinger then singled in Sanford, chasing Fowler with the Browns up 4 to 2.

Carl entered the game, and got Al Zarilla to fly out to deep left, far enough for Dillinger to tag and move to second. Johnny Berardino followed with a single, scoring Dillinger. Left fielder Jeff Heath then stepped into the box.

Heath had been an All-Star for Cleveland twice during the war years. He was in the midst of his best home run season, on his way to a career-high of 27. This afternoon, he turned on one of Carl's offerings and sent it into the bleachers for a two-run blast. The A's now trailed 7 to 2.

1947
Rookie year
4-6 ERA 5.04

Carl would give up one more run as he mopped up the loss. Fred Sanford improved his record to 6-13. Fowler fell to 10-11. Carl's ERA surpassed 5.00.

On Sunday, September 14th, the A's won the first game of a doubleheader 11 to 9 against Lou Boudreau's Indians. Sam Chapman had gone 4 for 4 with a home run to lead the Athletics' attack.

Connie Mack tapped Carl to pitch the second game. His opponent on the mound was rookie Bob Kuzava, recently promoted from Baltimore of the International League.

The two battled to a 2 to 2 tie by the 8th inning. In the top of the 8th, Hank Edwards homered off Carl to give the Indians the lead. The A's tied it up in the bottom of the inning on Chapman's RBI single, chasing Kuzava.

In the 9th, the Indians scored a run on an error, taking the lead again. In the bottom of the inning, the A's started to rally against Al Gettel. Valo and Handley were on second and third with two out. Boudreau summoned Bob Lemon to try to save the game.

The young right-hander was in his second season, just prior to his incredible stretch where he would win twenty games seven times in nine seasons and make seven consecutive All-Star appearances. The future Hall of Famer and future New York Yankees manager toed the rubber. Rookie left fielder Austin Knickerbocker stepped into the box. The 48 at bats he totaled in 1947 would be the only ones of his career. Lemon fired, and Austin ripped a ball up the middle into center field. Handley scored the tying run, and Valo moved to third.

Sam Chapman, who had six hits on the day, stepped in next. Valo was the winning run at third. Knickerbocker danced off of first. Lemon fired again, and Chapman drove the ball to center field, right into the waiting glove of George Metkovich to end the inning.

The game was then called after nine innings due to curfew. Carl had thrown a complete game, yielding only three earned runs. It was one of his best starts of the season. His ERA dropped to 4.85.

Carl's last appearance in 1947 was at Fenway Park, in the second game of a double-dip. The A's had won the first game 9 to 3 as Phil Marchildon ran his record to 18-9. Bill Dietrich took the hill for the A's in the second game versus Earl Johnson.

Dietrich fell behind the Red Sox and was pulled for a pinch hitter in the top of the 5th trailing 3 to 1. Carl entered the game for the bottom of the 5th and had a wild inning, walking two and giving up three singles en route to yielding three runs. He did not continue into the 6th.

The season had a lot of ups and downs for Carl, not unexpected for a twenty-year-old rookie. His performance flipped like a switch from exceptional to terrible, most likely due to tipping his pitches. He then struggled to work out of the problem, losing his control, and over-throwing at times. Through June 22nd, Carl was 3-0 with a 1.12 ERA. The rest of the way, he was 1-6 with a 7.85 ERA.

Imagine what would have happened had one of the coaches or players on his own team noticed what he was doing and helped him to correct it. He may have had one of the great rookie seasons in major league history. Instead, he plummeted to 4-6 with a 5.04 ERA.

"We didn't have a very good team that year," Carl recalled in 2006, "I won three in a row and ended up four and six. It was tough winning in Philadelphia. Later in my career, I wanted to be an outfielder. I wanted to play the outfield real bad, which I thought I could do real well. But they always needed pitchers, so I suspect there's some irony here."

The Athletics finished above .500 at 78-76, in 5th place behind the pennant-winning New York Yankees.

Sam Chapman led all hitters with 14 home runs, Eddie Joost trailing by one. Barney McCosky led the team with a .328 batting average.

On the mound, Phil Marchildon led the team with a 19-9 record. Russ Christopher contributed 12 saves.

8.

PENNANT RACE

Early in the year, the A's signed amateur free agents Billy and
BILLY +Bobby Shantz. The brothers, from Pottstown, Pennsylvania, were
battery-mates.

Just before Philadelphia's spring camp opened in March,
1948, at West Palm Beach, Florida, Carl, married Georgene
Umholtz, a hometown girl, on February 25th. The right-hander
then rode the train to spring training with his bride.

Now twenty-one, it had been five years since Carl's debut as a
sixteen-year-old. He had been to war, and was now married. He
had also survived the ups and downs of his 1947 season, and was
right back in the Athletics' starting rotation.

He made his first appearance on Sunday April 25th in the first
game of a doubleheader against the Washington Senators at Shibe
Park. The A's had started well, winning three of the first five
games of the season. Washington had won four of five. Veteran
Sid Hudson was on the mound for the Nats, fresh off of his 9 to 1
victory against the Yankees.

Neither team scored in the 1st. In the top of the 2nd, the
Senators' Mickey Vernon led off with a double. Mickey would play
twenty seasons in the big leagues, mostly for Washington. He was
a seven-time All-Star, five of them happening from age 35 and
onward. He would win a batting title at age 35, hitting .335. In
1948, his age 30 season, the lanky first-baseman would make his
second All-Star appearance. Carl managed to leave him stranded
in scoring position as he retired three of the next four batters,
only Leon Culberson reaching on a walk.

The A's rallied for Carl in the bottom of the 2nd, scoring four
runs. Ferris Fain singled, followed by Hank Majeski's free pass.
Sam Chapman then bunted them into scoring position. Buddy
Rosar then singled both of them home. Pete Suder followed with a
single to left fielder Gil Coan, who threw wildly into second,
allowing the runners to move up. Carl then stepped to the plate
and whacked another single out to Coan, scoring both Rosar and
Suder, increasing the lead to 4 to 0. This would be the final score.
Carl scattered six hits en route to the complete-game shutout.

On Saturday, May 1ˢᵗ, the A's were in Washington for an afternoon contest. Both teams were sporting 5-5 records. Carl's mound opponent that day was Early Wynn, who would go on to win 300 games and enter the Hall of Fame. Wynn had won 17 games the prior season, making his first All-Star appearance. He would be traded to Cleveland after 1948, where he went on to greatness.

The two exchanged goose eggs until the bottom of the 3ʳᵈ, when catcher Jake Early led off with a double. After striking out Wynn, lead-off hitter Eddie Yost ripped a double to left, driving in Early. It would be the only run of the day for the Senators, who could not solve Carl.

The A's cruised to a 5 to 1 victory, bolstered by home runs from Eddie Joost and Hank Majeski. Carl threw another complete game, scattering eight hits and three walks. He was now 2-0.

The Saturday May 8ᵗʰ game against the White Sox at Shibe Park may have been the most fun game of Carl's big league career. The first-place A's were 9-5, having just beaten Bob Feller 8-5 on Thursday. Carl was tapped to face Orval Grove.

The Sox did not get to Carl in the 1ˢᵗ, but the A's sure did wake up Orval! They batted around, using four singles, two walks, and two sacrifice bunts, including a suicide squeeze, to generate five runs. It would be all the action Grove saw that day.

The scored stayed 5 to 0 until the bottom of the 5ᵗʰ. After reliever Frank Papish loaded the bases with a single and two free passes, Jim Goodwin was summoned from the pen. He gave up a single to Pete Suder, scoring two. Carl then followed with a double, knocking in one more. The A's added yet another run in the inning, handing Carl a 9 to 0 lead.

Finally, in the 6ᵗʰ, the White Sox scored on a couple hits and a ground out. In the 7ᵗʰ, they looked like they would get to Carl again. Luke Appling and Tony Lupien started the inning with back-to-back singles. Taffy Wright was up next. He lined a ball to second baseman Pete Suder, who tossed to Eddie Joost covering second, catching Appling off the bag. Joost then fired to Fain at first before Lupien could return to the base. The A's had just pulled off a triple play! Surely the baseball gods were favoring Carl this day.

Bob Gillespie replaced Goodwin, and exchanged zeros with Carl for a couple innings, until the bottom of the 8ᵗʰ. Gillespie, who had pitched well in the Texas League for Dallas in 1946, was

1948
Great start
for Carl + A's.

a spot starter and long man for the Sox. He had been 5-8 with a 4.73 ERA in 1947 and was struggling to stay in the big leagues in 1948. The A's weren't helping matters for him, either.

Valo, Fain, and Majeski hit consecutive singles off of Gillespie, loading the bases. He then walked Sam Chapman, forcing in a run. Mike Guerra followed with a sacrifice fly, scoring Fain. Pete Suder then worked a walk, bringing up Carl with the bases loaded and no one out, his team leading 11 to 1. Carl turned on a Gillespie offering and pulled it over the left field wall for a grand slam home run!

The A's added another run before Carl went to the mound in the bottom of the 9th. He made quick work of the Sox, including getting Luke Appling for the final out.

The A's and Carl were on top of the world. They were now 10-5, and Carl was the ace with 3 of those wins.

The A's won their next four games, increasing their lead over the Yankees. Very fittingly, they were at Yankee Stadium on Friday May 14th for Carl's next appearance, this time against Vic Raschi. Vic, in the midst of his first All-Star season, would win 19 games in 1948. He would take a no-hitter into the 5th, when Hank Majeski singled. Raschi was superb, limiting the A's to only three hits and three walks en route to a complete game shutout.

Carl, on the other hand, limited the Yankees to only four hits and three walks. Unfortunately for him, two of those hits were home runs—by Johnny Lindell and Yogi Berra. The performance was good enough to win on most days and significantly better than his troubles the prior season. He was now 3-1, and the Yankees were a game closer in the standings.

By Thursday May 20th, the A's had slipped into second place, now 16-8. They were in Detroit to face the Tigers. Fred Hutchinson, just off a superb 18-win season for Detroit, was Carl's mound opponent.

Sam Chapman ripped a two-run homer in the 2nd to give the A's the lead. Carl, meanwhile, held the Tigers scoreless through three.

But, the Tigers figured him out in the 4th, getting a run, and in the 5th, taking the lead on a Bob Swift two-run homer. A run in the 6th was also charged to Carl who was replaced by Bob Savage, losing 4 to 2. It was a tough outing for Carl, giving up 12 hits in only five innings. Both he and Hutchinson sported 3-2 records at the end of the contest.

Five days later, on May 25th, Carl took his turn in Chicago against the White Sox. He was opposed by Bill Wight, who would end up losing twenty games in 1948. Carl only lasted four innings in this one, giving up six hits and two runs before he was replaced by Bob Savage. He did contribute a double at the plate. The A's won 4 to 3, Savage picking up the win. The A's were only a half game back in second place.

Next up for Carl, the Yankees were at Shibe Park for a doubleheader on Sunday May 30th. Carl started against Eddie Lopat who had been traded in the off-season from the White Sox for Bill Wight, Aaron Robinson, and Fred Bradley. He would be a steady force on the mound for the Yankees through 1954, including a 21-win season in 1951.

Carl and Lopat exchanged zeros until the top of the 3rd. Lopat and Bobby Brown started the inning with singles. Tommy Henrich then bunted them into scoring position. Charlie Keller hit a short fly to center into the waiting glow of Sam Chapman, the runners holding. It looked like Carl would get out of the inning, but Joe DiMaggio thought differently. He lined a single to left scoring both runners, and advanced to second on an errant throw. Yogi Berra followed with a triple, plating DiMaggio. Billy Johnson then drove in Berra with a double. Carl walked McQuinn, and ended the inning by getting Rizzuto to ground out. The Yankees took the field with a 4 to 0 lead.

The Athletics tied things up with two runs in the 4th, and two more in the 5th on a Peter Suder home run. But the Yankees were back on top in the 7th when they added a run. With one out, Henrich doubled and Charlie Keller singled him home. Carl ended the inning by inducing DiMaggio to ground into a double play.

The A's manufactured two runs in the bottom of the 8th, chasing Lopat from the game, and giving themselves a 6 to 5 lead. Valo and Majeski each had RBI singles, helped by two sacrifice bunts in the inning.

Carl took the mound in the top of the 9th with the chance to win the game. He got Johnny Lindell to fly out to center. Bobby Brown then fouled out to Majeski at third. Tommy Henrich stepped in the box. This season would be his finest, leading the league in triples and runs scored while hitting .308 and knocking in 100. The 35-year-old right fielder launched a Carl pitch into the right field seats to tie the game. He finished the inning when Charlie Keller flied out to center.

In the bottom of the 9th, Karl Drews retired Guerra and Suder, bringing Carl up to the plate with two outs and the game tied in the bottom of the 9th. Connie Mack allowed Carl to hit. Carl was batting over .300. He did not disappoint, hitting one the opposite way into right field for a single. Skeeter Webb was called upon to pinch run for Carl, ending his day.

Eddie Joost followed with a single, putting Webb in scoring position, but Rookie Don White grounded out to end the threat.

Nels Potter retired DiMaggio, Berra, and Johnson in order in the 10th. In the bottom of the 10th, with one out, Ferris Fain doubled. Following a walk to Majeski, Sam Chapman hit a walk-off single to right, winning the game for the Athletics.

Philadelphia was now 25-10 atop the American League. While Carl had a no-decision, his team had won, and he had contributed with the bat.

On Friday, June 4th, the White Sox were at Shibe Park. Carl was tapped to face Bill Wight. He lasted only three innings, yielding three hits, three walks, and three runs. He exited the game behind 3 to 1. Bob Savage and Lou Brissie both pitched three shutout innings. Brissie earned the win when the A's rallied for three runs in the bottom of the 7th. The Athletics won, improving to 27-14, still leading the American League.

Carl was on the mound again on June 9th. Detroit was in town, and it was Dizzy Trout's turn to take the hill. Carl blanked the Tigers in the 1st, but Dizzy gave up three in the bottom of the 1st. Carl was able to front-run until the top of the 6th.

Neil Berry and Eddie Lake singled against Carl. Former teammate and future Hall of Famer George Kell then followed with a three-run home run to tie the game.

"I had him struck out," recalled Carl years later, "but the ump called it a ball. When Kell hit the next pitch out, I called the ump an SOB, but he didn't hear me."

Carl then retired Wakefield, but walked Hoot Evers. At that point, Earle Mack pulled him in favor of Nels Potter. Nels ended the threat, but couldn't carry it through the next inning. In the end, the Tigers won 7 to 4. Carl received a no-decision. The A's had lost their fifth straight, and had fallen to third place.

On Sunday June 13th, the St. Louis Browns were in town for a doubleheader at Shibe Park. St. Louis won the first game 7 to 5,

Nels Potter giving up the lead as the Browns put up six runs in the 8th inning.

Carl took the mound in the second game. His opponent was Bryan Stephens.

The two exchanged zeros through the first three innings. In the top of the 4th, the Browns got to Carl for a run. Bob Dillinger led off with a triple. Sam Dente then knocked him in with a sacrifice fly. Carl escaped any further damage.

The A's tied things up in the bottom of the 5th as Chapman scored on Suder's single. The A's then took the lead in the bottom of the 7th. Ferris Fain singled, and moved to second on a wild pitch. Hank Majeski then singled, putting men on first and third. Guerra walked to load the bases, bringing Pete Suder to the plate. He hit a fly ball to center deep enough to score Fain. The throw from center fielder Paul Lehner was late. Catcher Les Moss threw to second to nail Guerra, ending the inning. The run counted.

The A's added an unearned run in the 8th, locking up the complete game victory for Carl. He was now 4-2 with a 3.07 ERA. Philadelphia was 31-20, three games out of first.

This same day, Babe Ruth's number three was retired at Yankee Stadium. It was the Babe's last public appearance.

Four days later, on June 17th, the Athletics were in Detroit to face the Tigers. Once again, Carl was to face Dizzy Trout.

Both teams were held scoreless until the 6th. The visiting A's scored once. In the bottom of the inning, the Tigers tallied two to take the lead, Dick Wakefield hitting a two-run single against Carl.

Philadelphia added four more runs over the final two innings, propelling Carl to a 5 to 2 victory. Carl helped his own cause with two hits and a run scored. On the mound, he pitched a complete game, yielding six hits, three walks, and two runs, though none were earned. His record improved to 5-2 with a 2.72 ERA. The A's remained in second, two games behind.

The following article by Clifford Kachline appeared in *The Sporting News* on June 18th:

Used in Bat Drills, Then as Reliever, Young Pitcher, Now 21, Off to Good Start for Second Season in Row

Connie Mack, 85-year-old manager of the astounding Athletics, has a question—a $6,400 question.

1948
can Scheib
be consistent?

If the answer is "Yes," no one will get the $6,400. If the answer is "No," more than 30 A's will win the pennant and get the $6,400.

The question: Is Carl Scheib's spectacular showing this year a flash in the pan, as it was last year, or does the 21-year-old right-hander have the poise, the experience, and the determination to continue his great work to the finish of the season?

Last year Scheib won his first three starts in magnificent fashion. Then he was whipped by the Yankees, his confidence was shaken and he never was able to get going again. This season he again won his first three starts and then was beaten by the Yankees and Tigers.

But the kid came back to win his next three starts—two against the Browns sandwiching one at Detroit and on two of these occasions, as on two earlier ones, his victory wrote an end to a Mack losing streak.

Thus the strong-armed Pennsylvania Dutchman loomed as that rare gem among pitchers, a "stopper" –one who is at his best when his team seems at its worst.

After his defeat by the New Yorkers last year, it was learned that Charlie Dressen, clever signal-stealing coach of the Yanks, had "called" every pitch made by the youngster—fast ball or curve—by the manner in which he held the ball.

After his defeat by the Yanks this year, a 3 to 0 setback, caused by home runs by Johnny Lindell and Yogi Berra, Dressen said he had been unable to "call" a pitch, that Scheib hid his pitches well and the Yanks were fortunate to win.

Tagged for McCahan Spot

If the youngster can keep rolling this season and contribute his share of victories, he should be able to take up the slack caused by the ailing arm of Bill McCahan. With Phil Marchildon, Joe Coleman, Dick Fowler, Lou Brissie, and Scheib able to work in turn, the A's will be in the scrap to the finish.

A new windup, a new way of bending and swinging his body on his right leg to get the full force of his 190 pounds behind his pitch, has been a big help to Scheib in his early victories.

He has the stuff, the size, and the experience to be a success this year. At 21 he has been a major league pitcher for five years.

Mack Gives Brucker Credit

Connie Mack takes no credit for the development of Carl in the past two years. "Scheib is strictly Coach Earle Brucker's property," said the boss of the A's. "He brought him along, taught him the tricks of pitching, how to hide his pitches, where to throw his stuff so that it would be most effective. All I do is ask Earle if he is ready. If he says he is, in goes Scheib."

Brucker, on the other hand, passes all the credit to *SCHEIB* Scheib himself. "All any coach can do is tell a fellow what is right," said Earle. "It is up to him to do it. And Scheib has been doing it. He learned a great change of pace overseas— I merely try to tell him when to pitch it. He's made the grade himself."

Before spring training this year, Scheib was married to Georgene Umholtz of Hegins, Pa., and took his bride to West Palm Beach.

For a time it looked as if the A's might have a brother battery, as Carl's brother Paul is a catcher. But Paul was shunted to Moline last year.

Connie Mack said Scheib reminded him of Red Ruffing, formerly of the Yankees. Ruffing won 15 and lost eight his sixth year in the big league. Mr. Mack will be satisfied if Scheib can do the same.

On June 22nd, the Athletics were at Sportsman's Park to play the St. Louis Browns. Rookie Ned Garver was tapped to face Carl.

The two battled to a 3 to 3 tie until the 8th inning, when the A's plated four runs. Carl then took a 7 to 3 lead into the bottom of the 9th. He gave up three more runs, narrowly escaping with a 7 to 6 victory. He scattered 12 hits and 3 walks in keeping the A's four games back in the pennant race. Carl improved his record to 6-2, his ERA rising a bit to 3.06.

The last place White Sox next played the Athletics at Comiskey Park. Orval Grove took the mound against Carl on June 27th in the first game of a doubleheader.

The A's jumped on Grove for two runs in the 1st. In the bottom of the 3rd, the White Sox, due to three hits and some sloppy

1948

defense, scored three runs to take the lead. The 3 to 2 score held until the top of the 4th when Philadelphia tallied four runs, one of them scored by Carl. The A's had handed Carl a 6 to 3 lead. In the bottom of the 5th, Luke Appling knocked in two with a double, to pull the Sox within a run, 6 to 5. But Carl would hold the lead the rest of the way.

Carl had pitched the A's back into first place, winning his 7th game. He was now 7-2 with a 3.05 ERA, two of the runs allowed were unearned.

Sunday July 4th, the Athletics were in Boston to face the Red Sox. Ellis Kinder was the starting pitcher matched with Carl. A late-bloomer, Kinder had been a 31-year-old rookie in 1946, after a long minor league career. He would peak the following season with 23 wins, and would pitch until age 42, becoming a dependable closer late in his career.

This was a game the A's would like to forget. The Sox jumped to a 1 to 0 lead in the 2nd, and added a run in the 5th. In the top of the 6th, Philadelphia handed Carl a 3 to 2 lead, thanks to a Hank Majeski home run.

Carl took the lead into the bottom of the 6th, but gave up three more runs, and was lifted with two outs. Bubba Harris ended the rally, but allowed an incredible 12 runs in the next third of an inning in the 7th. Bill McCahan allowed two more before putting out the fire. The Red Sox had exploded for 14 runs in one inning. They would win the game 19 to 5, dropping the A's to a game behind in the pennant race.

Johnny Pesky had five RBI in the game. Billy Goodman went 4 for 6 with 4 RBI. Even Ellis Kinder had three hits and three runs scored. Carl, who had given up Bobby Doerr's home run among the 5 runs he allowed, was not the losing pitcher. That was Harris. What a line for the rookie reliever: 2/3 of an inning, 6 hits, 5 walks, and 12 runs allowed. He faced 14 batters—12 of them scored.

The lack of a solid bullpen for the A's would continue to plague them. On July 8th, Carl was called to start against the Yankees at Yankee Stadium. Allie Reynolds was named the starter for New York. Allie, known as "Superchief," had won 19 games in 1947 and was on his way to a solid campaign. He would appear in five All-Star teams in his career, and would win 20 games in 1952.

George McQuinn gave the Yanks a 1 to 0 lead in the 2nd with a home run off of Carl. But the A's got two back in the 3rd. Carl led off with a triple. Joost and McCosky walked to load the bases. Reynolds walked Ray Coleman, scoring Carl. Ferris Fain then hit a fly to Joe DiMaggio in center, deep enough to score Joost.

The A's added on in the 5th. Elmer Valo singled and stole second. Buddy Rosar then doubled him home. Pete Suder followed with a sacrifice bunt, moving Rosar to third. Carl then followed with an RBI single.

Bucky Harris had seen enough of the Superchief that afternoon. He pulled him in favor of Gumpert. Randy must've given Bucky further fits when he unleashed a wild pitch, allowing Carl to sprint to second. Eddie Joost then grounded out, Carl moving to third. Bernie McCosky followed with a ground single to right, scoring Carl. The A's were now up 5 to 1.

Carl held the lead until the bottom of the 7th. Perhaps Carl was tiring a bit. After Billy Johnson singled, he was able to mix two walks between two outs, loading the bases for Tommy Henrich. Known as "Old Reliable" and "The Clutch," Henrich had been a tough out for Carl. He ripped a ball into the seats for a game-tying grand slam.

In the bottom of the 8th, the Yankees broke the tie on a Cliff Mapes sacrifice fly, plating McQuinn who had doubled and moved to third on a sacrifice bunt. The Yanks were ahead 6 to 5.

The A's were unable to get one back in the 9th, and lost by a run. Carl fell to 7-3, his ERA rising to 3.57. The Athletics fell to a game behind, in second place.

Just before the All-Star break, the A's were at home against the Red Sox on Sunday July 11th.

In the first game of a doubleheader, Lou Brissie was knocked out in the 4th. In the bottom of the 8th, with the A's losing 8 to 6, Carl pinch-hit for Joe Coleman against Boo Ferriss. He struck out, but entered the game as the pitcher in the top of the 9th.

Carl retired three of the four Boston hitters, giving up only a single to Bobby Doerr. In the bottom of the 9th, the A's rallied for two runs to tie the game.

Unfortunately for Carl, he was a little wild in the 10th. He had just thrown a complete game three days prior, and may have been a little tired. Billy Goodman led off with a triple. He then got Birdie Tebbetts to foul out to third. Boo Ferriss drew a walk, bringing Dom DiMaggio to the plate.

The younger brother of the Yankee Clipper was an All-Star in his own right, appearing in the Mid-Summer Classic seven times.

Dom ripped a ball into the gap, scoring Goodman for the go-ahead run, and putting men on second and third.

Carl walked Johnny Pesky to load the bases and then worked out of the jam, popping up Stan Spence to second, and retiring Vern Stephens on a fly to center.

Now trailing 9 to 8 in the bottom of the 10th, the A's tried to mount a comeback against Boo Ferriss. He struck out catcher Herman Franks. Pete Suder followed with a fly out. This brought Carl to the plate with two outs, but Ferriss proved too much, striking out Carl to end the game.

This relief appearance was booked as a loss for Carl, dropping his record to 7-4.

The A's won the second game 7 to 5 to stay a half game back of Cleveland entering the All-Star break.

The All-Star game was held at Sportsman's Park in St. Louis, on July 13th. Joe Coleman and Buddy Rosar both saw action in the game, The American League won 2 to 1.

The last place White Sox came to Shibe Park on Sunday July 18th for a doubleheader. Carl faced Frank Papish in the first game.

The A's jumped out to a 5 to 0 lead in the first two innings, chasing Papish, but Carl struggled to hold it. He gave up single runs in the 3rd and 4th. In the 5th, leading 5 to 2, he coughed up two more.

Pat Seerey was the main culprit in all of this. The power-hitting platoon left fielder was known to strike out a lot—leading the league in 1944, 1945, 1946, and 1948, despite playing part time. This day was one for the ages for Pat Seerey.

Carl struck him out to lead off the 2nd. In the 4th inning, he ripped a solo home run. In the 5th, he nailed a two-run four-bagger. Aaron Robinson followed with a single, chasing Carl. Bob Savage took the hill for the A's.

In the 6th, the Sox took the lead on a three-run blast from Seerey off of Savage. Bubba Harris retired him in the 7th, to end a rally. The Sox were up 11 to 7, but the A's came right back and tied it up at 11 in the bottom of the 7th. Eddie Joost had hit a three-run homer.

In the top of the 9th, Joe Coleman walked Seerey, and neither team scored. The game went into extra innings.

In the top of the 11th, with Lou Brissie on the mound, Seerey sent another pitch into the stands for his fourth home run of the day. The White Sox won 12 to 11.

At the time, Seerey was only one of five players to accomplish this feat: Bobby Lowe, Ed Delahanty, Lou Gehrig, and Chuck Klein. Over the years, eleven more players would hit four home runs in a game, including Willie Mays and Mike Schmidt, but no one had ever exceeded four. The Texas Rangers' Josh Hamilton was the last to do it in 2012.

For Carl, this was another shaky outing, albeit a no-decision. His ERA climbed to 3.75, and the team was 1½ games back in second place.

Later in this same series, Lou Brissie started against Marino Pieretti on July 20th. The Sox jumped on Brissie for five runs, chasing him in the 4th inning. Carl was called in to mop up, the team trailing 5 to 0.

In the bottom of the 5th, Carl doubled off of Pieretti, and was one of two runs Joost drove in with his triple in the next at bat, but it was the only offense the A's could muster that day.

Carl threw six scoreless innings, but they were for naught. His ERA was back down to 3.57, and the A's were a game behind again.

The A's were soon back on the winning side. In the first game of a doubleheader on Sunday, July 25th, the A's beat the Tigers 4 to 0 behind the complete game shutout by Joe Coleman. They were now back in first place.

The second game was one of Carl's worst of the season. He was set to face Fred Hutchinson. While he posted a scoreless 1st inning, Carl could not escape the second. He gave up four runs on two walks and three hits. Bubba Harris was called to relieve him.

The Tigers won this one 10 to 5, Carl dropping to 7-5. Fortunately, they still clung to a one game lead over the Red Sox.

On Friday, July 30th, the A's were in Detroit to face the Tigers before 45,996 fans. Joe Coleman was on the hill to face Fred Hutchinson. It was a hostile environment for the Mackmen.

Coleman gave up one in the 1st and two in the 2nd, before he was chased in a seven run 4th. Bubba Harris gave up two more before Carl took over in the 6th.

Carl pitched three innings, the rest of the way, but gave up seven more runs on seven hits and two walks. The A's lost 17 to 2, and were a game and a half back.

Carl's ERA ballooned to 4.21 due to the inconsistency.

It looked like Carl was in the dog house, now relegated to the bullpen. Perhaps he just needed a break from starting.

On August 5th, the A's were back in Chicago and back in first. Joe Coleman threw a shutout in the first game. Bill McCahan got the call for the second game, to face Frank Papish.

The A's scored four in the 1st, but the White Sox chipped away on McCahan, scoring one in the 2nd, one in the 3rd, and two more in the 5th to tie the game. Carl got the call with one out in the 5th. He threw 4 2/3 innings of shut-out ball. The A's rallied for three in the 9th, making a winner of Carl and keeping Philadelphia in first place.

The American League-leading Philadelphia Athletics were home August 11th against the Washington Senators. Phil Marchildon was on the hill, facing Sid Hudson.

With Washington up 3 to 2 in the 7th, Carl got the call. He retired the Senators in order. In the bottom of the 7th, Don White led off with a single. Pete Suder then intended to sacrifice himself by bunting White to second, but the runners were called safe. Herman Franks then bunted both runners into scoring position.

Carl was next to bat. He ripped a double to center field, scoring both White and Suder. The A's now led 4 to 3.

The Nats made two more pitching changes in the inning, and loaded the bases. Sam Chapman then blasted the game open with a grand slam off of Tom Ferrick, plating Carl, Valo, McCosky, and himself. The A's now led 8 to 3.

Carl sailed through the 8th and went for the victory in the top of the 9th. He struck out catcher Jake Early. Gil Coan was called to pinch-hit for Tom Ferrick. Carl struck him out too. Manager Joe Kuhel then called on Early Wynn to pinch-hit for lead-off man John Sullivan, who was normally on the bench. Wynn, like Carl, was known as a good-hitting pitcher. Carl got him to pop out to first to end the game.

The A's stayed a half game up on second-place Cleveland. Carl's record was now 9-5, and his ERA down to 3.97.

Friday, August 13th, would be a terrible day in Philadelphia baseball history. While 41-year-old "rookie" Satchel Paige was throwing a five-hit shutout for Cleveland, the A's were in New York, clinging to a half-game lead over the Indians. Paige made quick work of the White Sox, ending the affair in less than two hours, before 4 PM Central, 5 PM Eastern.

72

The Athletics were leading 5 to 0 going into the bottom of the 8th. It was about 5 PM Eastern when the Yankees came to bat for the bottom of the 8th.

Lou Brissie had been superb, shutting out the Yankees on four hits. It was a miracle Lou was even on the mound, let alone beating the New Yorkers in their own stadium. A rookie in 1948, he had narrowly survived a shattered leg caused by an artillery barrage during the war. Brissie insisted his doctors should save his leg and not amputate. He did not want to give up baseball. Connie Mack had been on to him in 1941 when he was 17. Had Brissie's father not insisted Lou finish high school, he may have been a teenager in the majors a year before Carl.

Connie had decided to give Lou a chance, despite his reconstructed leg. In 1947, he signed him to a contract and was rewarded with a 23-5 season at Savannah in the South Atlantic League. Brissie started a game for the A's in September and took the loss.

Brissie and Carl were roommates from 1949 through 1951, and Carl fondly recalled those days.

"He had to put salve on his leg to keep it from drying out," said Carl of Brissie, "He wore a shin guard too. I remember one time Ted Williams ripped a ball off of the leg. Lou laid on the ground awhile, but got back up and continued pitching."

Now, on that terrible August 13th, he was in the midst of his rookie campaign in the big leagues. He loaded the bases, walking Stirnweiss, yielding a single to Henrich, and walking Lindell.

Bubba Harris got the call—bases loaded and no one out. He walked Joe DiMaggio, bringing in a run. Yogi Berra then pinch-hit for Billy Johnson. Yogi ripped a single to right scoring Henrich and Lindell, moving DiMaggio to third. Bobby Brown then pinch-hit for Souchock and drew a walk, loading the bases again.

Earle Mack made a visit to the mound, wanting to preserve the lead. He replaced Harris with Alex Kellner. Phil Rizzuto then came to the plate. He lined a single up the middle, plating Dimaggio and Berra. The game was now tied 5 to 5. Kellner walked Gus Niarhos to load the bases again. Earle Mack then came to get him, calling on Carl.

Carl entered the game with the bases loaded and no one out. The game was tied 5 to 5, and the Cleveland victory was evident on the scoreboard.

Charlie Keller grounded a ball to Pete Suder at second, that should have been an out somewhere – maybe even at home, but

8/24/48
A's drop to fourth place

Suder couldn't handle it, and Brown scored the go-ahead run. The bases were still loaded, and no one was out.

Snuffy Stirnweiss was next. He hit a single to left, scoring Rizzuto and Niarhos. There were now men on first and second with no one out. The Yankees now led 8 to 5.

Tommy Henrich was next. He had been hitting Carl well, especially in the clutch. This time, Carl got him to ground into a double play. With Keller on third, he ended the inning by getting Johnny Lindell to fly out.

Though none of the runs were charged the Carl, four A's pitchers had coughed up eight runs in one inning, blowing a 5 to 0 lead in a critical game in the pennant race.

Spec Shea came in and shut down the A's in order. The final was 8 to 5. The A's slipped to 2nd place, a half game back.

That Sunday, the 15th, the A's were still in New York for a doubleheader. Phil Marchildon faced off against Eddie Lopat. There were over 72,000 in the seats at Yankee Stadium, the largest crowd of the year at that point.

The A's led 2 to 0 going into the bottom of the 9th. Once again, another A's starter was throwing a terrific game against the Yanks, only to get into trouble late.

Bobby Brown led off with a walk. Marchildon then retired Henrich on a pop out to second. The Yankee Clipper was next up. DiMaggio blasted a two-run home run to tie the score. After Berra singled and Keller walked, Carl got the call with two on and one out. The game was on the line.

Phil Rizzuto was first up against Carl. He tapped a ball to third and beat the throw. The bases were now loaded with one out.

With nowhere to put anyone, and no margin for error, Carl bore down on George McQuinn, striking him out for the second out. Next up was pitcher Eddie Lopat. Eddie was a decent-hitting pitcher, and could win his own game with a single. Carl got him to pop out to catcher Buddy Rosar.

In the top of the 10th, the A's used four singles against Lopat to take a 5 to 2 lead. Allie Reynolds was called to replace Lopat with two out. Suder was caught stealing to end the inning, with Buddy Rosar at the plate.

In the bottom of the 10th, Carl needed three outs to close out his tenth victory of the season. He got Stirnweiss to fly out. But Bobby Brown singled. After Henrich struck out looking. Joe DiMaggio stepped to the plate. The dangerous Yankee Clipper wasn't about to go quietly. He ripped a ball to deep center field,

74

plating Brown. It was a triple. Yogi Berra was up next, and the Yanks trailed by only two.

Earle Mack then called on Lou Brissie to replace Carl. The war hero was able to get Berra to ground out to end the game. The A's had won 5 to 3 and kept pace, 1½ back in second place. The Athletics also won the second game by the same score but couldn't gain on Cleveland, who had swept the White Sox in a doubleheader.

The next day, on August 16th, the A's were leaving New York when it was announced that Babe Ruth had died.

As the A's visited Fenway Park on Wednesday August 18th, they were in a four-way race for the pennant. The Indians were in the lead, with the A's two back, followed by the Red Sox, a game behind the A's, and the Yankees two games behind Boston.

Carl took the hill against Denny Galehouse. It would be a rough outing for the Gratz native.

After the A's jumped to a 1 to 0 lead, Carl got Dom DiMaggio to ground out in the bottom of the 1st. Johnny Pesky and Ted Williams then hit back-to-back singles. Vern Stephens next flew out to left. Williams advanced to second on the throw. With men on second and third and two out, Bobby Doerr singled, driving in two. Carl then ended the inning, getting Stan Spence to fly out.

Carl escaped some trouble in the 2nd, giving up no runs after two singles. In the 3rd, however, he wasn't so lucky. Williams led off with another hit. Vern Stephens followed with a single. Carl then walked Bobby Doerr to load the bases before he was pulled in favor of Bubba Harris.

Harris walked Spence to force in a run. Goodman grounded into a double play, scoring Stephens. Tebbetts then doubled in Doerr. The Red Sox now led 5 to 1. Galehouse made the last out of the inning.

The Sox would add five more against Bob Savage, winning 10 to 2. Carl's record dropped to 10-6. The team fell three games behind in the pennant race.

By August 24th, the A's had slipped to 4th place. The Tigers were at Shibe Park. Rookie Ted Gray was to face Lou Brissie.

Gray couldn't get out of the 1st inning. He lasted two outs, giving up two runs on three hits and a walk. Virgil Trucks was called in to stop the rally.

Brissie held the 2 to 0 lead until the top of the 3rd when the Tigers rallied for six runs. The inning included a bases-clearing triple by Pat Mullin, and a two-run home run by shortstop Johnny Lipon. Lou did not come out for the 4th inning. Carl entered the game in his place.

Trailing 6 to 2, Carl held the Tigers close, pitching the remaining six innings, giving up a run on four hits. The offense, however, could not do much with Trucks. Ultimately, the A's lost 7 to 4. They were now in 4th place, 3½ games out.

By Sunday August 29th, the A's were still hanging onto pennant hopes, only 3 games behind, in 4th place. Carl got the call to face the White Sox at Shibe Park. His opponent was fellow Pennsylvanian Randy Gumpert, who had been purchased from the Yankees the prior month. The Birdsboro High School graduate had been in a relief role for the Yanks. The White Sox made him a starting pitcher.

Gumpert and Carl traded zeros until the top of the 4th. Luke Appling had reached on a single. With two outs, Dave Philley doubled him home.

The A's tied it up in the bottom of the 5th. Pete Suder led off with a triple, Carl following with an RBI single.

The Sox were right back at it in the top of the 6th, scoring two to take the lead again. Dave Philley and Ralph Hodgin both singled in runs.

The lead was short-lived as the A's tied it up in the bottom of the 6th. Ferris Fain singled, followed by a Buddy Rosar double. Pete Suder then singled home Fain. Carl followed with a single, scoring Rosar.

In the bottom of the 7th, the A's took the lead as Rosar doubled-in Fain, but the Sox tied the game again in the top of the 8th. Taffy Wright doubled and later scored on a ground out. The game was knotted at 4 to 4.

Carl led off the bottom of the 8th. He ripped a Gumpert pitch to deep center field and ended up on third base with a triple. After Webb struck out and McCosky walked, Sam Chapman knocked Carl in with a single. The A's now had the lead, 5 to 4.

Carl made quick work of the Sox in the 9th, finishing off his 11th win of the season. The A's held their position in the standings.

By Friday September 3rd, the A's had lost four in a row and were now sliding to 5½ games out, still in 4th place. Carl got the call to face Joe Dobson and the 1st place Red Sox at Shibe Park. It would be one of Carl's best-pitched games of the season.

The Sox scored an unearned run in the top of the 1st on an errant throw by Hank Majeski at third. The play would have ended the inning, but Dom DiMaggio came in to score.

Neither side managed a hit until the top of the 4th. In that inning, Stan Spence doubled, but was stranded by Carl.

The A's finally got a hit in the bottom of the 4th when McCosky singled. But Ferris Fain grounded into an inning-ending double play.

Carl retired the Sox in order in the 5th. In the bottom of the inning, Hank Majeski singled to center. Sam Chapman then doubled, putting men on second and third with no one out.

Next up was Elmer Valo. He tapped a ball back to Dobson, who held the runners and threw over to first for the out. He then intentionally walked Rosar to load the bases. Pete Suder was up next. Suder popped up to shortstop, leaving the bases loaded with two outs. It was Carl's turn. Carl put a charge into one, sending a fly to center field, but it was corralled by Dom DiMaggio to end the inning. The A's had wasted an incredible opportunity.

In the top of the 7th, the Sox increased their lead to 2 to 0 on Birdie Tebbetts' home run.

The A's couldn't solve Dobson the rest of the way, falling 2 to 0. Dobson earned his 15th win, a complete game shutout. Carl took the loss but also pitched well, giving up one earned run on six hits over nine innings. His record dropped to 11-7, and his ERA to 3.97. The A's were now 6½ back with only 25 games to play.

When Carl next took the mound, the team was nine games behind the Red Sox in 4th place. The A's were at Griffith Stadium to play the Washington Senators on September 8th. Dick Weik was on the hill for the Nats, making his first major league start.

The A's took a 1 to 0 lead in the 2nd on a walk. Weik had walked the bases loaded and then walked McCosky.

In the bottom of the 3rd, the rookie helped his cause with a single. He then scored on Al Kozar's triple, tying the game at one apiece.

In the bottom of the 4th, Mickey Vernon drew a walk with one out. Sherry Robertson then singled, moving Vernon to third. While Mark Christman was at the plate, a right-handed hitter, Mickey Vernon took off for home, sliding in successfully before Carl could get the ball to Rosar. Buddy then threw down to second to get

Robertson, but the ball went into center, allowing Robertson to get to third. Carl got the next two batters to end the threat.

In the top of the 5th, Elmer Valo tied the game at two with a home run. Elmer played 20 years in the major leagues, never once making an All-Star team despite hitting .300 or better five times.

In the top of the 6th inning, Weik retired Suder and Carl on flies to the outfield. He then walked the bases loaded again. Hank Majeski singled in two, putting the A's up 4 to 2. Weik was then replaced by Forrest Thompson, having walked ten batters in 5 2/3 innings. Thompson got Chapman to pop out to short to end the inning.

The A's added on in the top of the 7th against Thompson. Mike Guerra singled with one out. After Pete Suder flied out to left, Carl came to the plate. He ripped a triple, scoring Guerra, putting the A's up 5 to 2. It was the final score.

Carl improved to 12-7, his ERA dropping to 3.84. The A's had won three in a row, and were still nine games back with 19 to play.

Sunday September 12th, the A's were at Fenway for a rematch of the Scheib vs. Dobson gem from the prior week. The A's still trailed the Red Sox by nine games.

The Athletics took a 1 to 0 lead in the 1st, Majeski doubling in Fain, who had walked. The score remained that way until the bottom of the 4th.

Carl led off the inning by walking Billy Goodman. Birdie Tebbetts grounded out, advancing Goodman to second. Billy Hitchcock then singled, driving in Goodman to tie the game. Next, pitcher Dobson sacrificed Hitchcock to second. With two outs, Dom DiMaggio drove in Hitchcock with a single. The Red Sox were now up 2 to 1.

In the bottom of the 6th, it looked like Carl was going to get himself out of trouble. Tebbetts and Hitchcock started the inning with singles. Dobson then came up and tried to sacrifice the runners up, but he bunted the ball right to Carl, who pivoted to third to nail the lead runner. Majeski then threw to Suder covering first to nail Dobson for a double play. Hitchcock was now the only runner on with two outs. Carl then pitched around Dom DiMaggio, putting him on first. Next up was Johnny Pesky. He hit a fly to right, but Elmer Valo dropped it, allowing Hitchcock to score. After walking the dangerous Ted Williams, Carl struck out Vern Stephens to end the inning.

The A's tied it up in the 7th. With one out, Valo walked, and Rosar doubled, putting two men in scoring position. Pete Suder then singled, driving in Valo, and putting men on first and third. Carl stepped in and lifted a fly to left, deep enough for Rosar to score, making it 3 to 3. Eddie Joost then doubled to right field, but Suder was nailed at the plate for the final out on a fine throw from Wally Moses.

The A's took the lead in the 8th on a Chapman double. They then added six more in the 9th off of three Boston relievers.

Buddy Rosar led off the inning with a single. After Suder made an out, Carl also singled. Eddie Joost followed with a single, scoring Rosar. The musical chairs continued as the A's scored five more on singles and ground outs. Carl went to the bottom of the 9th with a 10 to 3 lead. The Sox scored one in the 9th on a double play, but the A's hung on 10 to 4.

The win was Carl's 13th and pulled the A's back to nine games out. Carl was now 13-7. Dobson fell to 15-8.

On Sunday September 19th, the A's were in Cleveland to face the Indians in a doubleheader. Boston still led the American League, followed by the Yankees at two games back, Indians at 2 and a half back, and the A's at six and a half back. With only ten to play, it was now or never for Philadelphia. Carl was on the mound versus Bob Lemon.

Joe Gordon led off the bottom of the 2nd with a home run, giving the Indians the edge over Carl and the A's.

The A's tied it in the top of the 3rd on McCosky's RBI single, but Dale Mitchell's sacrifice fly scored Jim Hegan to take the lead in the bottom of the 3rd.

The Indians added on in the 4th, Wally Judnich singling home Lou Boudreau. It was now 3 to 1, Cleveland.

In the top of the 5th, off of future Hall of Famer Bob Lemon, Suder singled and Carl doubled to put men on second and third. Eddie Joost then grounded out, scoring Suder, and cutting the deficit in half.

Lemon and Scheib then traded zeros until the top of the 8th. McCosky doubled to right. After Fain grounded out, Majeski ripped a double, scoring McCosky. Lemon then intentionally walked Chapman to set up a force out. Valo singled to left fielder Dale Mitchell, who threw home to keep Majeski from scoring. On the throw, Chapman tried to advance to second but was nailed by catcher Jim Hegan, who threw to Joe Gordon for the tag.

1948
Best season
14-8 ERA 3.94

Pinch hitter Ray Coleman was intentionally walked to load the bases. Lou Boudreau pulled Bob Lemon in favor of Russ Christopher. Pete Suder ended the inning by popping out to the catcher.

In the top of the 9th, the A's tried to take the lead. Carl led off with a single, but Eddie Joost grounded into a double play. McCosky then singled but was caught trying to steal second with Fain at the plate.

Carl went to the mound in the bottom of the 9th in a tie game. Joe Gordon greeted him with a single, putting the winning run on base. Ken Keltner then bunted, moving Gordon into scoring position for Larry Doby. Doby, a future Hall of Famer, was in his rookie season with Cleveland. He was the second player, after Jackie Robinson, to break the color barrier in major league baseball. He was the first to do it in the American League. Larry would go on to seven All-Star seasons and would lead the American League in home runs twice. So, the first black player in the American League stepped in against the (former) youngest player in American League history.

"We had a loud-mouth in the stands named Pete Adelis," recalled Carl. "Philadelphia was a tough town in those days." In fact, the club had hired Adelis to heckle Doby during his at bats.

Discussing the integration of baseball, Carl empathized with the difficulties black players faced. "Jackie Robinson came up first in the National League, but in the American League, it was Doby and then Luke Easter. These guys took a beating. Guys spit on them and tagged them hard. On the road, they couldn't stay in hotels and had to stay with local families."

Larry, a left-handed batter, turned on a Carl offering and sent it into the right field bleachers for a walk-off two-run home run. Carl had matched Bob Lemon pitch for pitch, but he was no match for the slugger from South Carolina.

Carl's record fell to 13-8. The team slipped to 7½ back. The Indians also won the second game behind a three-hit shutout by Steve Gromek, who bested Dick Fowler 2 to 0. At the end of the day, the A's were 7½ behind the Red Sox with only eight to play.

On Tuesday, September 28th, the A's were now playing spoiler in one of the best pennant races in American League history. Before play began, Cleveland led both Boston and New York by only one game. Three horses were racing for a photo finish.

The Yankees were at Shibe Park this afternoon, sending 19-game-winner Vic Raschi to the mound against Carl.

The A's took the lead against Raschi in the 1st. Eddie Joost led off the inning with a triple, and was driven in on a single by McCosky.

In the bottom of the 3rd, three straight hits, including a triple by Ferris Fain, chased Raschi. The A's were leading 3 to 0 when Joe Page entered the game. Sam Chapman then doubled in Elmer Valo, putting Philadelphia up by four before Page ended the rally.

The A's added on another run in the 4th, Majeski singling in Joost, who had walked and advanced on McCosky's bunt. The A's were up 5 to 0.

Carl, meanwhile, was throwing a shutout against the Yankees, who were in a tight pennant race. He had scattered nine hits through eight innings. Only DiMaggio had reached him twice.

Johnny Lindell greeted Carl with a single, his second hit of the afternoon. Sherm Lollar walked. Joe Collins then pinch-hit for Snuffy Stirnweiss, and Hank Bauer was sent in to run for Lollar. The Yankees were not going to go quietly!

Joe Collins stepped to the plate for only his second major league at bat. He had just been called up from Newark in the International League where he had hit .273. He would go on for a ten year career, mostly as a platoon first baseman and right fielder. Whether Stirnweiss liked it or not, Bucky Harris's decision to use the rookie over the seasoned veteran paid off. Collins ripped a two-run double, scoring Lindell and Bauer. The score was now 5 to 2, and no one was out.

Billy Johnson stepped to the plate and flied to right for the first out. Phil Rizzuto was up next. He slapped a ball back to Carl off of his glove that was fielded by Joost. Eddie threw over to first to get the Scooter.

With two outs, Tommy Henrich came to the plate. Many times, it seems, Henrich had hit Carl in the past. This time, Carl kept him in the park. Henrich flied out to right.

Carl's record was now 14-8 after the complete game win. His final ERA was 3.94. The Yankees slipped to two games behind. Vic Raschi, 19-8, was charged with the loss.

The last two games of the season, the Senators were at Shibe Park. On Saturday October 2nd, Carl was the starting left fielder, batting 7th for the A's against rookie Dick Weik. Weik was wildly effective, winning 7 to 1 despite walking seven batters. Carl went 0 for 3 with a walk, dropping his batting average to .307. He had no chances in left, though two base hits came his way.

CARL On the final game of the season, October 3rd, Carl batted 6th and played right field. Ray Scarborough was on the hill against Phil Marchildon. Scarborough was at the end of his finest season. The Senators won again, 7 to 2, as Scarborough was tough to hit. Carl went 0 for 3, but drove in a run on a sacrifice fly. He also caught two flies in the outfield. His final batting average was .298 for 1948.

Recollecting 1948, Carl explained, "Now this is my opinion, but Connie Mack had a hard time getting his pitchers lined up in those years, you know, the steady starters. A lot of times he would start a pitcher, and if he didn't win, he was in the bullpen for a while, relieving. We didn't have specialists. We had long and short relievers. Every year that he let me start and if I lost, start again, I had fairly good seasons. You have to get regulated to pitching every four days, and you can't do that in the bullpen. In 1948, I had a 14-8 season when I started most of the season.

"In 1948 we had a pretty good bunch of starters, and we pitched well. We should have won the pennant, but we hit a bad streak late in September. We lost something like seven in a row, and that put us out of the race. In fact, we had to win the last game of the season to win fourth place."

The A's finished the season in 4th place, 12 games back. The Yankees finished third, two games back.

Eddie Joost led the team with 16 home runs. Hank Majeski blasted 120 RBI. Barney McCosky led the team with a .326 batting average.

On the mound, Dick Fowler led the team in wins with his 15-8 record. Joe Coleman, Lou Brissie, and Carl had 14 each.

Cleveland and Boston tied for the lead on the final game of the season. They played in the first play-off game in American League history, a one-game elimination at Fenway Park on October 4th. The Indians won 8 to 3 to go on to the World Series against the Boston Braves. They took the series in six games.

* Two months later, in December, Georgene gave birth to daughter Barbara Ann Scheib. It was a fitting end to a fantastic year for the young hurler.

9.
HOLD-OUT

The A's were optimistic about their prospects in 1949. During the off-season, they had purchased veteran outfielder Taffy Wright from the White Sox and signed veteran outfielder Wally Moses as a free agent.

Carl was an early hold-out before spring training. He wanted a raise after his 14-8 season, having made $8,000 in 1948. He wanted $10,000.

CARL

Carl was quoted in the *Harrisburg Telegraph* that January, "I spoke with Earle Mack last Friday, but I didn't sign. Earle said he would contact Mr. Mack, who is in Florida now."

The papers reported on February 11th that Carl had signed. Terms were not discussed, but Carl mentioned in a recent interview that he got his way.

Friday, April 22nd, the A's were in Washington, D.C., for the fifth game of the season. Carl was tapped to face Mickey Haefner for the Senators.

The A's scored two runs in the first on two singles and a sacrifice fly. Carl then proceeded to mow down the Nats.

Eddie Robinson was the first Senator to get a hit, leading off the 5th inning. Ralph Weigel followed by grounding into a double play. Only three other batters managed a hit the rest of the way. Only one runner reached second base until the 9th inning. To close out the game, Carl loaded the bases on a single and two walks but got Eddie Yost to ground into a game-ending double play.

In one of the finest starts of his career, Carl tossed a four hit, complete-game shutout. It was a nice way to start the season.

Ellis Kinder and the Red Sox were next up for Carl as the A's visited Fenway Park on April 27th. Kinder was making his second start in a season he would win 23 games.

The Red Sox got to Carl in the 1st, ending his streak of shut out innings at nine. Dom DiMaggio walked, followed by Johnny Pesky's single. Ted Williams made the first out of the inning, flying out to left. Vern Stephens then blasted a three-run home run.

*1949
Carl earns
$10,000 at age 22*

Stephens was a seven-time All-Star in his career. As a member of the Browns, he had led the league in RBI in 1944 and home runs in 1945. In 1948, he didn't miss a game, and blasted 29 home runs and 137 RBI. He would lead the league in RBI in 1949 and 1950, all while playing shortstop in Boston.

Carl managed to exit the inning without any further damage.

The A's jumped on Kinder in the 3rd. Pete Suder doubled to left. Carl followed with a single, putting men on the corners. Eddie Joost then grounded into a double play, Suder scoring the first run.

Elmer Valo and Ferris Fain next drew walks. Taffy Wright followed with a three-run home run. The A's were now up 4 to 3.

Wright had been purchased from the White Sox during the off-season. Now 37, Wright was a career .311 hitter in the majors, but never an All-Star.

The A's knocked Kinder out of the game in the top of the 4th. Catcher Joe Astroth led off with a single. After Pete Suder was struck out, Carl singled. Eddie Joost then hit a two-run double, chasing Kinder. Earl Johnson entered the game for the Sox, ending the rally.

Boston got one back in the 4th in exciting fashion. Birdie Tebbetts drew a walk. With two outs, Dom DiMaggio also drew a walk. Johnny Pesky then singled to right, scoring Tebbetts. Taffy Wright fielded the ball in right, and threw it in to Suder, who fired to third to try and nail DiMaggio, but he was already on his way home. Majeski then threw to Astroth at the plate, nailing DiMaggio for the final out.

Boston tied it up in the bottom of the 6th. Carl walked Ted Williams. Vern Stephens then blasted his second home run of the game, a two-run shot. Doerr next doubled deep to left. Mele bunted him to third. Walt Dropo then stepped in, and mid count, Carl was pulled for Bubba Harris. Harris walked Dropo, but the base on balls was charged to Carl. Bubba got the next two batters to end the threat.

The Sox went on to add four more, winning the game 10 to 6. Carl received a no-decision, but had yielded six runs on seven hits and seven walks. The A's dropped to 5-5, in 4th place.

On May 1st, the Senators were at Shibe Park for the first game of a doubleheader. Carl's opponent was Joe Haynes. Haynes had been part of one of the most lopsided deals in baseball history, traded by the Indians with Ed Klieman and Eddie Robinson to the Senators for Mickey Vernon and Early Wynn.

Haynes had led the American League in ERA in 1947, posting a 2.42 mark with winning fourteen games for the White Sox. He had slipped to 9-10, 3.97, for the Sox in 1948. This season would be even worse, dropping to 2-9, with a 6.26 ERA. Haynes would never be an effective major league starter again.

"Specs" Klieman would give up six earned runs in three innings before the Senators would waive him, and the White Sox picked him up. Klieman would only pitch one more season in the majors.

Eddie Robinson made the All-Star team for the Senators in 1949, but would be traded mid-season in 1950 to the White Sox for little in return.

Mickey Vernon would hit 18 homers for Cleveland in 1949, but was traded back to Washington in 1950 for wild Dick Weik.

Early Wynn, meanwhile, turned around his 8-19, 5.82 performance in 1948 with a winning record in 1949. He took the ERA crown in 1950 and won over twenty games five times on his way to the Hall of Fame.

The Senators started the scoring in the 2nd. Eddie Robinson blasted a home run off of Carl. They added two more in the 3rd on doubles by Clyde Vollmer and Robinson.

The Athletics exploded for four in the bottom of the 3rd. Suder singled, followed by walks to Carl and Joost, loading the bases. Elmer Valo then tripled, clearing them all. Ferris Fain drove in Valo for the go-ahead run on a sacrifice fly.

In the top of the 4th, Carl retired Al Evans on a ground out, but walked the pitcher, Joe Haynes. Lead-off hitter Gil Coan then tripled, Haynes scoring. Carl was then pulled from the game in favor of Jim Wilson. He got Buddy Lewis to ground out, but then gave up a two-run home run to Sherry Robertson. The Senators were up 6 to 4.

The A's proceeded to outscore Washington 11 to 3 the rest of the way, winning 15 to 9. Elmer Valo had four hits and seven RBI, and set a major league record with two bases-loaded triples. Joe Coleman earned the win in relief.

The game also marked the first major league appearance of Bobby Shantz. The Pottstown, Pennsylvania native pitched 2/3 of an inning, giving up one hit and no runs in his debut.

Carl, meanwhile, had another no-decision and saw his ERA balloon to 5.94.

The Athletics were in Detroit to face the Tigers on May 6th. Hal Newhouser was slated to face Carl. The two pitchers held their opponents scoreless for the first three innings.

1949

In the top of the 4th, the A's took a one-run lead, only to give it back in the bottom of the inning. Carl started the inning, but gave up three runs before he could get an out, including a home run to Vic Wertz. Bobby Shantz got the call to take his place.

Shantz and Newshouser then battled inning after inning. The A's finally added two more runs in the 8th, chasing Prince Hal, and tying the game.

Dizzy Trout and Shantz then battled for four more shutout innings, until the 13th. The A's got to Trout for two in the top of the inning. Shantz held on, giving up a run to close out the victory.

It was a remarkable outing for Shantz, his second in the majors. He had thrown nine shutout innings in relief before giving up a run in his 10th inning. He was credited with his first major league win.

Carl, meanwhile, had another ineffective no-decision and saw his ERA rise to 6.41.

Two days later, on May 8th, Carl was in the bullpen as the A's faced the White Sox in Chicago. Alex Kellner couldn't get out of the 2nd inning, the Sox posting an early four-run lead. Earle Mack replaced Kellner with Carl, who had been knocked out of his start earlier in the week.

Carl mopped up the next six and one-third innings as the Sox cruised to an 11 to 3 win. He struggled again, yielding seven runs, five earned, on eight hits and five walks. His ERA was 6.58.

The A's fell to 9-11 in 5th place.

Four days later, on May 12th, he finished the last two innings of a 9 to 3 loss to the Browns. Carl gave up four hits and two runs, worsening his ERA to 6.75.

While Carl wasn't used for the next eight days, the A's went on a winning streak and rose in the standings. They were now 16-14 and were facing the Tigers at Shibe Park on May 20th.

Phil Marchildon started for Philadelphia versus Marlin Stuart for the Tigers. Neither fared well, both failing to get through the 4th inning.

With the Tigers leading 6 to 0 in the top of the 4th, Marchildon gave up a single to the pitcher, Stuart. He then made an errant throw on the sacrifice bunt attempt by Johnny Lipon. Both runners advanced into scoring position. Marchildon was then pulled in favor of Carl. He retired the next three batters, one of the inherited runners scoring on a sacrifice fly. The A's were now down 7 to 0.

In the bottom of the 4th, the A's finally got things going. They scored four runs on five singles and two walks. Stuart was replaced by Art Houtteman in the midst of the rally.

The A's added six more in the 5th on three singles, three walks, and an error against three Detroit pitchers.

The A's tacked on four more in the 6th off of Dizzy Trout on a walk, four consecutive singles (including one by Carl), and an error. The score was now 14 to 7. Eddie Joost added a home run in the 8th to finish the scoring at 15 to 7.

(Carl) pitched six innings of one-hit ball. He gave up no runs in picking up his second victory of the season. His ERA dropped to 5.56.

The world champion Indians were at Shibe Park on May 23rd. Early Wynn was matched against Bill McCahan.

The Indians took a 1 to 0 lead off of McCahan in the 2nd on Mickey Vernon's RBI single.

In the top of the 3rd, McCahan left with an elbow injury. Bubba Harris was called to take his place.

In the top of the 4th, Ken Keltner led off with a home run. Larry Doby singled, and Vernon reached on an error by Valo, who dropped a fly ball. The Indians added four more runs, all unearned, as Eddie Joost also made an error. The Athletics now trailed 6 to 1.

(Carl) took over in the 5th and gave up a run, but he shut out the Indians the rest of the way.

The A's finally got to Wynn in the 9th. Hank Majeski reached on an error with one out. Elmer Valo drew a walk. Pete Suder then grounded out for the second out. Mike Guerra then ripped a ball into the gap, scoring Majeski and Valo. Guerra, meanwhile, tried to stretch it into a triple, and made the last out at third base, a cardinal sin.

In the 7 to 3 loss, Carl had thrown five innings, giving up one hit, one walk, and one run, which was unearned. His ERA dropped to 4.85. The A's finished the day 19-15, in second place, three games behind the Yankees.

May 30th, the A's were at Fenway Park to face the Boston Red Sox. Carl opposed Mel Parnell, who was already 6-1 in the early season. Parnell was in his first All-Star season and would go on to win twenty-five games in 1949, the first of two twenty-win seasons for him.

He held the A's scoreless until the 3rd when Wally Moses singled and Ferris Fain walked. Sam Chapman then singled home Moses.

Carl held the Red Sox scoreless until the 5th inning, when Dom DiMaggio singled home a run.

In the bottom of the 7th, Parnell helped himself with an RBI single, giving the Red Sox the lead, 2 to 1.

Eddie Joost walked to lead off the 8th. Wally Moses doubled to center, scoring Joost. Fain then bunted Moses to 3rd. Chapman followed with a single to drive in Moses. The A's now led 3 to 2.

In the bottom of the 8th, Ted Williams was pretty frustrated. He had grounded out three times. After Johnny Pesky walked to lead off the 9th, it was the Splendid Splinter's turn at the plate.

"I had retired him three straight times on curve balls," recalled Carl, many years later, "As Williams came to the plate, he said to Guerra who was catching, 'if he throws me one more God damn curve ball, I'm going to hit it out.' Of course, I did, and Ted Williams hit the ball out of the park to win the game. How dumb to throw him four of the same pitches in a row! Boy did his balls climb!"

The two-run homer by Williams gave the Sox a 4 to 3 lead. Parnell shut down the A's in order in the 9th to seal the victory.

Carl fell to 2-1 while Parnell went to 7-1. The loss dropped the A's to 21-19, 5½ games back in third place. For Carl, it was a pretty good game. He pitched a complete game, going eight innings, yielding eight hits, three walks, and four earned runs, but it was a game he could have won, if only he had mixed it up more against Williams.

June 2nd, the Athletics were in Detroit to face the Tigers. Lou Brissie started against Ted Gray. The A's had a 4 to 1 lead going into the bottom of the 8th.

Lou walked Don Kolloway and George Kell. He then struck out Vic Wertz, but Hoot Evers ripped a ball into the seats, scoring three and tying the game. Carl got the call in the pen, and got the last two outs and three more in the 9th to take the game into extra innings.

In the bottom of the 10th, Carl retired Kell and Wertz on fly balls but gave up a double to Evers. Johnny Groth was next up. He was a rookie center fielder who was hitting over .300, and had hit .340 for Buffalo in the International League in 1948. Groth ripped a single, scoring Evers to win the game.

Carl was the pitcher of record, falling to 2-2. Art Houtteman earned the win in relief. The A's were now 7½ games back in 5th place at 21-21.

Three days later, on June 5th, Carl got the call against the Indians in the second game of a doubleheader at Cleveland Stadium.

In the first game, Bobby Shantz got credit for the win, throwing 6 2/3 innings of one-hit relief to defeat Bob Feller, who had fallen to 1-5 to start the season.

In the second game, Carl was tapped to face Satchel Paige.

In the top of the 2nd, Carl faced Paige and flied out to center. In the bottom of the 2nd, after two walks, Jim Hegan lined a ball into center to score a run. Satchel Paige was next up. Carl got him to ground into a double play.

In the top of the 3rd, Joost and Majeski homered off of Paige. The A's were leading 3 to 1.

In the bottom of the 3rd, Carl got a little wild. He walked three to load the bases with one out. Bubba Harris got the call to replace Carl.

Mickey Vernon came to the plate. He popped a ball up to the catcher, but Guerra dropped it, and all of the runners moved up, including one across the plate. Harris managed to thwart the rally, though.

The A's added a run in the 8th off of Mike Garcia, making it 4 to 2, which was the final score. Harris was the winner and Paige the loser. Carl pitched 2 1/3 innings, giving up only one earned run, but he walked six.

Satchel Paige, now 42, had been a star in the Negro Leagues for many years, and continued to pitch into his 50s in the minor leagues, after his major league career was over. He would be inducted in the Hall of Fame.

On June 6th, the next day, Carl was called late in the game against the Indians. Cleveland was leading 9 to 5 in the bottom of the 8th with one out. He came in with the bases loaded and walked Lou Boudreau, forcing in a run. Ray Boone then hit a sacrifice fly to score another run. Carl ended the threat by getting Jim Hegan to fly out. The game ended 11 to 5, but Carl was not charged with the runs.

1949 mediocre start to season

The Athletics were in St. Louis to face the Browns on Sunday June 12th. Bobby Shantz and Carl were in the bullpen for the A's, who had sent Joe Coleman to the hill as the starter.

Coleman was pulled in the 6th when the Browns tied it at 2 to 2 and threatened for more. Shantz was next in the game, stopping the rally and putting them down in order in the 7th. In the 8th, however, Bobby got into trouble. Whitey Platt led off the inning with a single. Stan Spence walked. Sherm Lollar then doubled them home, tying the game at 4 to 4, and chasing Shantz.

Carl got the call with Lollar on second and no one out. The Browns swapped the speedier John Sullivan for Lollar. Rookie Roy Sievers was the pinch hitter for Tom Ferrick. He grounded out. Carl then retired Andy Anderson on a grounder to third. With two out, Carl was close to exiting without any further damage, but Bob Dillinger wouldn't go down easy. He singled, bringing in Sullivan for the go-ahead run. The Browns got another on an error by Joost, taking a 6 to 4 lead to the bottom of the 9th.

Ned Garver was called from the pen to close it out for the Browns. He stymied the A's to seal the victory.

Carl's line for the day was one inning, one hit, and one unearned run. Shantz was charged with the loss. The A's slipped to 27-24, five games back in third place.

Tuesday, June 14th, Carl ran into Virgil Trucks and the Tigers at Shibe Park.

Trucks was 8-3 on his way to a superb nineteen-win season in which he would lead the American League in shutouts and strikeouts. The three-time All-Star would win 177 games in the majors against 135 losses.

Carl handed the Tigers three in the top of the 1st. After Don Kolloway led off and popped to short, Paul Campbell tripled to center. Carl then plunked George Kell with a pitch, putting men on the corners. Up stepped the dangerous Vic Wertz. Vic was in his first All-Star season, en route to hitting .304 with 20 homers and 133 RBI. He was ready to put a charge into one. He hit a line drive to deep center, but it was right at Sam Chapman. Campbell tagged at third, and scored.

Hoot Evers followed with a single. Aaron Robinson then doubled home Evers and Kell. Carl retired Johnny Groth to end the inning.

Carl and Trucks exchanged zeros until the top of the 8th. Along the way, Virgil was nicked for only one hit in the 5th. Hank Majeski had mustered a single from the stingy Alabama native.

In the 8th, it was Vic Wertz again, driving in Campbell with a double, expanding the lead to 4 to 0.

The A's could not solve Trucks the rest of the way. Virgil had thrown a one-hit shutout, improving his record to 9-3. Carl also went the distance, giving up four runs on seven hits in nine innings. Carl's record was now 2-3. His ERA was 4.48.

The Tigers, at 31-22, improved their hold on second place, at three games behind the Yankees. The A's fell to 28-25, in third place, six games out.

The last place Browns were at Shibe Park on June 19th. Joe Ostrowski started against Carl. Dick Kokos greeted him with a two-run homer in the 1st. The 21-year-old slugger had been tearing up the American Association at Toledo in 1948 before getting a chance with the Browns for the second half of the season. Kokos hit 23 homers in 1949. It would be his career high. Kokos would lose three seasons to military service in Korea and was never the same afterward.

While Ostrowski held the A's scoreless for four innings, the Browns added on in the 5th. Catcher Les Moss took Carl deep for another home run. The A's now trailed 3 to 0.

In the bottom of the 5th, Nellie Fox flied out to right. Joe Astroth followed with a walk. Carl was next up. He knocked a single to center, putting two men on. Eddie Joost then followed with a three-run blast to tie the game. The veteran shortstop, now 33, was having his best season in 1949. He would score 128 runs for the A's, and hit 23 home runs, driving in 81 from the lead-off spot. Eddie would go to the All-Star game for the first time in 1949.

Carl and Ostrowski kept things scoreless in the 6th, but in the 7th, the wheels came off for Scheib. Jerry Priddy started things with a single. Carl then walked Moss and Anderson to load the bases. Pitcher Ostrowski followed with a single, plating Priddy. The Browns were now ahead 5 to 4, and the bases were still loaded with no one out.

Bill McCahan entered the game as Carl went to the dugout. He gave up a two-run single to Stan Spence. Dillinger sacrificed Ostrowski to third. After Kokos walked, Jack Graham scored Ostrowski on a sacrifice fly. McCahan then ended the inning, retiring Sievers, but the A's never recovered, losing 7 to 3.

Carl dropped to 2-4, his ERA hitting 5.00.

On June 22nd, the Indians were at Shibe Park. Joe Coleman faced Gene Bearden in a battle of second and third place teams.

1949
first 3 months
2-6   ERA 4.94

The two were knotted at 3 to 3 into extra innings. In the bottom of the 11th, with two outs, Carl pinch-hit for Bubba Harris against Bob Lemon. He popped out to first and took over pitching duties in the 12th.

Lemon and Carl exchanged zeros in the 12th and 13th innings. In the top of the 14th, the Indians got it going. Bob Kennedy walked. Jim Hegan singled. Bob Lemon came to the plate and intended to bunt but ended up safe at first, loading the bases. Dale Mitchell then broke it open with a bases-clearing triple. Ray Boone followed with a single, adding on a 4th run before Carl escaped further damage.

With a 7 to 3 lead, Lemon was able to close out the A's for the victory. Bob Lemon was credited with his 7th win, now 7-2 on the season. He had relieved Bearden in the 8th and pitched seven innings of one-run ball.

Carl fell to 2-5. He gave up four runs on six hits and three walks in three innings. His ERA was now 5.30.

Only two days later, Carl was asked to start against the White Sox in Philadelphia on June 24th. Randy Gumpert was on the hill for the Sox. The two were magnificent through six innings, locked in a scoreless duel.

In the top of the 7th, the Sox manufactured a couple of runs on a double, a walk, a single, and a ground out. The A's got one back in the bottom of the inning when, with one out and two men on, Taffy Wright, hitting for Carl, was safe on an error by shortstop Bobby Rhawn, allowing Nellie Fox to score.

Gumpert didn't budge the rest of the way, and the game ended 2 to 1 in favor of the White Sox.

Carl was the losing pitcher, but he had given up only four hits in seven innings. Only one of the two runs allowed was earned. His record dropped to 2-6, but his ERA improved to 4.94.

The A's, meanwhile, still held onto second place at 5½ back.

This time, Carl got a little rest between appearances. He was the starting pitcher as the A's took the field at Griffith Stadium in Washington on June 29th. His mound opponent was Ray Scarborough.

Carl was dinged in the 1st when the Senators scored a run on a double play.

No one else scored until the top of the 4th when the A's tied the game. Elmer Valo drove in Ferris Fain on a sacrifice fly.

In the top of the 5th, Philadelphia took the lead. With one out, Carl singled to center. After Eddie Joost made the next out, Taffy Wright was hit with a pitch. Ferris Fain walked to load the bases. Scarborough then walked in a run, giving a free pass to Sam Chapman, scoring Carl. Scarborough was replaced by Dick Welteroth, who escaped any further harm.

In the top of the 6th, the A's added on. Welteroth walked the bases loaded, issuing passes to Valo, Fox, and Carl. Lloyd Hittle was then called to try to end the threat. He got Eddie Joost to fly out, but Valo was able to tag up and score.

In the bottom of the 6th, things got a little rough for Carl. Bud Stewart greeted him with a triple. Clyde Vollmer then doubled him home. Eddie Robinson flied out to center, Vollmer taking third. Al Kozar then singled in Vollmer, tying the game at three.

The A's returned the favor in the 7th. Fain singled, and Chapman reached on an error, Fain reaching third. On the next play, Hank Majeski hit a grounder to third. Ferris Fain, off the bag at third, broke for home and was caught in a run down. With one out, Chapman was on second and Majeski on first. Elmer Valo then reached on an another error, loading the bases. Nellie Fox followed with an RBI single, scoring Chapman and Majeski.

Fox, from St. Thomas, Pennsylvania, had been signed as a 16-year-old in 1944, the year after Carl, but he was sent to the low minors to get some seasoning. After a full season at Lancaster, in the Interstate League where he hit .314, Nellie lost a year in 1946 to military service. In 1947, he returned around mid-season to Lancaster, and received a September call-up to the A's. In 1948, he was superb at Lincoln in the Western League and also got a September call to Philadelphia. This season, 1949, was his rookie year. Nellie "Mighty Mite" Fox would go on to a Hall of Fame career, though mostly with the White Sox.

Mike Guerra was next up for the A's. He also singled, driving in Valo, Fox scampering to third. Carl then followed with a sacrifice fly, scoring Fox. The A's now led 7 to 3.

Stewart added a home run in the 8th, but Carl hung on for a 7 to 4 victory. His record improved to 3-6 thanks to the complete-game victory. At 39-29, the A's were now knocking at the Yankees' door, only 4½ behind in the pennant race.

Independence Day, July 4th, 1949, the Athletics were at home against the Senators. Once again, Carl was tapped to face Ray Scarborough.

1949, then start, then believe!

The Senators jumped on Carl for three in the 1st. After Gil Coan walked, Sherry Robertson blasted a two-run homer. After getting Bud Stewart on a fly out, Carl loaded the bases, walking Vollmer, and allowing singles to Robinson and Kozar. Sam Dente then flied to right, Vollmer scoring.

The Athletics got two of them back in the bottom of the 1st. Eddie Joost walked. Taffy Wright then grounded out to the right side, advancing Eddie. Ferris Fain followed with a single, scoring Joost. Sam Chapman doubled, putting two men in scoring position. Scarborough pitched around Hank Majeski, walking him. Elmer Valo then plated Fain on a sacrifice fly.

The score remained 3 to 2 until the top of the 4th. Dente singled, and was doubled home by Evans. Ray Scarborough then singled, putting runners on the corners. Bubba Harris was called to end the threat, but he allowed both men to score, on an error and a sacrifice fly. The inning ended with the Senators up 6 to 2.

A seven-run 7th put the A's in the lead for good. They would win 9 to 7, Dick Fowler picking up the victory in relief.

For Carl, it was a rough outing, and a no-decision. His ERA climbed to 5.18. The A's held their position at 4½ back.

Four days later, on July 8th, the A's were at Fenway Park to face the Red Sox. The Sox were out to a 7 to 1 lead, when Carl was called in to mop up for Dick Fowler and Bubba Harris. He threw three innings of one-hit ball. He even struck out Ted Williams, but the A's couldn't mount a comeback against Joe Dobson.

The next day, the Sox again pounded the A's pitchers, getting out to a 7 to 3 lead. Carl was called upon to pitch the 8th, following Kellner and Harris. He pitched a scoreless inning, and the A's rallied in the 9th for two, but came up short, 7 to 5.

In the last game before the All-Star break, in a wild affair against the Red Sox, Carl was called to pitch for the third day in a row.

Bobby Shantz started for the A's, retiring lead-off hitter Dom DiMaggio, but Bobby couldn't get anyone else out. He walked Pesky and Williams. Stephens then doubled in Pesky. Doerr singled in Williams and Stephens. Goodman singled, putting two on for Tommy O'Brien. Bobby unleashed a wild pitch, Doerr moving to third. Earle Mack then pulled Shantz in favor of Carl. With runners on the corners, and only one out, Carl got O'Brien to pop to second, but Matt Batts doubled, scoring Goodman and Doerr. After walking the pitcher, Masterson, Carl faced Dom DiMaggio, who was batting for the second time in the inning. Dom doubled to center, scoring Batts and Masterson. Johnny Pesky flied out to end the frame, the A's leading 7 to 0.

In the top of the 2nd, Carl helped to get some of the runs back. With one out, Walt Masterson gave up a single to Majeski, and a double to Moses. Nellie Fox then singled them both home. Joe Astroth then walked, bringing Carl to the plate with the bases loaded. He ripped a double to center, plating Moses and Fox, and chasing Masterson.

Carl was relieved in the bottom of the 2nd by Dick Fowler. The Red Sox would go on to win a wild one, 11 to 10. Tex Hughson was the winning pitcher. Bobby Shantz got the loss.

Carl's 2/3 of an inning, allowing two runs, upped his ERA to 5.12 at the All-Star break.

The Yankees were solidly in first, 5½ games ahead of Cleveland, and 7 ahead of the A's.

The A's were in Detroit on July 17th. Carl was the starting pitcher versus Ted Gray. Things did not go well.

Carl walked two in the 1st but escaped any damage. In the bottom of the 2nd, he loaded the bases on two walks and a single. At that point, before any runs were scored, Carl was pulled in favor of Bubba Harris.

The strategy was looking pretty shrewd. Ted Gray, the pitcher, grounded back to Harris, who threw home for a force out. Paul Campbell then stepped to the plate. He drove a Bubba Harris pitch into the seats for a grand slam. The A's were down 4 to 0.

Gray would go on to pitch a three-hit shutout, the Tigers winning 8 to 0. Carl's record fell to 3-7, his ERA at 5.34. The A's were also slipping in the race, now nine back.

Something would have to give for Carl soon. His performance was well below his lofty results in 1948. With him struggling so much, there must have been talk about demotion or release.

After his very short outing the day before, Carl was called from the bullpen again against Detroit.

The A's were leading 8 to 7 in the bottom of the 7th when Carl replaced Alex Kellner. He allowed the tying run in the inning, but then pitched into extra innings. The A's scored five in the 10th off of Stubby Overmire to win the game 13 to 8. Carl was the winner, pitching four solid innings, yielding three hits and one run.

1949 200 pitches - no game - no pitch counts in a game

The A's improved to 46-39, eight games back in 3rd place.

The next day, at St. Louis, Carl entered his third game in a row.

Bobby Shantz had been chased again early. Bubba Harris then kept it close. Carl was called in the 8th, trailing 5 to 4. He put up a zero, but the A's couldn't score against Red Embree in the 9th.

Shantz fell to 3-7 with a 5.12 ERA. Carl, still 4-7, improved his ERA to 5.17. Both of the young hurlers were struggling equally.

On July 22nd, Carl took one for the team. The White Sox were in town, and Carl was named the starting pitcher, facing Randy Gumpert.

While Gumpert threw a four-hit shutout, Carl coughed up eight runs in the 1st on eight hits and three walks. Thirteen men came to the plate. The Sox hit six consecutive singles to start the inning. Despite all of the trouble, the A's brass let Carl pitch through it. Alex Kellner had just pitched a complete game, and it had been awhile since the last extra-inning affair. So, the management was not low on arms in the bullpen.

Carl rewarded them with six consecutive shutout innings. There were no pitch counts in those days, but Carl would end up facing 49 batters in this game. A typical major league pitcher, these days, lasts about six innings and throws 100 pitches. Usually, he has faced half that number of hitters. It's very likely Carl threw close to 200 pitches in this game!

In the bottom of the 8th, the White Sox got to him again. They added four runs to win 12 to 0. Carl's final line was nine innings pitched, eighteen hits, eight walks, and twelve runs allowed. Carl fell to 4-8, his ERA growing to 5.78. The listless A's fell to 47-43, now 10½ back in 4th place.

The last place Browns were in town on July 27th. Despite the tiring outing the last time out, the A's sent Carl to the hill on his usual turn. Cliff Fannin was Carl's opponent.

In the top of the 1st, Carl provided a near repeat performance of the prior start. Perhaps he was a little tight from the 200 pitch affair. The Browns jumped out to a five run lead on four hits and a walk, including two two-run homers from Roy Sievers and Les Moss.

The A's got three back in the bottom of the 2nd. Sam Chapman singled and Augie Galan walked. Pete Suder then tripled them both home. Joe Astroth followed with another triple, plating Suder.

The Athletics tied things up in the 4th. With one out, Carl singled to center. One out later, Elmer Valo singled, moving Carl to third. Ferris Fain then singled to right, scoring both runners. The game was now 5 to 5.

Carl gave up a run in the 7th when pitcher Cliff Fannin doubled in a run, but the A's came right back in the bottom of the 7th, scoring the tying run on Sam Chapman's single.

The A's put it away in the 8th. Carl walked, Joost singled, and Valo singled, loading the bases against Red Embree with no one out. Ferris Fain followed with a sharp grounder to first. Paul Lehner picked the ball and threw home to force Carl. Les Moss, the catcher, then threw wildly, allowing Joost to score, and the runners to move up. After Majeski was intentionally walked to load the bases and set up a force play, Sam Chapman beat the strategy by drawing a walk and forcing in the second run. The A's now led 8 to 6. It would be the final score.

Carl survived his horrid 1st inning, and ended up pitching nine innings, yielding six runs on six hits and three walks. His record was now 5-8. His ERA stayed at 5.80.

The A's, meanwhile, had won their fifth straight game, and were now climbing back in the race at 7½ back.

On Sunday, July 31st, the A's dropped both games of a doubleheader to the Tigers. Carl was called to mop up the last inning of the second game, the team losing 5 to 0. Carl gave up a run in the 8th, Johnny Groth doubling in Hoot Evers. The A's fell to 5th place, nine games back.

The White Sox were in town on Tuesday, August 2nd, and few seemed to care. Less than 5,000 fans were in the park to see Carl take the mound against Randy Gumpert.

Carl only allowed one in the 1st, Chuck Kress singling in Luke Appling. The A's got it right back in their at bat on Elmer Valo's sacrifice fly, scoring Joost.

The A's took the lead in the 4th. Sam Chapman led off with a single. Nellie Fox attempted to bunt him over, but Gumpert bobbled the ball, and both men were safe. Rookie first baseman Hank Biasatti tapped one back to Gumpert, who threw to third to force Chapman. Mike Guerra then singled, scoring Fox. Carl then grounded a ball to Appling at short, who flipped to Michaels at second for one, but Carl beat the throw to first. There were now runners on the corners with two outs. Eddie Joost doubled, scoring Biasatti. The A's were up 3 to 1.

The White Sox added on in the 6th. Cass Michaels tripled to lead off the inning and subsequently scored on a ground out.

In the bottom of the 7th, the A's added on. Nellie Fox singled. Biasatti bunted him over to second.

Hank Biasatti was an interesting character. He was born in Beano, Italy, in 1922. He had been signed at age 20 in 1942, playing in the Canadian-American League. He then lost three seasons to the war, returning to Sunbury, Pennsylvania in the Interstate League as a Yankee farm hand, hitting .343. He spent two more years in the minors before the A's called him up in 1949. Biasatti would be with the team all season but only batted 24 times in 21 games, hitting .083. It was his only big league experience. He would play six more seasons in the minors but never made it to the top again.

After Mike Guerra grounded out, Carl stepped to the plate with a man on second and two out. He singled to center, scoring Fox. The A's now led 5 to 2. It would be the final score.

Carl had one of his best games of the year, throwing a complete game, yielding only two runs on eight hits and five walks. His record was now 6-8. His ERA dropped to 5.55.

Carl got a little rest before his next start on August 9th. The A's were in Washington to face the Senators and Dick Weik.

Weik was wild, as usual. The A's scored two on bases-loaded walks in the 2nd. Weik had walked five in the inning.

They scored two more in the 3rd. Carl hit a sacrifice fly scoring Fox. Eddie Joost drove in Guerra with a single.

Another was added in the 4th as Suder doubled in Fain.

Wally Moses tacked on another run, hitting a sacrifice fly in the 5th. Weik had thrown four innings, giving up seven runs on six hits and ten walks!

The A's added an insurance run in the 8th to take an 8 to 0 lead. Carl had been superb the whole game. He had scattered five hits to no effect.

In the bottom of the 9th, the Senators finally opened up, scoring three runs on four straight hits before Carl shut them down for good.

Carl notched his 7th win and lowered his ERA to 5.39. Dick Weik fell to 1-5, his ERA now 6.38.

Dick Weik, in 1949, would give up 103 bases on balls in 95 innings pitched. He would never be able to harness his control, pitching five years in the majors with a 6-22 record and a 5.90 ERA. He would pitch 213.2 big league innings, giving up 203 hits and 237 walks.

The win put the A's back in 4th place, 7½ out with 48 to play.

The Yankees were in town on August 13th. In the bottom of the 7th, with one out and the game tied 5 to 5, Carl pinch-hit for Nellie Fox against Joe Page, who had just replaced Vic Raschi.

With Pete Suder on 3rd, Carl singled to deep short, driving in the go-ahead run.

Dick Fowler could not hold off the Yankees, and they won 9 to 7.

On Sunday the 14th, Carl again pinch-hit for Nellie Fox against the Yankees. He came to plate in the 7th with one out and no one on base against Bob Porterfield. The Yankees were winning 4 to 0. Carl grounded out, and the A's ended up losing the game 4 to 2.

On August 15th, Carl finally pitched against the Yankees. This would seem to indicate that the A's management had planned to keep Carl out of the games against the first division teams until he started to pitch better.

Carl took the mound in Philadelphia against Eddie Lopat. Phil Rizzuto, the "Scooter," was first up and earned his nickname. He slapped a single to left. He then stole second with Cliff Mapes at the plate. Catcher Mike Guerra's throw went into center field allowing the Scooter to scoot to third. Mapes then hit him home with a sacrifice fly. Carl ended the inning, getting Gene Woodling and Joe DiMaggio to fly out.

In the bottom of the 3rd, against Lopat, Nellie Fox walked. Mike Guerra then tried to bunt him over to second, but hit the ball too close to Yankee catcher Charlie Silvera, who was able to throw to second to force Fox. Carl was next up. He doubled to deep center field. The Yankee Clipper sailed to the ball and threw it to the cut-off man, Rizzuto, who pivoted and threw home to Silvera just in time to nail Guerra at the plate. Eddie Joost followed with a single to left plating Carl just before Eddie was caught in a run down between first and second. The A's had tied the game at 1 but should have gotten a lot more.

The Yankees took the lead again in the 4th. Cliff Mapes led off with a triple. One out later, DiMaggio singled him home.

In the bottom of the 4th, the A's loaded the bases against Lopat. Nellie Fox then singled to right, scoring Elmer Valo. Ferris Fain also tried to score on the play, but the throw from right fielder Cliff Mapes was on the money. The game remained tied at two.

With two outs in the 5th, the A's took the lead. Eddie Joost walked and Don White singled. Elmer Valo then walked to load the bases. Ferris Fain followed with a single scoring Joost and White. Lopat then walked Sam Chapman to load the bases. Casey Stengel came to the mound, in his first season as the Yankees manager, and pulled Lopat in favor of Duane Pillette.

Stengel, "The Old Perfesser," had managed for nine years in the National League for the Brooklyn Dodgers and the Boston Bees and Braves. He had only one season slightly above .500 before he became the Yankees manager. He would win five consecutive World Series titles from 1949 through 1953 and three more pennants and two more titles through 1960. He ended his career managing the expansion Mets from their founding in 1962 through 1965. As a player, he had played 14 years as an outfielder in the National League, batting .284. Stengel would be elected to the Hall of Fame for his years managing the Yankees.

Pillette ended the threat by striking out Suder. The A's led 4 to 2.

The Yankees caused some trouble for Carl in the 6th. With one out, DiMaggio singled and Tommy Henrich walked. After Bobby Brown made the second out of the inning, Charlie Keller walked, loading the bases for Billy Johnson. Johnson ripped a double to right, clearing the bases. Carl then retired Pillette to end the threat. The Yanks were ahead 5 to 4.

With one out in the bottom of the 6th, Mike Guerra doubled and Carl walked. Eddie Joost singled scoring Guerra, and chasing Pillette. Stengel brought in Ralph Buxton with two men on and one out.

Buxton walked Moses, loading the bases. Elmer Valo then hit a hot grounder to first. Tommy Henrich picked it and fired home to Silvestri to force Carl at the plate. Ferris Fain then singled, knocking in two. Sam Chapman followed with a double, plating two more. The A's were up 9 to 5. It would be the final score.

The 61-51 A's were now nine games behind the 69-41 Yankees, still in 5th place. Carl evened his record at 8-8, lowering his ERA to 5.30.

Carl took his regular turn and was at Yankee Stadium on August 20th for a rematch with Eddie Lopat.

The Yankees got out to a one run lead in the 1st. With two outs, Gene Woodling ripped a home run to left center.

Woodling had played briefly for Cleveland and Pittsburgh before the Yankees purchased his contract from San Francisco in the Pacific Coast League after the 1948 season. He would play 17 years in the majors, reaching the All-Star game once in 1959 for Baltimore.

The Yankees added two more in the 4th. DiMaggio singled in a run and later scored on a ground out.

In the bottom of the 5th, Gene Woodling was at it again, blasting a three-run home run to give the Yanks a 6 to 0 lead. Carl was then replaced by Bobby Shantz.

Carl took the loss, dropping to 8-9. He pitched five innings, yielding six runs, two earned, on four hits and three walks. His ERA dropped to 5.25.

Eddie Lopat improved his record to 12-5. The A's were now 12 back in 5th place.

Carl struggled on August 27th in St. Louis against the Browns. His opponent on the mound was Joe Ostrowski.

The two exchanged zeros until the 4th when the A's notched a run.

In the bottom of the 4th, St. Louis scored four, chasing Carl from the game. Bubba Harris relieved him and gave up six more runs over his four innings of relief.

The A's lost 11 to 3, dropping to 66-55, nine games back in 5th place. Carl pitched only 3 1/3 innings, giving up four runs on seven hits and a walk. His record slipped to 8-10 and his ERA increased to 5.37.

On Thursday, September 1st, the A's were in Cleveland. The Indians were in the thick of the pennant race, 4½ games out. They sent Bob Lemon to the mound to face Carl. The two proceeded to unleash a classic old-time pitchers' duel.

After a scoreless 1st, Lemon set the A's down in order in the 2nd. The Indians then manufactured a run in the bottom of the 2nd off of Carl. Joe Gordon walked. Lou Boudreau then reached on an error. The two runners tried a double steal, but Guerra nailed Gordon at third. Bob Kennedy followed with a single, driving in Boudreau.

That would be the only run until the A's batted in the 9th. Bob Lemon was working on a shutout. Carl had given up an unearned run in the 2nd.

In the top of the 9th, with the game on the line, Sam Chapman nailed a home run off of Lemon to tie the game.

1949
inconsistent
8-10, ERA 5.17

The Indians could not score against Carl in the bottom of the 9th. Both teams were scoreless again in the 10th.

In the top of the 11th, Lemon was still on the mound to face the heart of the A's line-up. He mowed them down 1-2-3.

Carl took the mound for the bottom of the 11th. Finally, one of the hurlers had run out of gas—or luck. Thurman Tucker singled to center. With Larry Doby at the plate, Carl uncorked a wild pitch, allowing Tucker to move up. Doby then singled to left, scoring Tucker. It was the second time Carl had experienced a walk-off hit by Larry Doby. The Indians won 2 to 1 in eleven innings.

Bob Lemon improved his record to 17-9, his ERA dipping to 2.87. Carl slipped to 8-11, but his ERA improved to 5.09.

The A's were now 67-60, in 5th place, twelve behind with 27 to play.

Four days later, on the 5th, the Yankees were at Shibe Park. Lou Brissie faced-off against Vic Raschi.

The Yankees knocked Brissie out after the 3rd, taking a 5 to 0 lead. The A's got one back in the bottom of the 3rd. Carl entered the game trailing 5 to 1.

Charlie Silvera singled to lead off the inning. Carl then walked Vic Raschi, the pitcher. Phil Rizzuto grounded into a double play, moving Silvera to third with two out. (The 1949 Athletics set the all-time record for turning double plays: 217. This mark still stands to this day.) Bobby Brown walked to put men on the corners. Carl then gave up consecutive singles to Hank Bauer, Joe DiMaggio, and Billy Johnson, each one driving in a run. Carl finally ended the inning on a line-out to second by Charlie Keller.

Carl would bat in the bottom of the 4th and drive in a run with a single. But his day was done.

The Yanks went on to a 13 to 4 win. Vic Raschi improved to 18-9. Lou Brissie dropped to 13-9. Carl pitched one inning, giving up three runs on four hits.

On Sunday, September 11th, the Red Sox were at Shibe Park, hot on the tail of the league-leading Yankees. The A's had won the first game of the doubleheader 6 to 4, Joe Coleman defeating Joe Dobson. The Red Sox were in 2nd place, two games back.

For the second game, Carl got the call against Chuck Stobbs. It would be one of Carl's finest games of his career.

Eddie Joost blasted a solo home run in the 3rd. Sam Chapman added on with a two-run shot in the 5th.

Carl, meanwhile, did not give up a hit until Matt Batts singled in the 5th.

The A's would add an insurance run in the 6th as Carl cruised to a two-hit shutout.

The top of the Red Sox line-up—a list of All-Stars comprised of Dom DiMaggio, Johnny Pesky, Ted Williams, Vern Stephens, and Bobby Doerr—went a combined 0 for 14 against Carl.

Carl's record improved to 9-11. His ERA dropped to 4.96. The A's, meanwhile, had swept a doubleheader, but were still 14½ games out with 16 to play.

By Carl's next start on September 17th, the A's had been eliminated from the pennant race. The White Sox were in town, sending Mickey Haefner to the hill against Carl.

Carl would not get out of the 3rd inning, leaving with one out. The Sox built an 8 to 3 lead before sealing the victory 8 to 5.

Carl fell to 9-12. His ERA nudged up to 5.09.

On Carl's last start of the season, only 1602 fans were at Shibe Park to see the Tigers and Ted Gray take on the A's.

The Tigers notched a run in the 1st, but both pitchers settled in after that.

The A's then took the lead 4 to 1 with a two-run 4th and a two-run 5th.

The Tigers scored two in the 6th and two more in the 7th. Carl was chased with no one out, and the game tied at five apiece.

The A's went on to win with a three-run 8th, winning 8 to 6. Lou Brissie picked up the win in relief. Carl gave up ten hits and seven walks in his six innings. His season ERA ended at 5.17.

Carl's last appearance of the season was as a pinch hitter in the last game of the season against the Senators at Griffith Stadium.

With the Senators up two to nothing in the 8th, Carl pinch-hit for Nellie Fox but made an out. The Senators won 3 to 0.

The A's finished the season a respectable 81-73, in 5th place, sixteen games behind the pennant-winning Yankees.

Carl's batting average for 1949 was .236. He drove in ten runs in 72 at bats.

Sam Chapman led the team with 24 home runs and 108 RBI. Eddie Joost hit 23. Elmer Valo led all hitters with a .283 average.

On the mound, Alex Kellner went 20-12. Lou Brissie was 16-11, and Dick Fowler 15-11.

After the season, the team traded catcher Buddy Rosar to the Red Sox for Billy Hitchcock. They also, unfortunately, traded Nellie Fox to the White Sox for Joe Tipton.

On December 13th, the Athletics traded Rocco Ippolito, Ray Coleman, Billy DeMars, Frankie Gustine, and $100,000 to the St. Louis Browns for Bob Dillinger and Paul Lehner.

The next day, Hank Majeski was sent to the White Sox for Ed Klieman.

Carl Scheib's lifetime pass to the Major Leagues. (Photo by Tammi Knorr)

Carl's father, Oliver Scheib
(1896-1953)

Carl's mother, Pauline Scheib
(1899-1984)

The Scheib home as it looked in the summer of 2014. (Photo by the author)

Close-up of the Scheib home as it looked in the summer of 2014.
(Photo by the author)

Carl in his early teens.

Ad for the Indianapolis Clowns troupe from the 1940s.
Previously known as the Ethiopian Clowns, this group toured
the nation, including Gratz.

Carl as a lad in Gratz, riding a bike circa 1941.

The Gratz High School baseball team, 1942.

Carl in high school, 1942.

The shop in Gratz where Hannah Clark met Al Grossman and discussed the young hurler.

Carl on the mound as a rookie.

Carl circa 1944

Carl circa 1945

Carl circa 1945

Carl and brother Paul Scheib in A's uniforms. Paul was a catcher who played minor league ball.

Paul Scheib in his Navy uniform during WW2.

Carl in his Army uniform circa 1945.

Carl takes the mound in Germany in 1946.

Newlyweds off to spring training.

Carl by his car, likely in Gratz after the War.

Carl signing his contract after his hold out in 1949.

Carl on the mound at Shibe Park.

Carl with a bat.

The A's dugout during the national anthem at Shibe Park.
Carl is on the far right.

Banquet honoring Connie Mack.

SPRING IS HERE—Another year, another baseball season rolls around. Getting the grounds in shape, only because they were the first to arrive at the Philadelphia A's Went Palm Beach, Fla., training camp are, left to right: coach Augie Galan; pitcher Bobby Shantz; pitcher Carl Scheib; coach Rollie Hemsley and pitcher Charles Bishop. (AP Wirephoto from The News-Review (Roseburg, Oregon) • Fri, Feb 19, 1954 • Page 7)

Cartoon of Carl Scheib.

The author and Carl explore his memorabilia cabinets at his home in San Antonio, 2014. (photo by Tammi Knorr)

Game ball from the double play record in 1949.
This record still stands.

Display of Carl's baseball cards courtesy of the Philadelphia Athletics Historical Society.

Game ball with the signatures of Pete Suder, Ferris Fain, and Eddie Joost.

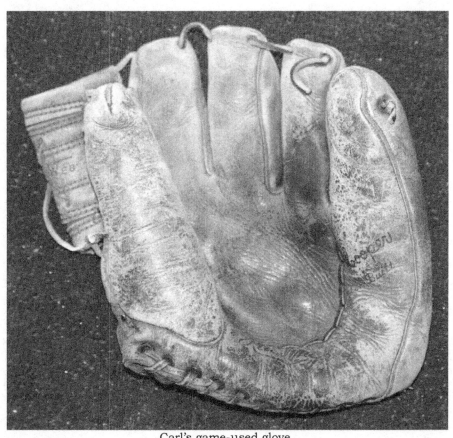

Carl's game-used glove.

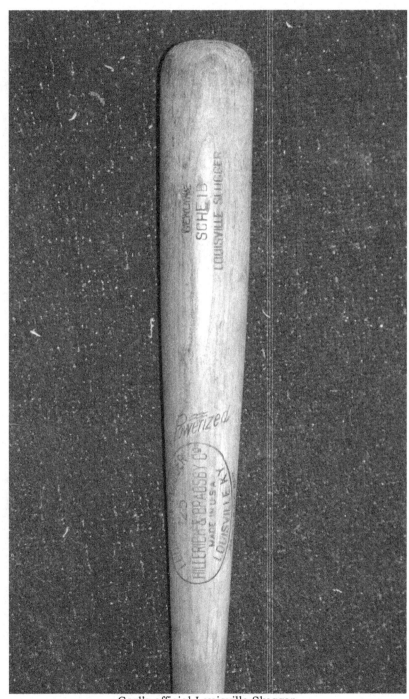
Carl's official Louisville Slugger.

131

Carl's spikes and other A's memorabilia.

Ballfield in Gratz, PA (photo by Lawrence Knorr)

Carl in 2014 (photo by Tammi Knorr)

1950

Plaque honoring Carl Scheib in Gratz (photo by Lawrence Knorr)

10.

OPENING DAY STARTER

Carl worked on the family's Pennsylvania farm in the off-season.

Tuesday, April 18th, the Senators and Athletics opened the 1950 season at Griffith Park in Washington. Carl was named the opening day pitcher versus Ray Scarborough. His off-season was probably one day too short!

Following two ceremonial pitches by the ambidextrous President Truman, who tossed one right-handed and one left-handed, Scarborough put up a zero in the 1st. Carl didn't fare so well. Gil Coan started the inning with a single. Sam Dente followed with a double. Irv Noren then singled home Coan, putting men on the corners. Eddie Robinson walked to load the bases. At that point, with no one out and one run in, Carl was pulled in favor of Bobby Shantz. Bobby gave up singles to Bud Stewart and Eddie Yost, both plating two runs. The A's were behind 5 to 0. Four of the runs belonged to Carl.

When rain started falling in the 6th inning, President Truman donned a raincoat and remained to the end.

The Senators hung on for an 8 to 7 win. Carl took the loss.

Three days later, on the 21st, Carl got the last two outs in the 9th in an 8 to 2 loss to Boston at Shibe Park.

On April 26th, the Senators were in Philadelphia. Bobby Shantz was facing Sid Hudson. Shantz gave up a run in the 1st and gave up a three-run homer to Al Evans with no one out in the 2nd. Carl got the call to return the opening day favor. The A's were trailing 4 to 0.

Carl did everything he could to win this game, with his arm and bat. He put down the Nats in order in the 2nd and 3rd. In the bottom of the 3rd, he led off the inning with a single and came around to score the A's first run of the day on Sam Chapman's sacrifice fly.

He gave the run back in the 4th, as the Senators opened the inning with a walk and two singles.

Ferris Fain hit a two-run homer in the 5th to close the gap to 5 to 3. Carl put the Nats down in order in the 6th and then singled in the bottom of the inning with two outs. He was stranded on first.

Carl pitched eight innings, giving up only one run on five hits and three walks. The A's lost 5 to 3, but Carl dropped his ERA from 54.00 to 5.19! He went 2 for 4 at the plate with a run scored.

On Sunday April 30th, the A's lost the first game of a doubleheader in Boston 19 to 0 as Joe Dobson bested Dick Fowler. The second game pitted Hank Wyse for the A's against Chuck Stobbs for the Red Sox.

Wyse had fallen behind 5 to 0 by the time Carl was called in the 4th with one out and the bases loaded. Carl got Bobby Doerr to pop out to first and Al Zarilla to pop out to the catcher to end the inning without any further damage.

In the top of the 5th, Carl helped with the bat, driving in a run on a single. He and Pete Suder then scored on Paul Lehner's double making it 5 to 3.

In the 7th, Eddie Joost singled in Pete Suder to make it a one-run game, 5 to 4.

The Sox got one back in their 7th, pitcher Chuck Stobbs singling in Bobby Doerr.

The A's erased that one in the 8th, scoring a run on a double by Dillinger, a passed ball, and a ground out. The A's were down 6 to 5.

In the bottom of the 8th, Johnny Pesky singled off of Carl, but he got Ted Williams to ground into a double play. The one-run deficit was preserved.

In the top of the 9th, Pete Suder singled. Next up was Carl, but he was called back for pinch hitter Wally Moses. Moses popped out to third, and Stobbs retired two more en route to the win.

The A's fell to 4-8, in last place. Carl threw 4 2/3 innings giving up one run on four hits. His ERA plummeted to 4.12. He was 1 for 2 at the plate, scoring a run and driving one in.

Thursday May 4th, before only 1901 fans, the A's hosted the Tigers at Shibe Park. The Tigers were up 8 to 5 in the 9th when Carl was called to keep it close. He retired the Tigers in order, and the game ended 8 to 5.

Three days later, on May 7th, rookie Bob Hooper was throwing a shutout into the 9th against the White Sox at Shibe Park. In that inning, things got tough for Hooper. The White Sox plated two, and loaded the bases with only one out. Carl got the call from the pen, the A's leading 4 to 2.

First up was lead-off hitter, center fielder Herb Adams. Adams had shown promise in 1949 as a 21-year-old rookie, batting .293 in part-time duty. Carl got him to pop out to third for the second out.

Next up was Dave Philley. He would play 18 years in the majors, batting .270. In 1950, he was on his way to his best power performance at 14 homers and 80 RBI. He had been hot so far this season, batting over .330 coming into the game.

Philley grounded a ball to the right side, fielded by first baseman Ferris Fain, who flipped to Carl covering. The game was over. Carl was credited with what, today, would be his first major league save (saves weren't a statistical category until 1969). Carl's ERA dropped to 3.60. This was the lowest it would go in 1950.

On May 9th, the Indians were at Shibe Park, trailing the A's 8 to 4 in the 8th inning with two outs and the bases loaded. Hank Wyse was pulled in favor of Carl.

First up was Dale Mitchell. As he swung, the runners took off, there being two outs. Mitchell singled to center field, plating all three runs, which were charged to Wyse. The Indians now trailed 8 to 7.

Henry Conyers then pinch-hit for Thurman Tucker. Conyers lined a ball into the glove of Pete Suder to end the threat.

The A's added an insurance run in the bottom of the 8th. Eddie Joost hit a home run.

In the top of the 9th, it was up to Carl to hold the lead. First up was Luke Easter. The first baseman was in his rookie year at age 34, having been one of the early players to break the color barrier in 1949. Easter hit for power, as evidenced by his 86 home runs from 1950 through 1952. Easter would play in the minors until he was 48 in 1964, ten years after his last major league appearance.

This day, the great former slugger from the Homestead Grays struck out against Carl for the first out.

Next up was right fielder Allie Clark. He struck out too.

Then came rookie third baseman Al Rosen. Al would be an All-Star four times in his career, and would lead the American League in home runs twice, 1950 being the first time.

Rosen was hot, and already had three hits on the day. He ripped a Carl offering over the wall for a home run. The A's were now leading only 9 to 8.

1950 terrible start

Joe Gordon was next up, pinch hitting for Ray Boone. The former Yankee second baseman was in the final year of his career, following nine straight All-Star appearances. Gordon would one day be elected to the Hall of Fame. He would also hit 19 home runs in his final year to end his career at 253, second to only Rogers Hornsby among second basemen until Joe Morgan would come along.

This day "Flash," as he was known, stepped in against Carl with two outs, down by a run. Carl struck him out looking to end the game and save the victory. It was Carl's second save.

May 13th, at Yankee Stadium, the Yankees jumped on Hank Wyse for four runs, including home runs by Yogi Berra and Bobby Brown. With two outs in the 2nd, Carl got the call. After walking Cliff Mapes, he struck out Tommy Henrich to end the inning.

In the bottom of the 3rd, Carl gave up a triple to Joe DiMaggio. Yogi Berra walked. With Bobby Brown at the plate, Carl balked, allowing DiMaggio to score and Berra to move to second. Carl then walked Brown and was pulled in favor of Dick Fowler.

Carl's line for the day was 1/3 of an inning pitched, allowing one run on one hit and three walks. The A's lost 9 to 3 and fell to 7-14 on the season.

The A's were in Cleveland to play the Indians on May 16th. Early Wynn started for the Indians against Alex Kellner. In the bottom of the 5th, with one out and a man on third, the Indians had built a 3 to 1 lead. Kellner was pulled in favor of Carl.

Joe Gordon made the second out of the inning on a fly to short right field, not deep enough to score Al Rosen on third.

Ray Boone then stepped to the plate with two outs. The father of Bob Boone and grandfather of Aaron and Brett Boone was the starting shortstop for the Indians. He would be a two-time All-Star in his career, playing for six different teams over thirteen seasons.

Boone singled to left scoring Rosen. The Indians led 4 to1, all of the runs charged to Kellner.

In the top of the 6th, the A's got to Wynn. Bob Dillinger led off with a double. Sam Chapman followed with a single to center, scoring Dillinger. Pete Suder then ripped a two-run home run to tie the score at four. Wynn retired the next three batters in order, including Carl on a line drive to center.

Carl took the mound in the top of the 7th. Early Wynn was first up. He laced a single to right. Dale Mitchell followed with another hit. After Bob Kennedy flied to right for the first out, Luke Easter stepped into the box. He put the Indians up by a run, hitting a single into center, putting runners on the corners. Larry Doby was next up. He had hit a game-winning home run in the bottom of the 9th off of Carl in 1948. He had another walk-off hit on his resume against Carl. In fact, Doby would tally five home runs against Carl in his career, the most by any batter against the Gratz native.

This at bat, Carl kept him in the park. Doby ripped a triple to center field, plating two runs. The A's now trailed 7 to 4. Bob Hooper was called from the pen to replace Carl. He would strand Doby on third.

The Indians went on to blow out the A's 15 to 4. Carl was tagged with the loss, his second. His ERA ballooned to 5.60. The team was now 8-15 in 6th place.

The next day, the series continued with Bob Feller facing Dick Fowler. Neither starter figured in the final decision, as the game went to the bottom of the 9th with the A's up 7 to 5, but the Indians in the midst of a rally against Bobby Shantz. Dale Mitchell had just doubled in a run, and men were now on second and third with only one out when Carl got the call. He got Bob Kennedy to pop up to the catcher for the second out. Luke Easter followed, and hit a fly to left into the waiting glove of Paul Lehner. The A's won 7 to 5, and Carl earned another save.

On May 19th, the Athletics were in Detroit to face the Tigers.

"When we'd go from Cleveland to Detroit in those days," recalled Carl, "we'd take a ferry boat across Lake Erie. We could stay on the boat awhile, after arriving."

In the bottom of the 5th, with no one out, the Tigers had rallied for two runs, narrowing the A's lead to 5 to 4. Carl was called to replace starter Hank Wyse with two men on base.

With Johnny Groth at the plate, Carl threw a wild pitch, allowing Vic Wertz and Hoot Evers to move up. Groth then walked to load the bases.

Catcher Joe Ginsberg made the first out, flying to left deep enough to score Wertz, who tagged up at third base.

First baseman Dick Kryhoski was next up, batting 8th. He singled to right, plating Evers,

Fred Hutchinson, who had relieved Virgil Trucks, stepped into the box. He would win 95 games as a pitcher, making the All-Star game once in his career. Like Carl, he was also a good hitter, batting .263 over his ten seasons, including four home runs.

1950 Connie Mack is retired. Jimmy Dykes new mgr.

Hutchinson ripped a double to left, clearing the bases. He advanced to third on an error.

Light-hitting shortstop Johnny Lipon was next up. Hutchinson took off from third as Carl pitched to Lipon. Johnny dropped a bunt, the ball rolling to Carl close to the mound. Carl had no choice but to throw to Suder covering, Hutchinson having scored on the suicide squeeze. There were now two outs, but the A's trailed 9 to 5.

Jerry Priddy reached second base on a play in which first baseman Ferris Fain made two errors: one handling the ball hit at him and another on a throw.

George Kell followed with a single, putting men on the corners. Vic Wertz then doubled, scoring Priddy. At that point, Carl was pulled for Harry Byrd.

Byrd gave up a double to Hoot Evers, allowing both of Carl's runners to score. The inning ended with the Tigers up 12 to 5. They had scored ten runs in the 5th off of three A's pitchers. The Tigers would win 14 to 8, Hank Wyse taking the loss and Fred Hutchinson earning the win.

Carl, in two-thirds of an inning, gave up six runs, three earned, on four hits and a walk. His ERA was now 6.63. The A's dropped to 9-17.

In a battle of two second-division teams, Carl finally made his second start of the season against the St. Louis Browns at Sportsman's Park. He was opposed by Al Widmar.

It's hard to believe the A's opening day starter would be held out for over a month, but on May 23rd, he took the hill again in the 1st inning.

Carl fell behind 2 to 0 in the 2nd. Second baseman Owen Friend, batting 8th, blasted a two-run home run. Friend, a rookie in 1950, had shown some pop in the minor leagues, but would hit only .227 over five seasons, playing for five different teams. This season, 1950, would be his best, as he hit eight home runs and knocked in 50 while batting .237.

The A's got one back in the top of the 5th. Carl, who had reached base on a fielder's choice, came around to score on Dillinger's single.

The Browns added a run in the bottom of the 5th on Ray Coleman's solo home run.

They increased their lead to 5 to 1 with two runs on three hits and a walk in the 6th.

Wally Moses pinch-hit for Carl in the 7th, ending his day. The Browns won 7 to 1, Carl falling to 0-3. He gave up five runs in six innings. His ERA increased to 6.84. The A's record was now 10-20.

"I loved the Chase Hotel in St. Louis," recalled Carl. "It had a fancy club on top of the roof. The ballplayers would rush back after the game. Tommy and Jimmy Dorsey and Spike Jones would perform there. I talked to Tommy Dorsey a lot about baseball. He was a big fan."

On May 26th, the A's board of directors met and announced some surprising decisions, notably that coach Jimmy Dykes would be the club's assistant manager and would take over for Connie Mack when the season ended. Also, Mickey Cochrane, the great catcher on Mack's pennant-winning teams from 1929 to 1931 and the current pitching coach, was named general manager. Earle Mack, Connie's longtime heir apparent, became chief scout. In fact, Connie Mack's 50-year managerial career was over, and Dykes was the new pilot.

The Yankees were in town for Carl's next turn in the rotation on Sunday May 28th. The Yankees had won the first game, Vic Raschi defeating Bob Hooper, who had relieved Dick Fowler. Joe DiMaggio and Cliff Mapes had three hits for the Yanks, but the go-ahead run came on a bases-loaded walk of Rizzuto by Bob Hooper in the 8th.

In the second game, Carl was tapped to start against Fred Sanford.

Sanford lost 21 games in 1948 for the Browns, but the Yankees thought enough of him to pick him up that December in a five-player trade. Sanford would pitch mostly from the pen and as a spot-starter.

The top of the 1st was a little shaky for Carl. After retiring Phil Rizzuto to start the game, he loaded the bases on a single and two walks. Gene Woodling then grounded out, driving in a run.

The A's got the run back in the bottom of the 1st, Dillinger and Chapman both doubling.

In the top of the 3rd, with two outs, Joe DiMaggio singled to score Rizzuto, who had led off the inning with a walk. Gene Woodling then doubled to put the Yanks up 3 to 1.

The A's pulled close in the bottom of the 3rd on Paul Lehner's sacrifice fly.

1950
Carl has a
poor start

In the top of the 6th, Carl loaded the bases with one out for pinch hitter Tommy Henrich. Old Reliable drove in two with a single. The Yanks were now up 5 to 1.

The A's rallied in the bottom of the 6th off of Sanford and Joe Page. Joe Astroth tripled in Ferris Fain. Billy Hitchcock, batting for Carl, hit a two-run homer. Bob Dillinger added another home run to give the A's a 6 to 5 lead.

Alex Kellner retired the Yankees in the 7th, before the game ended early. Carl was credited with his first win, now 1-3. He had yielded five runs on six hits and five walks in six innings. His ERA increased to 6.97.

6.97

Carl's next start was on June 4th at Shibe Park against the St. Louis Browns. His mound opponent was Ned Garver.

Carl escaped some trouble in the 1st, stranding Dick Kokos on third, but in the top of the 2nd, the flood-gates opened. The Browns loaded the bases, and then Garver singled in a run, followed by Tom Upton's two-run safety. Right fielder Dick Kokos then hit a three-run blast to put the Browns up 6 to 0. Carl wiggled out of the inning, stranding men on the corners.

In the bottom of the 2nd, Carl participated in the A's two-run rally singling in a run, but he was replaced by Hank Wyse in the 3rd.

The Browns went on to win 12 to 5, Carl dropping to 1-4. His ERA exploded to 8.18. It would be the last time he started a game for awhile. The team was now 14-28.

The next day, veteran and former star Phil Marchildon was released.

On June 6th, Hank Wyse of the A's was unable to hold a 5 to 3 lead in the 7th inning against the St. Louis Browns at Shibe Park. The Browns scored three with no one out. Carl was called in to put out the fire. He pitched three scoreless innings the rest of the way, giving up only two hits and two walks. The Browns won 6 to 5, dumping the A's into last place at 15-29.

The Indians were at Shibe Park on Saturday June 10th. Lou Brissie fell behind Mike Garcia, 5 to 3. Hank Wyse relieved Brissie and gave up two more. Carl entered the game to pitch the 9th inning, losing 7 to 3. He put the Indians down in order, including getting Luke Easter to fly out for the final out. Carl's ERA was inching down, now at 7.30.

ERA

On June 15th, the Athletics were in Detroit to face the Tigers. Bobby Shantz fell behind Fred Hutchinson 6 to 3 after seven innings. Carl pitched the bottom of the 8th, and gave up a run on two hits and a sacrifice fly. The A's lost 7 to 3.

The next day, the Athletics started a series against the Indians at Cleveland Stadium. Early Wynn and Alex Kellner faced-off. Kellner was pulled, tied 1 to 1, in the 5th inning with one out. Carl got the call with a man on second. He was able to get Bob Kennedy to hit into a fielder's choice for the second out, but Luke Easter followed with a two-run blast to put the Indians up 3 to 1. The A's got one back in the top of the 5th on Elmer Valo's home run. Carl did not yield a hit the rest of the way, but the A's couldn't rally against Wynn. Kellner was tagged with the loss because he was responsible for the base-runner who scored ahead of Easter on the homer run. Carl pitched 3 2/3 innings of shut out ball. His ERA dipped to 6.91.

The next afternoon, June 17th, the A's took the lead late in the game, scoring two in the 8th to go up 7 to 6. In the bottom of the 8th, Bobby Shantz retired Dale Mitchell, but gave up a double to Bob Kennedy. Carl then got the call to preserve the lead.

He induced Luke Easter into a ground out, Kennedy moving to 3rd. Carl then pitched around Larry Doby and Al Rosen, walking them both to load the bases with two outs. Next, he got Joe Gordon on a fly to center to end the threat.

The A's went in order in the top of the 9th, and Carl returned to the hill attempting to hold a one-run lead. Ray Boone greeted him with a single.

"Take that man out and bring in Byrd," barked Connie Mack to Jimmy Dykes.

Dykes replied, "You can't bring in Byrd."

"Why can't Byrd pitch?" asked Connie.

"You sent him to Buffalo three days ago," answered Dykes.

Carl stayed in the game and struck out Jim Hegan. Thurman Tucker was then called to pinch-hit. He singled to center, but the ball got away from Sam Chapman for an error, allowing Boone to score and Tucker to get to third.

With the winning run on third and only one out, Carl set up a force by intentionally walking Dale Mitchell. Indians' skipper Lou Boudreau then inserted himself to pinch-hit for Kennedy. He hit a ball to second baseman Kermit Wahl, who bobbled it. Everyone was safe, and Tucker scored the winning run.

Carl was charged with a tough loss, dropping to 1-5 on the season. If only Harry Byrd hadn't been sent down!

On Sunday June 18th, the Indians won their third in a row against the A's in the first game of a doubleheader. Bob Feller threw a two-hit shutout as the Indians won 7 to 0.

In the second game, Lou Brissie started against Mike Garcia.

Brissie was in trouble from the start. Dale Mitchell doubled to lead off the inning, but after Bob Kennedy lined out, Lou walked five batters in a row, bringing in three runs. Jim Hegan followed with a two-run single and pitcher Mike Garcia, the ninth batter in the inning, singled in another. The Indians led 6 to 0.

Lou then walked Dale Mitchell to load the bases. Connie Mack had seen enough. Carl was summoned from the bullpen to calm things down. He didn't fare much better.

He started out by walking in a run, issuing a pass to Bob Kennedy. Luke Easter then singled in two, followed by Larry Doby's RBI single.

It was now 10 to 0 with men on the corners and no one out, and no one was coming to get Carl. At this point, he was taking one for the team.

Al Rosen was next up. He slapped a ball at Eddie Joost that should have been an inning-ending double play. Instead, it went through his wickets for an error. Another run scored.

With men on first and second, Carl got Joe Gordon to fly out to center. Finally, there were two outs!

Ray Boone stepped into the box, the Indians now leading 11 to 0. He blasted a three-run homer to increase the lead to 14-0.

Mercifully, Jim Hegan popped out to first to end a very brutal inning. Seventeen men had come to the plate. Fourteen of them had scored. It was a record in the modern era that would be equaled several times, but not surpassed.

Carl was right back out there in the 2nd. He allowed two more singles with one out, but got Luke Easter to ground into a double play to end the inning.

Carl remained in the game for the 3rd inning. Things got ugly again as he loaded the bases on a single and two walks. With one out, Jim Hegan stepped in with the bases loaded. Hegan would have his third of five All-Star appearances in 1950. He would play 17 years in the majors, hitting only .228. But he was a solid defender with some power.

"Shanty," as he was known, stepped into one and pulled it over the fence for a grand slam. The Indians were now up 18 to 0.

Pitcher Mike Garcia followed with a single, as did Dale Mitchell, the runners advancing on an error by Barney McCosky in left.

With runners now on second and third and one out, Bob Kennedy stepped to the plate. He lined a ball at shortstop Eddie Joost, who quickly flipped to Suder at second, catching Mitchell off the bag for a double play.

Moe Burtschy pitched the rest of the game, giving up three more runs.

Mike Garcia was the beneficiary of a 21 to 2 win. Lou Brissie fell to 2-9, his ERA rising to 5.17. Carl pitched 2 2/3 innings, charged with nine runs, five earned, on nine hits and three walks. His ERA ballooned to 7.54.

The A's had been swept in a four-game series. They were now 19-38, 20½ games out in 8th place.

Having pitched four days in a row to little benefit, Carl was kept out of games for five days. One June 23rd, he pitched in relief against the White Sox in Chicago.

Alex Kellner fell behind Randy Gumpert 6 to 1 after four innings. Carl relieved for the 5th and the 6th, giving up two runs on one hit and three walks. The White Sox won 11 to 5.

On June 28th, the Red Sox were at Shibe Park for a wild affair. Bob Hooper was the starting pitcher for the A's versus Chuck Stobbs. Despite the A's poor record, Hooper had been 7-4 to that point. Neither pitcher would escape the 1st inning.

In the top of the 1st, Hooper was wild, giving up six runs, five earned, on two hits and six walks. Trailing 6 to 0 with two outs, Carl got the call. He was able to get the final out in the inning without further damage.

The A's erupted for four runs in the bottom of the 1st, knocking Stobbs out of the game.

Carl returned to the hill for the 2nd, only trailing by two. He did not record an out. He gave up four runs, three earned. Dick Fowler replaced him and gave up four more runs before retiring the side.

Now trailing 14 to 4, the A's rallied for three in the bottom of the 2nd, but they could not catch up. The Red Sox won 22 to 14—a football score. There were 35 hits and 11 walks in the game but only one home run—a two-run blast by Ted Williams.

Carl's ERA was back up to 8.12. The A's were 22-44.

145

On July 5th, the A's were at Yankee Stadium. Alex Kellner faced Tommy Byrne. Kellner fell behind again, and was knocked out after the 4th, trailing 6 to 2.

The A's got two back against Byrne in the 6th before an out was recorded. Casey Stengel called on Joe Ostrowski to end the threat. He did, holding the score to 6 to 4.

After the Yankees got two more off of Hank Wyse in the 6th, Carl got the call, trailing 8 to 4.

In the top of the 7th, he pinch-hit for Ostrowski, but grounded into a rally-killing double play. The A's did manage one run, pulling to within 8 to 5.

Carl then took the mound in the bottom of the 7th. He walked Cliff Mapes but got pitcher Ostrowski to ground into a force play at second. Phil Rizzuto followed with a double, putting two men in scoring position. Gene Woodling then hit a sacrifice fly, plating Ostrowksi for the 9th run. Carl ended the inning by getting Yogi Berra to fly out to left.

The A's went in order in the 8th. The Yankees did not. After Joe DiMaggio grounded out, Johnny Mize walked. The Yanks then loaded the bases on a single and another walk. Cliff Mapes followed with a two-run single. Ostrowksi was next, grounding out, but driving in a run.

Carl then retired Phil Rizzuto to end the inning. The Yankees now led 12 to 5.

In the top of the 9th, the A's started a rally with two outs. Mike Guerra singled. Carl followed with a triple, scoring him. After Bob Dillinger walked, Elmer Valo tripled in both runners, making the score 12 to 8. Paul Lehner then flied out to left to end the game.

Carl had pitched two innings, giving up four runs on three hits and three walks. His ERA hit a season-high 8.52. The A's were 25-46.

On July 16th, the first-place Tigers were in Philadelphia for a doubleheader. The A's won the first game 5 to 2 behind Alex Kellner.

In the second game, Bob Hooper started against Ted Gray.

The A's got out to a 4 to 0 lead by the top of the 4th. In that inning, Hooper gave up six runs, including home runs by George Kell and Hoot Evers. With two outs, Hooper was yanked in favor of Carl. Carl walked a batter but struck out George Kell, the 11th batter in the inning, to end the threat.

Now trailing 6 to 4, the A's got a run in the bottom of the 4th, chasing Gray.

146

Carl proceeded to mow down the first-place Tigers through the 8th. In the top of the 9th, Jerry Priddy hit a solo home run to put Detroit up 7 to 5.

In the bottom of the 9th, with two outs, Ferris Fain singled in a run and was the tying run on base, but Pete Suder flied out to end the game. The final score was 7 to 6.

Carl threw 5 1/3 innings, giving up a run on three hits and three walks. It was his best outing since April.

The next day, despite having thrown over five innings in the last 24 hours, Carl was again called in relief of a struggling starting pitcher against the Tigers.

Lou Brissie was nursing a 6 to 3 lead going into the 5th inning. With one out, he gave up two more runs, allowing the Tigers to close the gap to 6 to 5.

Carl was summoned from the bullpen to face Johnny Groth with men on first and second. He singled to load the bases.

Next up was Don Kolloway. Carl got him to roll into a double play to end the inning.

Going into the 8th inning, Carl maintained the tight 6 to 5 lead. Hoot Evers started the inning with a single. Pat Mullin pinch-hit for Johnny Groth and added another single. With Charlie Keller at the plate, catcher Joe Tipton threw down to first after a pitch to nail Mullin, but Keller followed with a triple to score Evers. The game was now tied at 6.

Aaron Robinson pinch-hit for Bob Swift. Carl intentionally walked him to put runners on the corners with one out.

Fred Hutchinson was then called to pinch-hit for Hal Newhouser. He singled, driving in the go-ahead run. Carl then got the hook, Bob Hooper taking his place.

Next, Johnny Lipon lined out to center, Aaron Robinson tagging and taking third. Jerry Priddy then followed with a single scoring Robinson, but Hutchinson was thrown out at home to end the inning.

The Tigers were now up 8 to 6. Neither team scored the rest of the way. Hal Newhouser was credited with his 10th win. Carl was the losing pitcher, falling to 1-6. He gave up three runs in three innings on five hits and two walks.

On July 19th, the Indians were in Philadelphia, sending Bob Feller against Dick Fowler.

7/21/50
2-6, ERA 7.74

Feller threw a four-hit shutout for his 9th win of the season. Carl pitched a scoreless 9th with the A's trailing 4 to 0. He started the inning by striking out Bob Feller.

The White Sox were in Philadelphia on July 21st. Lou Brissie started the game and got into trouble in the 8th inning, holding a 5 to 2 lead. He gave up two runs with no one out and was pulled in favor of Carl.

Carl entered the game with a one-run lead. He could not get out of the inning, coughing up two more runs on two hits and two walks in two-thirds of an inning. Hank Wyse came in to shut the door, the A's now trailing 6 to 5.

The A's tied the game in the bottom of the 9th and won it in the bottom of the 11th, 7 to 6.

Two days later, in the same series, Carl was called to pitch the 8th, the White Sox winning 4 to 2. He pitched two scoreless innings.

In the bottom of the 9th, the A's mounted a rally. Luis Aloma walked the first two batters. Pete Suder pinch-hit for Carl, and got to first on an infield single. The bases were now loaded.

Aloma then walked Eddie Joost to drive in a run. The score was now 4 to 3, no one out, and the bases still loaded.

Mickey Haefner was summoned to try to stop the rally. He pitched too carefully to Wally Moses, forcing in the tying run. Paul Lehner then singled to right, driving in the game-winner.

Said Carl of Paul Lehner, "He was our top pinch hitter. I was number two. He was a skinny guy who could really hit, and could drink a case of beer a night."

The A's had won 5 to 4, Carl was the beneficiary of the late rally, improving his record to 2-6. His ERA dropped to 7.74.

On July 25th, the A's were in Cleveland to face Bob Feller and the Indians. Alex Kellner took the mound for the A's, and yielded six runs in the first three innings. The A's entered the 4th trailing 6 to 1. They added two runs in the top of the inning to close the gap to 6 to 3.

Carl was called from the bullpen. He walked Jim Hegan, but then retired Feller and Dale Mitchell. Lou Boudreau followed with a single scoring Hegan. The A's were now down 7 to 3.

In the top of the 5th, Carl faced Bob Feller with one out. He singled to center, but was stranded on third at the end of the inning.

In the bottom of the 5th, Al Rosen singled, but Carl escaped any trouble.

Bob Feller then mowed down the A's in the top of the 6th. Carl returned the favor in the bottom of the 6th, retiring Feller, Mitchell, and Boudreau in order.

In the 7th, Joe Tipton started the inning with a home run, pulling the A's to within 7 to 4. Carl followed with another single versus Bob Feller. Eddie Joost walked, but Rapid Robert ended the inning with two strikeouts.

In the bottom of the 7th, Carl escaped without any trouble, stranding Luke Easter who had singled.

In the top of the 8th, Ferris Fain led off with a double. The next two batters flied out to left, but Fain got to third. Joe Tipton followed with a walk, putting men on the corners with two outs for Carl.

Carl had been 2 for 2 against Bob Feller in the game. Feller would win 266 games in his career, entering the Hall of Fame. He would lead the American League in strikeouts seven times, and wins six times. Now 31, Bob had been signed by the Indians when he was only 17 years old. If anyone symbolized the expectations for Carl when he came up at 16, it was fellow-teen phenom Bob Feller. Feller lost three seasons to the war and very likely would have won over 300 games in his career.

Carl hit a bullet to the hot corner, but Al Rosen picked it and fired to second for the force out to end the inning.

In the bottom of the 8th, Carl retired three in a row, including Feller for the final out on a pop-up to second.

In the top of the 9th, Feller began to struggle. Eddie Joost walked. After Wally Moses popped out to second, Paul Lehner singled to put men on first and second. Sam Chapman then singled to center, scoring Joost, and chasing Feller.

With only one out and two men on, Bob Lemon got the call to shut things down. The A's were trailing 7 to 5. Ferris Fain was next up. He coaxed a walk from Lemon. The bases were now loaded.

Billy Hitchcock stepped into the batter's box against Lemon. He hit a fly to left deep enough to score the run. It was now 7 to 6 with two outs and two men on.

Kermit Wahl was next up. He hit a hard grounder to Rosen near the bag. Rosen, who was guarding the line, scooped it up and stepped on third for the final out.

Bob Feller won his 10th game. Bob Lemon earned his 3rd save. The A's lost, but Carl had held them close with five innings of one-

1950
Eddie Robinson
Carl's nemesis

run ball. He had also produced two hits against one of the greatest pitchers of all-time.

On July 29th, at Briggs Stadium, the A's faced the Tigers. Ted Gray started for the Tigers against Bobby Shantz. Neither allowed a run in the 1st.

In the top of the 2nd, the A's took a 2 to 0 lead on Kermit Wahl's two-run single.

In the bottom of the 2nd, Johnny Groth singled off of Shantz, who was then replaced by Carl. Carl walked the bases loaded, but escaped with a strikeout and double play. The score was still 2 to 0.

In the top of the 3rd, Carl came to bat against Ted Gray. Ted had been called to his first and only All-Star game in 1950. He had won ten games in 1949, and was on his way to another ten-win season in 1950. Carl turned on a pitch and drove it into the seats for the third run of the game. Eddie Joost followed with a home run to make it 4 to 0.

In the bottom of the 3rd, the Tigers got one back on Vic Wertz's RBI double.

Two innings later, in the bottom of the 5th, Wertz ripped a pitch into the seats for a solo home run. The lead was now 4 to 2.

The Tigers scored an unearned run in the 6th to pull within one, 4 to 3.

Carl batted in the top of the 7th, reaching on an error, but he was stranded.

Hank Wyse picked up the pitching duties for the A's. He gave up the lead in the 7th and 8th. The Tigers went on to win 8 to 5 to remain in first place.

Carl pitched five innings of three run ball. He also hit a solo home run in three at bats.

The A's visited Comiskey Park in Chicago on August 2nd. Carl was back as a starting pitcher, facing Ray Scarborough.

In the bottom of the 1st, with two out and two on, Eddie Robinson hit a three-run home run to give the White Sox an early lead.

EDDIE

Of all the players Carl faced in his career at least forty times, Eddie was his nemesis. Robinson hit four home runs and batted in 12 in 48 plate appearances, hitting .432 against him. The big first baseman was a four-time All-Star in his 13 year big league career. Robinson hit 20 or more home runs in four seasons and 100 or more RBI three times.

The A's tied it up in the 3rd. With one out, Carl singled and scored on Eddie Joost's home run. Elmer Valo hit the game-tying home run later in the inning.

The A's took the lead in the 4th when Joe Tipton knocked in Ferris Fain, who had doubled.

Philadelphia padded their lead with four runs in the 5th, chasing Scarborough. The A's had four hits, an intentional walk, a sacrifice fly, and scored a run on Carl's ground out. They now led 8 to 3.

They added insurance runs in the 8th and 9th on RBI singles.

Carl, meanwhile, was enjoying front-running for once. He didn't give up a run the rest of the way, scattering eight hits and four walks, earning the win. His record improved to 3-6. His ERA dropped to 6.69. It would be his only complete-game in 1950.

Sunday, August 5th, the Browns were in St. Louis for a battle of teams deadlocked for last place. Carl started against Ned Garver.

Once again, Carl gave up three runs in the bottom of the 1st.

The A's got one back in the 2nd, but the Browns rallied in their home 3rd. Carl gave up a run before he was pulled in favor of Bobby Shantz. Bobby then gave up three more in the inning, the Browns ahead 7 to 1. They went on to win 10 to 3.

Carl was the loser, giving up four runs in two innings on three hits and two walks. He fell to 3-7. His ERA was back up to 6.97.

The Browns had nudged past them into 7th.

Carl got another chance to start against the Yankees in New York on August 12th. He faced Allie Reynolds.

The A's got out to a 1 to 0 lead in the 1st on Sam Chapman's RBI single.

Carl put the Yankees down in the 1st, allowing a runner on an infield error.

In the 2nd, Carl singled against Reynolds but was stranded.

In the bottom of the 2nd, Carl got into trouble. Yogi Berra bounced a ball into the stands for a ground-rule double. Bobby Brown drew a walk, bringing up Cliff Mapes. He put down a sacrifice bunt, moving the runners into scoring position. Carl then intentionally walked Jerry Coleman to load the bases and set up a double play.

Pitcher Allie Reynolds was next up. Superchief was not a good hitter, but he got a hold of a Scheib pitch, sending into right field for a single, scoring Berra and Brown. Gene Woodling then followed with a single scoring Coleman.

The Scooter, Phil Rizzuto stepped up. He slapped a double, plating Reynolds and putting two men in scoring position.

At that point, Carl was pulled in favor of Bobby Shantz. Shantz didn't fare much better. He intentionally walked Hank Bauer to load the bases and set-up a double play.

Johnny Mize then stepped in. "The Big Cat" had been purchased by the Yankees from the Giants in August of 1949. His nine All-Star appearances straddled three years of war service. Mize led the National League in home runs four times, and RBI three times. The 37-year-old first baseman produced 25 home runs and 72 RBI in 113 games in 1950 on his way to an eventual election to the Hall of Fame. Mize hit 359 home runs in his career, and may have approached 500 if not for his war service.

Mize tapped a ball back to Shantz, who turned and threw to 2nd for the force, but Mize beat the throw to 1st, allowing the runner on third to score.

Yogi Berra ended the inning on a ground-out.

The Yankees won the game 7-2, Reynolds improving to 10-10, while Carl dropped to 3-8. Carl's ERA was back up to 7.39.

Four days later, on August 15th, the A's were at Fenway to face the Red Sox. Bob Hooper started against Walt Masterson. Neither would be around at the end.

The A's took a 7 to 4 lead in the 3rd, chasing Masterson. The Red Sox, however, chipped away, scoring one in the 4th, two in the 5th, and three in the 6th, taking a 10 to 7 lead on Hooper. Bob was pulled in favor of Carl for the 7th. Carl went the rest of the way, giving up two runs on five hits as the Red Sox won 12 to 7.

The next day, 29-year-old rookie Joe Murray made his major league debut against the Red Sox. He had been called up following his 20 win season at West Palm Beach in the Florida International League. Murray had been in the minors since signing at age 19.

Ellis Kinder took the hill for the BoSox.

The Red Sox manufactured two runs in the 2nd off of the rookie. In the bottom of the 3rd, he couldn't get an out. Johnny Pesky walked and Billy Goodman reached on an error. Vern Stephens then hit a double, scoring Pesky. Bobby Doerr walked to load the bases. Clyde Vollmer followed with a single, scoring Gooodman. The bases were still loaded and no one was out.

Carl was called from the bullpen to replace Murray. He gave up a double to Al Zarilla, plating two. After an intentional walk, Ellis Kinder helped himself with a sacrifice fly. Carl then ended the inning on a double play by Dom DiMaggio. The A's now trailed 7 to 0. All of the runs were charged to Murray.

Carl pitched four innings, yielding two more runs in the 6th. The Red Sox won 10 to 6.

On August 20th, Carl pitched the last two innings at home against the Yankees in a 6 to 4 defeat. Eddie Lopat won his 4th game for the Yanks.

Five days later, on August 25th, Carl spelled Alex Kellner again as the A's lost to the Indians at home 6 to 2. Carl pitched the final 2 2/3 innings without giving up a run, but the A's could not rally against Mike Garcia.

In the 7th inning, Carl batted against Garcia and drove in a run on a single.

Two days later, against the Tigers at home, Carl mopped up an 8 to 1 loss, pitching the last two innings, yielding three runs, one earned.

On Wednesday August 30th, the two worst teams in the American League, the Browns and A's faced off in a doubleheader. Only 1356 fans attended.

In the first game, the Browns won 2 to 1, Ned Garver besting Alex Kellner in a pitchers' duel. The second game pitted Hank Wyse against Al Widmar.

The teams were knotted at a run apiece until the top of the 5th, when the Browns scored three. Carl entered the game in the 6th, losing 4 to 1, and pitched the next four innings, yielding two runs run on five hits.

The A's were losing 6 to 1 in the bottom of the 8th when they scored twice, narrowing the deficit. They then tied the game in the bottom of the 9th, Al Widmar unable to close the deal.

Joe Murray took over in extra innings and coughed up a run in the 10th. The A's couldn't match it against Don Johnson in the bottom of the 10th, losing 7 to 6.

Murray was now 0-2. Carl's ERA improved to 6.79. The A's were 43-83, one game behind the Browns.

Carl was the starting pitcher on September 2nd against the Red Sox in Philadelphia. Mel Parnell was his opponent.

1950, ERA 7.22
3-10, worst complete season
Carl wants a trade!

The Sox jumped ahead 3 to 0 in the 2nd. In the 3rd, they added two more before Joe Murray got the call to replace Carl with only one out, the team trailing 5 to 0.

The A's could not catch up, though Murray pitched well, giving up only two runs in 5 2/3 innings. Carl, on the other hand, had yielded five runs on eight hits in 2 1/3 innings. His ERA was back up to 7.08. He fell to 3-9.

On September 6th, Sandy Consuegra of the Senators threw a six-hit shutout against the A's at Griffith Stadium in Washington. Bobby Shantz had coughed up an early lead, and was tagged with the loss, though he pitched well for seven innings. Carl pitched the 8th inning, and did not give up a run or a hit. The A's lost 3 to 0.

Two days later, with the A's still in Washington, Cuban Julio Moreno made his first major league start against Joe Murray.

The Senators gave Moreno a three-run lead in the bottom of the 1st, and extended it to 6 to 0 through the 4th. Murray was pulled in favor of Carl for the 5th.

Carl gave up three runs in the 6th and was yanked and replaced by Joe Coleman in the 7th.

The A's finally got to the rookie in the 8th with a run. They rallied in the 9th for three more, but Moreno held on for a complete-game victory, 10 to 4.

Carl gave up three runs on three hits and three walks in only two innings. His ERA increased to 7.13.

Joe Murray fell to 0-3. His ERA ballooned to 7.97. It would be his last decision in the major leagues.

Carl was called into a tie game against the Browns at Sportsman's Park to pitch the 9th. The game was locked at 3-3, Lou Brissie battling Ned Garver the whole way.

Rookie right fielder Ken Wood was the first batter of the inning. He ripped a pitch into the seats to end the game, 4 to 3. Carl did not record an out and was tagged with one run and the loss. He fell to 3-10. His ERA finished at 7.22. It was Carl's worst complete season. He had been the opening day starter, but faltered in most of his games. In 106 innings pitched, he gave up 138 hits and 70 walks, totaling 208 base runners—nearly two per inning. Ninety-six of those runners scored.

"After the first couple years," Carl recalled, "Connie Mack went to relieving me quite a lot, and that had a tendency of giving me a sore arm. Later, I had a lot of arm problems. Of course, the ball clubs didn't know what to do about sore arms in those years. Most of the relieving happened in the beginning of a season, when Mr. Mack was trying to regulate his four or five starters."

At the plate, Carl hit .250 in 52 at bats. He hit one home run and drove in six.

The team finished 52-102, a distant 8th in the American League.

Sam Chapman led the team with 23 home runs and 95 RBI. Paul Lehner and Bob Dillinger both hit .309.

On the mound, Bob Hooper was 15-10, but with a 5.02 ERA. He pitched more than half of his games in relief. Alex Kellner lost 20 games. Lou Brissie lost 19.

Connie Mack, who was eighty-eight on December 22nd, 1950, retained the title of club president, but he no longer owned or controlled the team.

Reflecting on those years in 2006, Carl said, "I wanted to be traded so badly. I really wanted to pitch for Detroit, or for Boston. I almost made it to Detroit, but Joost was in the deal, and the A's wouldn't let him go. I just wanted to pitch for a better team."

11.

FIREMAN

Carl turned twenty-four on January 1st, 1951 and became a father for the second time that month. Georgene gave birth to another daughter, Sandra Lee Scheib.

The A's were at Fenway Park in Boston on Sunday April 22nd, 1951. Dick Fowler started against Ray Scarborough.

The A's took a 1 to 0 lead in the 1st on Ferris Fain's RBI single.

In the bottom of the 1st, Ted Williams hit a two-run home run to put the BoSox ahead.

The score remained 2 to 1 until the bottom of the 3rd. Dom DiMaggio doubled with one out. Billy Goodman followed with a single, putting men on the corners. Fowler then walked Ted Williams to load the bases.

Next up was Lou Boudreau. The Indians former player-manager had been released after the 1950 season. The Sox picked him up as a free agent. The 34-year-old shortstop was nearing the end of a Hall of Fame career. Lou had been a seven-time All-Star during his 15-year career, winning the MVP Award in 1948 when the Indians won the World Series. Lou hit .355 that year with 18 home runs, 116 runs scored, and 106 RBI. He owned one batting title, and led the league in doubles twice. He would be a utility player for the Sox.

Boudreau slashed a single into center scoring two. The Sox were now up 4 to 1 with one out. Carl got the call from the pen.

Vern Stephens was first to bat against Carl. He hit a shot to third baseman Kermit Wahl, who threw to second sacker Billy Hitchcock for the force. Hitchcock then threw wildly to first attempting to get the double play. Ted Williams scored the fifth run on the play.

Carl ended the inning by getting Taffy Wright to fly out to left.

In the bottom of the 4th, the Sox got another run on Dom DiMaggio's RBI single, plating Bobby Doerr.

Eddie Joost made it 6 to 2 in the 5th, blasting a home run. Scarborough and Carl then traded zeros until the 9th.

"I remember Joe Tipton being able to make home plate umpire Bill McGowan and Ted Williams bust up laughing," said Carl. "Ted was trying to hit and Tipton kept asking him if he had noticed the beautiful blonde sitting 'over there.' It worked because Ted popped out to second!"

In the top of the 9th, Barney McCosky led off with a double. Wally Moses pinch-hit for Carl and drew a walk. Scarborough was pulled for Ellis Kinder with no one out.

Eddie Joost singled to left, scoring McCosky. The score was now 6 to 3. Kinder was recalled for Mel Parnell.

Elmer Valo greeted Parnell with an RBI single, plating Moses. The lead was down to two and there were men on first and third with no one out.

Paul Lehner was next. He grounded into a 3-6-3 double play, Joost scoring the 5th run.

Parnell then got Sam Chapman to ground out to win the game. The final score was 6 to 5.

Carl pitched 5 2/3 innings, giving up only one run on six hits and four walks.

On April 27th, Carl and the A's were at Griffith Stadium in Washington to face the Senators. Sandy Consuegra was Carl's opponent.

Both teams used extra-base hits to score runs in the 1st inning. Carl, however, game up an additional run in the 2nd on Eddie Yost's RBI single.

Neither team scored in the 3rd or 4th innings, but Carl got into trouble in the 5th. With two outs, the Nats had two on base. Second baseman Gene Verble came to the plate, and hit a grounder to Kermit Wahl at third. Kermit threw wildly to first for an error, scoring a run and putting two men in scoring position. Sam Dente followed with a single plating two. The inning ended with the A's trailing 5 to 1.

Carl was pulled for the 6th, replaced by Morrie Martin. The Senators went on to win 6 to 1. Carl was the losing pitcher, falling to 0-1. The Senators were 7-1 in 1st place in the American League. The A's were last at 1-10.

On April 30th, as part of a three-team trade, the Chicago White Sox sent Dave Philley and Gus Zernial to the Philadelphia Athletics. The Philadelphia Athletics sent Paul Lehner to the Chicago White Sox. The Philadelphia Athletics sent Lou Brissie to the Cleveland Indians. The Cleveland Indians sent Minnie Minoso to the Chicago White Sox. The Cleveland Indians sent Ray Murray and Sam Zoldak to the Philadelphia Athletics.

1951

On May 1ˢᵗ, Carl faced Dizzy Trout and the Tigers in Detroit. What a pitchers' duel! The two hurlers each threw seven shutout innings before the A's came to bat in the 8ᵗʰ.

With one out, Carl came to the plate and ripped a single right at center-fielder Johnny Groth. The ball was playable but bounced through Groth's hands and rolled to the wall. Carl, meanwhile, chugged around the bases, making it home before Groth could retrieve the ball. The play was ruled a single and an error, allowing Carl to score. It was the only run the A's would score in the inning. They were now up 1 to 0.

In the bottom of the 8ᵗʰ, the Tigers started to make some noise. Jerry Priddy led off with a single. George Kell followed with a line-drive right at shortstop Eddie Joost, who threw across the diamond to first baseman Ferris Fain to nab Priddy for a double play. Carl then got Vic Wertz to pop out to third.

In the top of the 9ᵗʰ, Fain greeted Trout with a single to center. Dizzy then walked Sam Chapman to put two men on. Kermit Wahl followed with a shot to third baseman Kell, who stepped on the bag for the force and threw to Priddy at second for the second out. Priddy could not nab Wahl for a triple-play at first, but the rally was effectively ended. Pete Suder grounded out to end the inning.

In the bottom of the 9ᵗʰ, Carl needed three outs for the complete-game shutout. He got Hoot Evers to tap back to him. Carl flipped to first for the first out.

Next up was Charlie Keller, pinch hitting for Johnny Groth. The former Yankee All-Star had hit .314 as a pinch hitter in 1950, but he had only gone 1 for 5 in limited duty in April—all pinch hitting appearances. Carl walked him.

Catcher Joe Ginsberg was next. He slapped a single just past second-baseman Suder. Neil Berry, who was pinch-running for Keller, scooted to third. Now there were men on the corners with one out.

Pat Mullin was announced as the pinch hitter for Johnny Lipon. Jimmy Dykes opted to go with Hank Wyse, pulling Carl.

Wyse got Mullin to fly out to right field, but it was deep enough for Berry to score the tying run. After a single to Dick Kryhoski, Dizzy Trout grounded out to end the inning.

Trout and Wyse each posted zeros in the 10ᵗʰ inning, but in the top of the 11ᵗʰ, the A's broke out. They scored eight runs against Trout and Gene Bearden, including a three-run double by Lou Limmer, a two-run triple by Dave Philley, and a two-run single by Eddie Joost.

The A's won 9 to 1 in eleven innings. Wyse was the winner, Carl getting a no-decision. Carl pitched 8 1/3 innings of one-run ball, yielding only five hits and four walks. His ERA dropped to 1.89. It wouldn't be any lower for the rest of the year.

The win ended a ten game losing streak for the A's, who were now 2-12 in last place, already 7½ games back.

The next day, the A's sold Bubba Harris to the Indians. On May 4th, they sold Barney McCosky to the Cincinnati Reds.

Carl's next start was against the White Sox in Chicago on May 6th. His opponent was Ken Holcombe.

The game was scoreless until the bottom of the 5th. Gus Niarhos led off with a walk. Pitcher Holcombe then singled to short, Eddie Joost throwing wildly to first. Both runners moved up. Chico Carrasquel flied out to right, deep enough to score Niarhos. Floyd Baker grounded-out for the second out, but Holcombe made it to third. Carl then hit Minnie Minoso with a pitch. He stole second to put two men in scoring position. Eddie Robinson then singled to right scoring Holcombe. As Robinson was caught in a run-down between first and second, Minoso flew home for the third run, Robinson tagged out to the end the inning.

The game ended with a 4 to 1 White Sox victory. Carl was tagged with his second loss despite pitching well. He pitched a complete-game, eight innings, giving up only three earned runs on five hits and five walks. He was now 0-2 despite pitching well enough to win his last two starts. The A's fell to 3-15, 11½ back.

The A's made it up to Carl on May 9th at Sportsman's Park in St. Louis. The A's and the Browns, the two worst teams in the league, were tied at one going into the bottom of the 8th. In that inning Alex Kellner, gave up the go-ahead run, the Browns now ahead 2 to 1. However, in the top of the 9th, Eddie Joost hit a game-tying home run.

Carl then took over on the mound for the A's in the bottom of the 9th. He did not allow a run.

In the top of the 10th, the A's exploded for six runs against Stubby Overmire and Al Widmar. Carl was a key player in the rally with a run-scoring double. He also came around to score a run.

1951 Carl faces Mantle for first time

Carl shut down the Browns in the 10th for the victory. He was now 1-2, and the A's and Browns were tied for 7th place in the American League at 5-16.

CARL

The next day, the Cleveland Indians traded Allie Clark and Lou Klein to the Athletics for Sam Chapman.

Three days later on May 13th, the Yankees were at Shibe Park. Alex Kellner threw the first six innings for the A's, giving up three runs, including a two-run home run to nineteen-year-old Mickey Mantle in the 6th. He handed the ball to Carl with a 4 to 3 lead.

In the top of the 7th, Carl walked the bases loaded while also mixing in two fly outs. Mantle was the third walk, a wise move after his blast in the 6th.

Hank Bauer came up with the bases loaded and two outs. Carl got him to pop out to first base to end the inning.

In the bottom of the 7th, Carl helped pad the lead by singling in a run.

To start the 8th, Yogi Berra doubled. Then, with Jack Jensen batting, Carl threw a wild pitch, allowing Berra to get to third. Jensen popped out to the catcher.

Gene Woodling, pinch hitting for Gil McDougald, singled in Berra. Carl then struck out Joe Collins, catcher Joe Tipton nailing Woodling trying to steal second. The inning ended with the A's up 5 to 4.

Carl took the mound in the top of the 9th with a one-run lead and Billy Martin at the plate.

Martin, still a rookie after appearing in only 34 games in 1950, had been put in the game as a defensive replacement at second base in the 7th. He rolled a single to third base.

Cliff Mapes followed, tapping back to Carl, who threw to first for the first out. Martin moved into scoring position on the play.

Phil Rizzuto flipped a single into right field. Martin rounded third while Elmer Valo got to the ball and fired it home to Tipton to clip Martin at the plate. Rizzuto scooted to second on the play. There were now two outs, and the lead preserved for the moment.

Next up was right fielder Mickey Mantle. Young Mickey would go on to a Hall of Fame career, blasting 536 home runs, winning four home run titles and a triple crown. He would be an All-Star from 1952 through 1965, missing in 1966, before earning the honor twice more in the twilight of his career.

Mickey had been hot, hitting over .300 in the early going in 1951. He stepped in against Carl for the first time with the

Scooter on second. When a ball got past Tipton, Rizzuto zipped to third, only ninety feet away from tying the game. Carl, however, got Mickey to pop out to him on the mound to end the game.

Thus ended the first encounter between Carl and Mickey Mantle. The A's won 5 to 4, Carl earning the save with three innings of one-run relief.

"I never had too much trouble with Mantle," recalled Carl. "He'd strike out a lot, and he couldn't play the outfield very well."

On May 16th, the two worst teams in the American League went at it again at Shibe Park. Carl started the game against Cliff Fannin. The A's handed Carl a 5 to 0 lead in the bottom of the 2nd. Carl made the best of it through three, putting up zeros, but in the 4th, the Browns caught up.

Until Jerry Berardino batted in the top of the 4th, Carl had not yielded a hit or a run, but the second time through the batting order was not going to be the same. Berardino beat out an infield single. Ray Coleman followed with another single. Sherm Lollar grounded into a force at second, putting men on the corners. Carl then got Roy Sievers on strikes. There were now two outs.

Up stepped Don Lenhardt, the Browns' left fielder. Lenhardt had hit 22 home runs as a 27-year-old rookie in 1950. He had hit 26 homers for San Antonio in the Texas League in 1949. Never an All-Star, Lenhardt would never improve upon his rookie season, but he had Carl's number this day. Lenhardt stepped into a pitch and sent it sailing out of Shibe Park. Three scored.

After Hank Arft and Tom Upton singled, Jim Delsing was called to pinch-hit for Cliff Fannin. Carl uncorked a wild pitch, allowing the runners to move up. Delsing then doubled to right field scoring both men. The game was tied at five.

Jimmy Dykes had seen enough. He pulled Carl in favor of Bob Hooper. Despite the excellent first trip through the lineup, Carl faltered terribly in the 3rd. He had given up five runs on six hits in 3 2/3 innings. His ERA jumped to 3.28.

The Browns ultimately went on to win this one 10 to 9, scoring two runs in the 8th. The A's slipped back into last place, behind the Browns, at 7-19.

Carl was back in the bullpen when the Indians were in town for a doubleheader on Sunday May 20th.

After winning a 2 to 1 pitchers' duel behind Dick Fowler in the first game, the A's and Indians were tied at three through six innings when Carl got the call to replace Morrie Martin in the 7th.

Carl put down the Indians in order in the 7th, but got into trouble in the 8th. After getting Larry Doby to foul out to left, he walked Al Rosen and gave up a single to Harry Simpson. Bob Kennedy followed with a single to left, scoring Rosen.

Next up was Sam Chapman. The veteran had been traded by the A's to the Indians only ten days prior. Chapman had been a solid performer in center field for the A's since the 1938 season, but he had gotten off to a slow start in 1951, hitting only .169, when the A's decided to try to get something for the 35-year-old fading former All-Star.

Chapman, who had already been in the military when Carl debuted as a sixteen-year-old in 1943, stepped into the box against his former mate. He hit a shot to third-baseman Kermit Wahl, but Wahl threw across the diamond to nail Chapman. Simpson scored on the play.

Carl ended the inning by striking out pinch hitter Luke Easter. However, the Indians were up 5 to 3. Carl was tagged with the loss, falling to 1-3 on the season.

Four days later, on the 24th, Carl pitched the final two innings of a 5 to 2 loss to the White Sox at Shibe Park. He gave up two hits and two walks but no runs.

Two days later, on the 26th, the A's were at Yankee Stadium. Dick Fowler started and faltered in the 2nd. With the bases loaded, one out, and the Yankees winning 2 to 0, Mickey Mantle cleared the bases with a triple. Jimmy Dykes came out to get Fowler, replacing him with Carl. The Yanks now had a 5 to 0 lead with Mantle standing on third base.

Next up, and the first to face Carl, was Bobby Brown. Brown was a left-handed hitting third baseman, who platooned at the position for Casey Stengel. He took Carl's pitch into the right field corner seats for a two-run home run. It was now 7 to 0.

Joe DiMaggio was next up. The Yankee Clipper, now 36, was in his last year in the major leagues. The skills were fading, and his batting average showed. Carl got him to ground out to third for the second out.

"I had a lot of respect for DiMaggio," said Carl. "But he was at the end of his career. I could throw a fastball by him, and he would swing late. He was a competitor though. He'd yell at any of his guys who loafed."

Yogi Berra had been hitting Carl well since he came into the league. Today was no exception. Berra ripped a double, hoping to extend the rally.

Carl then walked Hank Bauer, putting two men on with two outs. Joe Collins stepped into the box. The Yankee first baseman was retired on a long fly to center.

In the top of the 3rd, Carl came to bat against Vic Raschi, who was on his way to his third consecutive twenty-win season, and would lead the league in strikeouts in 1951. Carl singled to deep short, beating the throw to first. He would later be stranded on second.

In the bottom of the 3rd, Carl put Coleman, Raschi, and Rizzuto down in order.

In the top of the 4th, the A's scored four runs, closing the gap to 7 to 4. Carl had an RBI single in the inning, scoring on Eddie Joost's double.

In the bottom of the 4th, in Yankee Stadium, Carl faced Mickey Mantle, Bobby Brown, and Joe DiMaggio. He put them down in order.

The A's stranded two in their 5th. Carl retired Berra, Bauer, and Collins.

Carl led off the top of the 6th against Raschi. He put a charge into a pitch, blasting it into the left-center field gap. Carl raced around the bases, arriving safely at third. Eddie Joost followed with a fly to left, deep enough to score Carl. It was now 7 to 5.

In the bottom of the 6th, a little luck prevented another Yankee run. Carl walked Jerry Coleman. Raschi then bunted him over to second. The Scooter, Phil Rizzuto followed, lining a ball right at right fielder Wally Moses, who fired to shortstop Eddie Joost at second to double-off Coleman.

Dave Philley doubled for the A's in the 7th but was stranded. In the Yankees' 7th, Carl walked Mantle to lead off the inning, but with Bobby Brown at the plate, Mickey was caught stealing. Carl then retired Brown and DiMaggio.

In the 8th, Carl got another chance at the plate but popped out to the catcher. The A's stranded a runner and entered the bottom of the 8th still trailing 7 to 5.

Carl started strong in the 8th, retiring Berra and Bauer on pop flies, but Johnny Hopp, who took the place of Joe Collins in the 7th, blasted a solo shot. The veteran had been purchased from the Pirates near the end of the 1950 season. He had hit over .300 three consecutive seasons as a platoon outfielder. With the

*1951 in
Carl is
losing some good
games with good pitching*

Yankees, Casey Stengel used him primarily as a pinch hitter. It worked this time. The score was now 8 to 5.

The Yankees then locked up the victory, improving to 25-9 in first place in the American League. The A's slipped to 9-25, 16 games back in last place.

Carl pitched very well, going 6 2/3 innings in relief of Fowler, yielding only two runs on four hits and three walks. His ERA dipped to 3.23.

On Wednesday May 30th, the A's were in Washington, D.C. to face the Senators. Carl got the final two outs in the 8th inning, after replacing Alex Kellner with one out, one on, and the A's losing 5 to 2.

The A's were in St. Louis, at Sportsman's Park on Saturday June 3rd. In the second game of a doubleheader, Carl was the starting pitcher versus Stubby Overmire. The two pitchers only had one win between them, but they dueled for nine innings.

The game was scoreless until the bottom of the 4th, when the Browns nicked Carl for a run. They added another run in the 7th.

With the A's trailing 2 to 0, Carl came to bat in the top of the 8th. He stepped in against Overmire, who was only 5'7" tall, thus the nickname. Carl turned on one of the little lefty's offerings, knocking it out of the park for a home run. The A's had two more singles in the inning, but Stubby struck out Dave Philley to end the threat.

Carl put the Browns down in order in the 8th.

In the top of the 9th, Overmire got two quick outs. Catcher Joe Astroth singled to center, and was replaced by pinch runner Wally Moses.

With Moses as the tying run on base and two outs, Carl stepped to the plate. He had hit a home run in his last at bat against Overmire. This time, Carl grounded out to second base to end the game.

Carl threw a complete game, giving up only two runs on six hits and three walks. His record fell to 1-4, but his ERA improved to 3.05. *TO 3.05*

Overmire improved to 1-4, his ERA dropping to 3.24.

The next day, the team traded Kermit Wahl to the Chicago White Sox for Hank Majeski.

On June 8th, Carl and the A's were at Tiger Stadium to face Dizzy Trout.

Carl fell behind 1 to 0 in the 2nd, giving up a run on three singles.

The Tigers exploded for eight runs in the 3rd, five of them off of Carl. He was pulled with no one out and two men on base, trailing 4 to 0. Both of the inherited runners scored off of Morrie Martin, and then some.

The A's lost 9 to 2. Carl was the losing pitcher, falling to 1-5.

Two days later, on the 10th, Carl was called upon to pitch the 8th inning with the team losing to the Tigers 9 to 7.

He retired Jerry Priddy, but walked George Kell. Vic Wertz was next up, blasting a two-run homer off of Carl. The lead expanded to 11 to 7. Carl got Pat Mullin and Johnny Groth to end the inning.

June 12th, at Shibe Park, Bob Feller and the Indians faced Alex Kellner. Rapid Robert was in the midst of his last twenty-win season.

The Indian's dinged Kellner for a run in the top of the 1st. They followed up with four more in the 2nd, including a three-run home run by Al Rosen.

With the Indians up 5 to 0, the A's got four back in the bottom of the 2nd on six hits and a hit batter. It was now 5 to 4, and Carl was called to replace Kellner in the 3rd.

Neither team scored in the 3rd.

The Indians added two runs in the 4th without a hit. Sam Chapman started things with a walk. Carl then hit Al Rosen. Ray Boone bunted them over to scoring position. With Bob Kennedy at the plate, Carl threw a wild pitch, allowing Chapman to score and Rosen to move to third. Kennedy then hit a sacrifice fly to score Rosen.

With one out in the bottom of the 4th, Carl faced Feller and grounded out. Eddie Joost followed with a home run. The A's were now down 7 to 5.

Both teams were quiet in the 5th.

The Indians added an unearned run in the 6th on a sacrifice fly.

Feller took the 8 to 5 lead into the 9th but gave up two singles. Eddie Joost then hit a deep fly ball for an out, allowing a runner to move up to third. Al Lopez had seen enough, lifting Feller in favor of Lou Brissie.

Brissie had been part of the three-way trade back on April 30th. Lou got Ferris Fain to fly out, but it was deep enough to

1951

score Billy Hitchcock. He then walked Elmer Valo to put the tying run on.

Al Lopez came to the mound again and brought in Mike Garcia to face Gus Zernial. Gus would lead the league in home runs and RBI in 1951, his best season. Garcia got him to fly out to center to end the game.

Thus ended the game where Carl pitched better than Bob Feller, allowing only two runs in seven innings. Feller, who yielded six in 8 1/3, improved his record to 9-1. Alex Kellner took the loss for the A's, who fell to 15-34, mired in last place.

Five days later, on June 17th, Carl was back in the starting rotation against Randy Gumpert and the White Sox. Both starters threw well, pitching complete games. Carl game up four runs in nine innings, scattering ten hits and five walks. Gumpert was better, yielding only one run on eight hits and one walk. The Sox won 4 to 1. Carl fell to 1-6, while Gumpert improved to 6-0.

On June 21st, the A's were home at Shibe Park against the Detroit Tigers. Carl started against Bob Cain.

Detroit scored two in the top of the 1st, but left the bases loaded.

In the bottom of the 3rd, Carl stepped to the plate against Cain. He ripped a home run to close the gap to 2 to 1.

The Tigers got it right back, plus another, in the 4th on three walks and a single. They added another in the 5th on a sacrifice fly. They now led 5 to 1.

Carl batted in the bottom of the 5th and doubled off of Cain, but he was stranded on second.

Neither team scored in the 6th, but the Tigers added another on a sacrifice fly in the 7th on a Vic Wertz triple followed by Pat Mullin's out.

Carl got the first man out in the 8th but gave up three consecutive singles to load the bases before he walked George Kell to drive in a run. Jimmy Dykes finally pulled him, trailing 7 to 1.

Vic Wertz immediately greeted Morrie Martin with a two-run single, expanding the lead to 9 to 1.

The A's added a couple in the 9th, but it was too little, too late. They lost 9 to 3.

Carl was the losing pitcher, dropping to 1-7. He gave up eight earned runs in 7 1/3 innings.

The A's were at Fenway Park on June 27th to face Ray Scarborough and the Red Sox.

Carl gave up a run in the first on Billy Goodman's RBI single. However, he was able to escape the inning, retiring Ted Williams on a grounder to first and Vern Stephens on strikes.

Lou Klein hit a homer for the A's in the 2nd, evening the score at one.

This score held until the bottom of the 4th. Ted Williams and Vern Stephens singled. Bobby Doerr then singled home Williams. After a sacrifice bunt, Les Moss singled home Stephens to increase the lead to 3 to 1.

Facing Willard Nixon in the bottom of the 6th, the A's scored three on a Dave Philley RBI single and Gus Zernial's two-run homer.

Carl took the 4 to 3 lead into the bottom of the 7th. Charlie Maxwell singled. Dom DiMaggio then tripled, driving in the tying run. Johnny Pesky then plated Dom on a sacrifice fly.

Now trailing 5 to 4, Carl gave up a triple to Billy Goodman, and was pulled for Morrie Martin.

Martin faced Ted Williams, who singled in Goodman for a 6 to 4 lead.

The A's got one more run, but still lost 6 to 5. Carl was the losing pitcher, falling to 1-8. He gave up six runs in 6 1/3 innings.

Carl was back in the pen for the game against the Senators on July 1st. Bob Hooper and the hometown A's were enjoying a 3 to 0 lead in the 8th. Hooper walked the first two batters but retired Gil Coan on a line drive. Irv Noren then knocked in a run with a double, making it 3 to 1 with two men in scoring position and only one out.

Jimmy Dykes then replaced Hooper with Carl.

Carl got Sam Mele to ground out, trading an out for a run.

With a man on third and two outs, leading 3 to 2, Carl faced Mickey Vernon. He got him to foul out to third to end the inning.

The A's did not score in the 8th, and Carl retired the Senators in order in the 9th for the save. He threw 1 2/3 perfect innings. It was his second save of the season.

On July 4th, the Red Sox were at Shibe Park. Carl started against Willard Nixon. It would be a rough outing.

The A's plated two in the bottom of the 2nd. Carl came to bat with a man on second and two out, but struck out to end the rally.

1951 ERA 5.36
1-10, ERA 5.36
at all Star Break

In the top of the 3rd, with two men on, Johnny Pesky cleared the bases on a single to right and an error by Hitchcock, which also allowed Pesky to score.

In the top of the 6th, Bobby Doerr hit a two-run home run with no one out. After Carl retired Billy Goodman, he gave up four consecutive hits and two more runs.

With two on and one out, he was pulled in favor of Johnny Kucab.

Johnny Pesky was up again. He ripped Kucab's pitch into center, plating two more runs. The score was now 9 to 2.

While the A's mustered three more, they fell 9 to 5. Carl was the losing pitcher, again, dropping to 1-9.

Carl and the A's were in Washington to face Sid Hudson and the Senators on July 8th.

Something wasn't right with Carl. In the bottom of the 1st, he started the inning by hitting lead-off hitter Ed Yost. After walking Gil Coan, Jimmy Dykes called for Bob Hooper. Hooper got Irv Noren, but gave up a triple to Mickey Vernon.

The Senators went on to win 8 to 2. Carl was tagged with the loss, his tenth, and did not record an out. His ERA was 5.36, the highest it would be in 1951.

After the All-Star break, Carl next pitched against the Tigers at Briggs Stadium on July 18th. In the bottom of the 7th, with the A's winning 10 to 6, Dick Fowler faced Vic Wertz with the bases loaded and one out. Wertz singled in two runs, and Jimmy Dykes went to the pound to pull Fowler in favor of Carl. The score was now 10 to 8.

Carl got Dick Kryhoski to line out for the second out. Johnny Groth followed with a single, plating another run. Charlie Keller was then called upon to pinch-hit for Hoot Evers. He popped out to short to end the inning. Carl had preserved the lead.

In the top of the 8th, Carl came to bat and singled with two outs. He later scored on Dave Philley's single. The A's added six runs, three of them on Hank Majeski's three-run home run. Carl proceeded to mow down the Tigers the rest of the way, retiring six of the final eight batters, including Kell on a fly and Wertz on a strikeout. The final was 16 to 9, with Carl earning his third save.

On July 22nd, Philadelphia was in Cleveland to face the Indians. Dick Fowler squared off against Bob Lemon. Unfortunately for Fowler, he gave up four runs over the first two innings and did not look sharp. Carl pinch-hit for him in the top of the 3rd inning. He then took over duties on the mound.

Carl's first batter was Larry Doby. The limber center fielder turned on a pitch and sent it into the seats, giving the Tribe a five-run lead. Carl then settled down, retiring Easter, Rosen, and Simpson on grounders.

He went the rest of the way and was at the plate with two outs in the 9th with the A's trailing 6 to 4. He grounded out to short to end the game.

Carl registered six innings, yielding only five hits and two runs.

Three days later, on the 25th, the Browns were in Philadelphia. With two outs in the 7th, Sherm Lollar had doubled home the go-ahead run, chasing starter Sam Zoldak, giving St. Louis a 4 to 3 lead. Carl was summoned from the bullpen and ended the rally, getting Jack McGuire to ground out to third, stranding two runners in scoring position.

In the bottom of the 7th, Carl participated in the rally, knocking a single off of Ned Garver. Eddie Joost later plated Dave Philley to tie the game. Carl was left standing on third base when the inning ended.

Carl mowed down the Browns in the 8th, 1-2-3, but the A's could not score in their half.

In the top of the 9th, shortstop Bill Jennings, batting 8th, singled off of Carl to start the inning. He was bunted over to second by pitcher Garver. Lead-off hitter Bobby Young then singled to left, putting runners on first and third. Jim Delsing followed with a sacrifice fly to put the Browns up. Carl ended the threat by getting Lollar to pop out to third.

In the bottom of the 9th, Wally Moses pinch-hit for Carl, but the A's could not score, going down 5 to 4. Carl was the losing pitcher, falling to 1-11 on the season. He had only given up one run in 2 1/3 innings.

The next day, Carl was summoned in the 9th inning with the A's trailing 6 to 3. He walked a couple batters but escaped unscathed. He then watched from the dugout as Satchel Paige nailed down his first save of the season, getting the last two outs for the victorious Browns.

Two days later, on the 28th, Carl was once again called to pitch the 9th inning of a losing affair against the Tigers. With Detroit up

6 to 3, Carl retired Kryhoski, Wertz, and Mullin in order. The A's rallied for two in the bottom of the 9th, but came up short 6 to 5.

The next day, July 29th, the Tigers and A's went at it again at Shibe Park. In the first game of a doubleheader, starter Sam Zoldak fell behind 6 to 2 after five innings. Carl pinch-hit for Zoldak in the bottom of the 5th and struck out against Dizzy Trout. He then took over mound duties for the remainder of the game.

Carl put the Tigers down in order in the 6th and 7th, but gave up a couple runs in the 8th before escaping with the bases loaded.

He then put Detroit down in order in the 9th, but the A's could not rally, falling 8 to 4. Carl had pitched four innings, yielding two runs on two hits.

With the White Sox winning 4 to 3 in the bottom of the 10th at their game in Philadelphia on August 2nd, Carl was called to pinch-hit for Joe Coleman with one out. He singled to left field against Randy Gumpert, who was then pulled for Frank Dorish.

Eddie Joost greeted Dorish with a single, moving Carl to second, but Dorish got Valo and Philley to make outs, ending the game.

On August 3rd, the Cleveland Indians were in Philadelphia. In the top of the 8th inning, Sam Zoldak was chased in a close 3 to 2 ballgame, leaving with two outs and two in scoring position with Ray Boone stepping up to the plate. Carl was summoned from the pen. He got Boone to pop out to the catcher to end the threat.

In the 8th inning, the A's got a couple of hits off of Mike Garcia before Early Wynn was summoned to shut things down.

In the top of the 9th, Carl was able to retire everyone but Wynn, who doubled. Wynn then completed the save, retiring the A's in the bottom of the inning, including Wally Moses, who pinch-hit for Carl and made the last out.

Two days later, on August 5th, the Indians sent Bob Lemon to the hill at Shibe Park to face the A's and Alex Kellner in the first game of a doubleheader.

The game was tied at one into the 6th, when Kellner tired, giving up a home run to Al Rosen and RBI singles to Bob Lemon and Dale Mitchell.

Carl entered the game with two on and one out, trailing 4 to 1. He induced a double play to end the inning.

In the top of the 7th, Carl gave up two runs on two hits and a walk, but in the bottom of the inning, Carl singled in a run to make it 6 to 2.

Following Bob Lemon's triple to lead off the 8th, Carl retired the last six Indians in order. Unfortunately, the A's could not close the gap, falling 6 to 3.

Carl worked 3 2/3 innings, yielding two runs on three hits.

On August 9th, at Fenway Park, the A's were leading the Red Sox 6 to 2 in the 9th inning. Bobby Shantz had replaced Morrie Martin, and had held the Sox in check.

Shantz started the inning by striking out Ted Williams, but Vern Stephens doubled to right, and Billy Goodman drew a walk. Walt Dropo then hit a fly ball to the deepest reaches of center field, pulled in by Dave Philley for the second out.

Next up was Clyde Vollmer, in the midst of his best season, when he would hit 22 home runs. Shantz grooved a pitch to him, and he did not miss it, sending it over the left-center field wall for three runs. It was now 6 to 5 and two were out.

Charlie Maxwell was called to pinch-hit for catcher Buddy Rosar, and Carl was summoned to get the last out. He got Maxwell to pop out to short to end the game and earn his 4th save.

With the Yankees leading 3 to 1 in the 9th inning at Shibe Park, Carl was called to pinch-hit for Joe Coleman with two outs and a man on. Carl stepped in against Eddie Lopat, and was hit by a pitch. He took his base.

The next batter, Eddie Joost, then lined back to Lopat to end the game.

The Yankees continued at Shibe Park on August 12th. In the top of the 7th, the A's were leading 7 to 0, but Bob Hooper had begun to tire. The Yankees jumped on him for four runs. With one on and two out, Carl was summoned to end the threat. Unfortunately, he gave up consecutive singles to Johnny Hopp and Gil McDougald, the latter plating another run.

Carl was pulled in favor of Alex Kellner, not having recorded an out. Kellner was able to end the inning without further damage, sparing Carl any negative consequences. The A's ultimately won 9 to 5.

The next day, August 13th, Carl was much sharper against the Yankees. In the 8th inning, leading 16 to 8, he retired Billy Martin,

Gil McDougald, and Bobby Brown in order. He then finished the game, yielding only a single, and getting Joe DiMaggio to pop out to second.

Carl pitched for the third day in a row, on August 14th against the Red Sox at home. Losing 7 to 4, Carl entered the game in the 9th inning. He yielded singles to Ted Williams and Fred Hatfield, but got Goodman, Dropo, and Vollmer in order to end the threat, stranding the Splinter at third base.

In the bottom of the 9th, Carl made the last out of the game, grounding into a force play at second.

The next day, August 15th, Carl appeared in his fourth game in a row, pitching a scoreless 9th in a losing cause against the Red Sox. He put down the side in order, but the A's could not rally from a 4 to 2 deficit.

The A's were back at Yankee Stadium on August 17th.

"One time the Yankees organized a batting contest between me and Spec Shea, one of their relief pitchers," said Carl. "We took turns trying to hit the ball into a barrel in center field. I hit in into the barrel and won a $50 War bond."

The A's trailed 3 to 1 in the bottom of the 7th when Carl was called to replace Bob Hooper. He retired the 8-9-1 hitters in order.

In the bottom of the 8th, still 3 to 1, Carl retired 2-3-4 in order, including Joe DiMaggio on a pop to first base.

In the top of the 9th, with two men on and two out, Carl came to bat against Stubby Overmire. Stubby had been traded by the Browns to the Yankees back in June, not long after he had given up a home run to Carl.

Hoping for a repeat, Jimmy Dykes let Carl in to bat against Overmire. He did not disappoint, knocking an RBI single, scoring Pete Suder, and putting the tying run on third base.

Next up was Eddie Joost, the A's trailing 3 to 2. Joost sent a fly into center, but DiMaggio was able to run it down to end the game.

The next day, August 18th, Carl pitched for the fifth time in six games. With the A's losing 4 to 1 to the Yankees at Yankee Stadium, Carl replaced Alex Kellner in the 8th inning. He retired Johnny Mize, but gave up a double to Hank Bauer. After striking out Jerry Coleman, Carl faced pitcher Vic Raschi with two out. Raschi lined a single to center, scoring Bauer. Carl ended the inning by retiring McDougald. The Yankees held on for a 5 to 1 victory.

Carl did not pitch again until August 23rd, when the A's were in Chicago to face the White Sox. In the bottom of the 8th with the A's winning 6 to 3, Dick Fowler started the inning by walking the first two batters. Carl entered the game and induced a double play from Jim Busby. He then retired Don Lenhardt on a fly.

In the bottom of the 9th, Carl closed out the save, retiring Fox, Dillinger, and Minoso on ground-outs. It was Carl's 6th save of the season.

On August 25th, the A's were in St. Louis to face the Browns. Carl was called to replace Morrie Martin with two out in the 8th inning, the A's ahead 4 to 1. The A's added five more runs in the top of the 9th, and Carl made quick work of the Browns in the bottom of the inning to close out the 9 to 1 victory. It was Carl's 7th save.

Five days later, on the 30th, the A's were in Cleveland to face the Indians. With the A's leading 6 to 2 with one out in the bottom of the 8th and the bases loaded, Carl replaced Morrie Martin. He faced the dangerous Al Rosen, who had led the league in home runs in 1950. Rosen hit a shot to shortstop Eddie Joost, who flipped to Pete Suder at second for out one. Suder then relayed on to Ferris Fain at first to complete the rally-killing double play.

In the bottom of the 9th, the Indians, who were tied with the Yankees for first, sent four pinch hitters to the plate to try to get something going against Carl.

Barney McCosky, batting for Clarence Maddern, popped to shortstop.

Dale Mitchell, hitting for Bob Kennedy, fouled out to third base.

Harry Simpson, batting for Birdie Tebbetts, drew a walk.

Paul Lehner, hitting for Lou Brissie, grounded to first baseman Fain, who tossed to Carl covering for the final out.

Carl's 8th save dropped the Indians a half game back.

On September 3rd, the 2nd place Yankees were at Shibe Park. In the top of the 9th with the Yankees leading 3 to 1, Carl was called in place of Alex Kellner. He held the Yankees scoreless despite walking two. He ended the inning by getting Joe DiMaggio to ground out.

1951
ERA 4.41
1-12) .396 BA
11 saves)

The Yankees held on for a 3 to 1 win, Johnny Sain earning the victory.

On September 7th, the Red Sox were at Shibe Park, leading 7 to 5 in the top of the 9th when Carl replaced Joe Coleman. The Sox manufactured another run on a walk, stolen base, and Lou Boudreau single. Boston won 8 to 5.

Two days later, on the 9th, Carl earned his 9th save by pitching a scoreless 9th inning with a 10 to 4 lead. Ted Williams made the first out, fouling out to first. Carl also retired Vern Stephens and Clyde Vollmer, in between which Billy Goodman reached on an error. The A's won 10 to 4.

On September 11th, the first place Indians were in Philadelphia, battling into extra innings, tied 5 to 5.

Carl took the ball in the 11th, replacing Morrie Martin. He walked Bob Kennedy but got Ray Boone to pop out to first. Jim Hegan then dropped a sacrifice bunt to move pinch-runner Harry Simpson up to second. Early Wynn was next up. He ripped a triple to center, scoring Simpson. Dale Mitchell was then retired to end the inning.

Wynn shut down the A's in order in the 9th to improve his record to 18-12. Carl recorded his 12th loss against only one victory.

Five days later, on the 16th, the Browns were at Shibe Park. Carl replaced Alex Kellner on the mound for the top of the 6th, leading 7 to 4.

After two hits and a walk, the Browns closed to 7 to 5. Carl retired the next eight batters in order before yielding a two-out single to Ken Wood in the 9th. He then got Mike Batts for the final out, earning his 10th save, 7 to 5.

The Tigers were in town on September 18th, leading 8 to 6 in the 9th. Carl pitched a scoreless 9th despite allowing two base runners. The A's failed to rally, coming up short 8 to 6.

Carl's last appearance on the mound in 1951 was on September 23rd against the Senators at Shibe Park.

Carl relieved Sam Zoldak in the 6th, leading 5 to 0. He gave up a run on Mickey Vernon's bases-loaded sacrifice fly, but escaped further trouble in the inning.

He put Washington down in order in the 7th but gave up a two-run inside-the-park homer to Irv Noren in the 8th. The score was now 6 to 3.

In the bottom of the 8th, Pete Suder led off with a single. After Joe Astroth popped to second, Carl whacked a ball to deep center, reaching third on a triple, scoring Suder. Eddie Joost then knocked Carl home with a single.

Carl, now staked to an 8 to 3 lead, put the Nats down in order in the bottom of the 9th, earning his 11th save.

On the mound, Carl finished the season 1-12 with 11 saves and a 4.41 ERA. It was the highest save total of his career, finishing second to Ellis Kinder for the league lead.

At the plate, Carl hit .396 with 21 hits in 53 at bats, including two home runs. It was the highest batting average of his career.

The A's finished 70-84, in 6th place, 28 games behind the first-place Yankees.

Gus Zernial led the team with 33 home runs and 125 RBI. His 33 home runs and 129 RBI led the American League (he had played four games with the White Sox at the beginning of the year).

Ferris Fain led all hitters with a .344 average. This won him the American League batting title.

Bobby Shantz led the hurlers with an 18-10 record. Carl led the team with 11 saves.

On November 19th, the A's plucked Kite Thomas from the New York Yankees in the Rule V Draft.

On December 5th, Shoeless Joe Jackson died in Greenville, South Carolina.

12.
THE YEAR BOBBY SHANTZ
WON 24

Another Carl Scheib entered the world in January, 1952. Georgene gave birth to their first son, and third child, Carl Alvin Scheib, Jr. *SCHEIB, JR.*

Carl, a favorite of manager Dykes because he was always ready and willing to take the mound as a starter or reliever, trained hard and got better prepared for the 1952 season. He enjoyed a solid spring training. His arm felt strong.

On opening day, April 16th, the Yankees were at Shibe Park. With the bases loaded, one out, and the Yankees leading 2 to 0 in the top of the 8th, Carl was called to relieve Alex Kellner. Gil McDougald was the first batter to face him. McDougald tapped a ball back to the mound. Carl turned and fired to second to get the force, but there was no chance for a double play at first, and Rizzuto scored. Jackie Jensen was caught in a rundown and made the last out on the play. The Yanks led 3 to 0.

In the 9th, Carl was knocked around as the Yankees increased their lead to 8 to 1, scoring five runs on five singles, two walks, and a double by Mickey Mantle. It was an ugly game for Carl, who also went 0 for 1 at the plate.

Nursing a sore elbow since spring training, Carl only made pinch hitting appearances for a couple weeks.

On April 20th in New York, with the Yankees winning 9 to 6, Carl batted for Alex Kellner against Johnny Sain. There was a man on third. Carl made the second out, popping out to shortstop.

The next day, at New York, he batted for Pete Suder in the top of the 6th with two on and two outs. Vic Raschi was on the hill for the Yanks. Carl popped out to second.

Once again, on the 22nd, Carl batted in Yankee Stadium. In the top of the 8th, with the Yankees winning 2 to 1, one out, and the bases loaded, Carl came to plate against Johnny Sain. He grounded to short, causing a double play to end the inning.

A week later, on the 29th, while losing 14 to 2 against the Indians, Carl pinch-hit in the 6th for Harry Byrd. There was one man on and no one out. Carl hit into another double play.

Finally, on May 2nd, Carl was called into a game against the White Sox in the top of the 8th with the score tied at 12. He retired the Sox 1-2-3 on fly balls.
In the bottom of the 8th, Carl singled to help the cause, but was stranded. The game remained 12 to 12.
Carl mowed down the Sox in the 9th, retiring them in order.
In the bottom of the 9th, Hank Majeski singled in Gus Zernial to walk-off the win 13 to 12.
Carl was the winning pitcher, now 1-0. He threw two scoreless innings.

Saturday, May 4th, the Tigers were in Philadelphia at Shibe Park. In the top of the 8th, with the Tigers leading 5 to 4 with two outs, Carl was called to replace Bob Hooper. The bases were loaded. The very dangerous Vic Wertz was the batter. Carl got him to ground out to end the threat.
The A's tied the game in the bottom of the 8th, and Carl set the Tigers down in order in the 9th.
In the bottom of the 9th, Dizzy Trout was on the mound for Detroit, having relieved Hal Newhouser in the 6th. Elmer Valo raked him for a double to lead off the inning. Dave Philley then put down a sacrifice bunt to move Valo to third. Trout followed by intentionally walking Zernial and Fain to load the bases and set up a force out at home.
Hank Majeski was next to face Trout. He ripped a single into right field, scoring Valo to end the game. Carl nabbed his second win thanks to the late-game heroics. He was now 2-0, doubling his 1951 win total.

On May 8th, only a few over 1200 fans were on hand to see the Browns face the A's on a Thursday afternoon at Shibe Park.
In the top of the 6th, with the A's leading 7 to 6, reliever Dick Fowler gave up a two-run triple to put the Browns ahead 8 to 7. Carl was summoned with a runner on third and only one out. He retired

1952
Carl loses
to Satchel Paige

Marty Marion on a grounder to third. The runner held. He then retired pinch hitter Jim Rivera on a fly to left field to end the inning.

Carl mowed down the Browns in the top of 7th, 1-2-3. The A's then tied the game in the bottom of the inning, 8 to 8.

In the top of the 8th, the Browns threatened. After Darrell Johnson struck out, Bobby Young beat out a single to shortstop. Satchel Paige, who had relieved in the 6th inning, contributed a sacrifice bunt. Carl then intentionally walked Jim Delsing to face Marty Marion, whom he retired on a pop-up to second.

The A's failed to score in their 8th inning, and Carl took the mound in the 9th with the game still tied 8 to 8. Jim Rivera was up first. The New York City native, son of Puerto Rican immigrants, was a rookie, finally breaking through at age 30. The tall, fleet center fielder would soon be known as "Big Jim" and then "Jungle Jim" for his aggressive unorthodox play. Rivera would be a steady performer for the White Sox in coming years, balancing power and speed.

He stepped to the plate against Carl, facing him for the second time in the game. This time, Rivera would not disappoint. He ripped a ball over the fence for the go-ahead run. Carl set down the Browns quickly after that.

Now trailing 9 to 8, the A's went after 45-year-old Satchel Paige. After Dave Philley grounded out, Gus Zernial singled to left. Ferris Fain then reached on an error by first baseman Gordon Goldsberry. The A's now had two men on with only one out. Hank Majeski, who had hit a walk-off single on Carl's behalf only a few days ago, came to the plate.

The venerable former Negro League star tossed one to "Heeney," who hit a shot to short. Marty Marion picked it and started a rally-killing 6-4-3 double play.

Satchel Paige won the first game of what would be his best season in the major leagues, improving to 1-1. Carl was the losing pitcher, falling to 2-1.

The Senators were in town on May 11th. Alex Kellner and Julio Moreno had battled to a 2 to 2 tie after nine innings.

Carl was called from the pen in the top of the 10th and held Washington scoreless, despite allowing a couple base runners.

The A's didn't score in the bottom of the inning, and Carl came to the mound in the 11th.

Following Mickey Vernon's double, Carl retired Pete Runnels on a grounder to third and Cass Michaels on a pop to short. Vernon was still standing on second with two outs.

Carl intentionally walked Mickey Grasso to set up a force play and to face pitcher Bob Porterfield. Porterfield tapped a ball to second and beat the throw, loading the bases.

The flood gates then opened after right fielder Elmer Valo and first baseman Skeeter Kell let a high foul pop by Eddie Yost fall between them behind first base. Both men came charging towards the spot where the ball would drop, yelling "I got it." Neither one did. With new life, Yost then singled in two, followed by an RBI single from Jim Busby. Carl struck out Jackie Jensen to end the inning, but the A's were now losing 5 to 2.

The loss dropped Carl's record to 2-2. His ERA ballooned to 7.59. The A's were now in 7th place, at 8-13.

Said Jimmy Dykes after the game, referring to the Valo-Kell confusion, "Those things happen. The boys hesitated and you know that he who hesitates is lost. We lost."

On Sunday May 18th, the A's were in Cleveland to face the Indians. Mike Garcia and the Tribe held a 3 to 0 lead into the bottom of the 7th when Carl replaced starter Sam Zoldak. He put the 7-8-9 hitters down in order.

In the bottom of the 8th, the Indians added three more runs, though only one was earned. Elmer Valo failed to make a play in right, allowing a run to score. Larry Doby followed with a single to score another run. After walking Dale Mitchell, Luke Easter popped out to second. Bob Kennedy then doubled in Easter to make the score 6 to 0. Carl retired Birdie Tebbetts to end the threat.

In the top of the 9th, Carl came to the plate with two outs and a man on. He singled up the middle off of Mike Garcia, but Eddie Joost grounded out to end the game.

Carl next appeared on the mound on May 30th against the Yankees in New York. Bob Hooper was throwing a shutout, leading the Yankees 4 to 0 before they started a two-out rally.

Gil McDougald singled. Gene Woodling followed with a triple, driving in McDougald. Irv Noren then singled in Woodling to make it 4 to 2. Bobby Brown stepped to the plate as the tying run.

Out of the bullpen came Carl to try to seal the deal. He stretched and threw a pitch to Brown, who tapped it to first baseman Billy Hitchcock to end the game, much to the chagrin of the 30,000+ fans in attendance.

It was Carl's first save of the season.

On June 6th, Carl was summoned from the pen in the 9th inning to help mop up a game with the Indians at home. First up was second baseman Bobby Avila, in his first All-Star season. Avila, a former Mexican League star at Puebla, would lead the league in triples in 1952 and win a batting title in 1954. He ripped a Scheib pitch into the seats for a home run.

Carl then got Al Rosen to fly out to right-center before Larry Doby ripped a triple. Dale Mitchell singled in Doby before Luke Easter bounced into a double play to end the inning.

Bob Lemon then shut down the A's in the 9th for the complete-game 11 to 4 victory.

Carl's season finally started to turn for the better as the White Sox came to town on June 12th.

After Dick Fowler was chased in the top of the 7th by a bases-loaded triple from Chico Carrasquel, Carl got the call to settle things down.

Chuck Stobbs hit a ball at first baseman Ferris Fain, who threw home to nail Carrasquel trying to score. Carl then retired Nellie Fox on a fly to right.

Behind 10 to 4, Carl tossed two shutout innings, scattering two hits. In the bottom of the 9th, he singled off of Chuck Stobbs. But Eddie Joost grounded into a double play to end the game. Carl's ERA dropped to 6.48.

On Sunday June 2nd, the A's were in Detroit to face the Tigers in the second game of a doubleheader. The Tigers had won the first game 4 to 3 in twelve innings, Hal Newhouser throwing seven shutout innings in relief for the win.

Carl got the call to start against Art Houtteman. It would be a laugher as the A's won 10 to 0. Carl scattered seven hits and two walks in the complete-game shutout. His record improved to 3-2, while his ERA plummeted to 4.21. Gus Zernial hit two home runs for the victors.

June 25th, the A's were in Cleveland, leading 11 to 9 into the 8th inning. Carl was summoned to protect the lead. He retired Harry Simpson on a grounder and Bobby Avila on a fly to center, before striking out Larry Doby.

In the bottom of the 9th, still 11 to 9, Carl quickly got two outs, retiring Al Rosen and Dale Mitchell, but Barney McCosky and Luke Easter singled to put the tying runs on base. Jim Hegan was next up, but Carl retired the All-Star catcher on a fly to left.

Carl was credited with two shutout innings and his second save. The A's improved to 26-31.

On July 1st, Carl was called to pinch-hit in the 9th inning of a game against the Senators at Shibe Park. Washington was winning 6 to 5, and there were two outs. Carl singled to center field off of Don Johnson, but Eddie Joost ended the game, popping out to first.

Carl was asked to start against the Red Sox on Thursday, July 3rd at Shibe Park.

Eddie Joost led off the bottom of the 1st with a home run off of Ike Delock.

In the bottom of the 4th, the A's extended their lead to 3 to 0. Carl's only blemish to this point was a single by Billy Goodman.

In the top of the 5th, the Sox threatened. Hoot Evers singled to left. Carl then walked George Schmees to put men on first and second with no one out, but he got Ted Lepcio to ground into a double play. He ended the inning when Sammy White grounded out.

In the top of the 6th, rookie Faye Throneberry, the brother of Marv Throneberry, singled with one out. Throneberry then stole second, and advanced to third on Joe Astroth's throwing error. Billy Goodman drew a walk to put men on first and third with one out.

Next up was Dick Gernert, the rookie first baseman from Reading, Pennsylvania. He had been struggling so far, barely hitting .200 with only one home run. The righty-hitting first-sacker stepped into a Carl pitch and sent it over the fence for a three-run game-tying blast.

Carl retired Vern Stephens and Hoot Evers to end the inning.

In the bottom of the 6th, Pete Suder and Joe Astroth led off with singles. Carl came to plate and grounded into a force, nailing Suder at third base. With one out, Eddie Joost stepped in to face reliever Ralph Brickner. Both runners took off, Carl reaching second safely on the back end of a double-steal. It would be Carl's only stolen base in the major leagues. It was all for naught, though, as Joost struck out, and the A's failed to score.

Carl faced the minimum nine batters over the final three innings, benefiting from double plays in the 7th and 8th.

The A's came to bat in the bottom of the 9th with the score tied at 3. After Eddie Joost flied out, Ferris Fain and Dave Philley singled, chasing Brickner. Al Benton entered the game for the Red

1952 (handwritten)

Sox, and got Gus Zernial to hit into a force at second. With men on first and third with two outs, Benton intentionally walked Elmer Valo to set up a force at any base.

Veteran utility man Billy Hitchcock was next up. The light-hitting infielder was a .243 hitter in the majors, playing for five different teams over nine seasons. Like many players of his era, Hitchcock lost the prime of his career to World War II, missing 1943 through 1945. He knocked a single to right to beat the strategy and give the A's and Carl a 4 to 3 victory.

Carl's record improved to 4-2, his ERA falling to 3.68.

On Sunday July 6th, the Yankees were in town for a doubleheader. The Bombers had won the first game 5 to 2, Tom Morgan defeating Bobby Shantz before 30,000+ fans at Shibe Park. Shantz, who lost for only the third time against fourteen victories, was the big draw. While he would go on to win 24 games and win the MVP, today the Yankees got the better of the diminutive 5'6" lefty.

In the second game, despite pitching a complete game only three days prior, Carl got the call to start against Eddie Lopat.

In the 1st, he gave up a solo homer to Hank Bauer, as the Yanks took a 1 to 0 lead.

After Mickey Mantle lined out in the 2nd, and Gene Woodling grounded out, Bobby Brown singled and Gil McDougald walked. Pitcher Eddie Lopat then helped himself with a single, scoring Brown. It was now 2 to 0.

Rookie Kite Thomas halved the lead with a solo shot off of Lopat.

Carl came to hill in the 3rd inning behind only 2 to 1, but Joe Collins and Hank Bauer hit back-to-back doubles to score another run and chase Carl.

Sam Zoldak got the call to face Yogi Berra whom he retired on a line drive to right, but Mickey Mantle followed with a single to left, scoring Bauer, and ending Carl's line for the day—an ineffective four runs in two innings.

Fortunately for the rubber-armed Carl, the A's would rally and win 7 to 6, Bob Hooper picking up the victory.

On July 11th, at Shibe Park, the Indians jumped on starter Harry Byrd for four runs in the 1st. After Harry Simpson hit the second triple of the inning, knocking in two, Carl was called with one out and a man on third. Joe Tipton tapped a ball to third baseman Billy Hitchcock, who threw home to nail Simpson. Carl then ended the inning by retiring Merl Combs.

The score held at 4 to 0 until the bottom of the 3rd, when Carl stepped to the plate against "Rapid Robert" Bob Feller. Feller had led the league in victories with 22 in 1951, but was struggling a bit in 1952. Carl proved the point, singling off of him to start the inning.

After Eddie Joost walked, Ferris Fain singled in Carl for the first Athletics run. Elmer Valo then walked, and Gus Zernial grounded into a double play, plating the second run.

But, Feller couldn't get another out, giving up two singles, a walk and a triple before Carl stepped to the plate for the second time in the inning. Joe Astroth was on third, and the A's were now winning 6 to 4.

Carl knocked a single into center field scoring Astroth, putting the A's ahead 7 to 4. Feller was yanked at that point in favor of former Athletic Lou Brissie. One has to wonder how many times a pitcher batted twice against Bob Feller in an inning and reached base both times on hits?

The score remained 7 to 4 until the top of the 6th inning. Hank Majeski drew a walk against Carl. "Heeney" had been purchased by the Indians from the A's the prior month.

Barney McCosky pinch-hit for Brissie, and doubled to right, scoring Majeski. Carl retired the next three batters in order to end the rally.

In the top of the 8th, McCosky was at it again, doubling with one out. After Bob Lemon lined-out, pinch hitting for Mickey Harris, Bobby Avila singled home McCosky, closing the gap to 7 to 6.

The A's again failed to pad their lead. Carl took the hill in the 9th. Al Rosen led off with a game-tying solo home run. Larry Doby followed with a shot to right field that got away from Elmer Valo, allowing Doby to circle the bases for an inside-the-park homer, and an 8 to 7 lead. Carl retired the next three batters in order, but the A's could not score in the 9th, falling 8 to 7.

It was a tough loss for Carl, his record dropping to 4-3. Carl threw 8 2/3 innings, yielding four runs.

Four days later, on July 15th, Carl started against the Browns at home. The game was scoreless until the top of the 4th, when the Browns took a 1 to 0 lead. They extended their lead to 2 to 0 in the 5th.

Carl was chased in the 6th in favor of Johnny Kucab after he gave up four more runs, only two earned.

Duane Pillette took a 6 to 1 lead into the bottom of the 9th. Kite Thomas started the inning with a home run. After Billy Hitchcock walked, Satchel Paige was summoned to close out the game. The A's knocked three consecutive singles to pull within 6 to 3 when Eddie Joost stepped to the plate with the bases loaded and no one out. Joost blasted a Paige pitch into the seats for a game-winning walk-off grand slam. The sudden change in fortune made a winner of reliever Ed Wright and spared Carl the defeat. It was the second walk-off grand slam yielded by Paige this season, a major league record.

On July 19th, at Shibe Park, Carl and the Tigers' Billy Hoeft battled through seven innings, Hoeft with a 4 to 2 edge.

The A's tied the game in the bottom of the 8th on a two-run double by Ferris Fain. The A's then won it in the 9th on a walk-off single by Ray Murray. The final score was 5 to 4, Carl receiving a no-decision.

The A's were in Chicago on July 25th for a doubleheader against the White Sox. Billy Pierce blanked the A's for his 11th win in the first game, improving to 11-7 as the Sox won 5 to 0.

Carl got the call in the second game to face Saul Rogovin.

The Sox scored a run in the second on a wild pitch, Sam Mele scooting home.

Rogovin didn't last the 3rd, giving up three hits and three walks en route to a five-run A's rally. Pete Suder's bases-loaded triple was the key hit.

After shutting down the Sox in the bottom of the 3rd, Carl started the 4th with a single off of Howie Judson, but the A's could not score.

In the bottom of the 7th, Sherm Lollar led off with a solo home run off of Carl, but he escaped further damage in the inning.

In the top of the 8th, Joe Astroth singled. Carl then sacrificed him to second, but the A's could not plate him.

Leading 5 to 2 in the bottom of the 8th, Carl walked Nellie Fox to start the inning. Minnie Minoso grounded out, moving Fox to second. Tom Wright then flied out for the second out, bringing up Eddie Robinson. The All-Star first baseman had knocked in 117 runs in 1951, blasting 29 home runs. He was in the midst of another 100+ RBI season in 1952. He liked one of Carl's offerings, launching it into the stands for a two-run dinger.

184

Bob Hooper was then summoned to relieve Carl with the A's up 5 to 4. They would hold on for the victory. Carl's record improved to 5-3. The A's pulled to 42-44, nearing .500 in 6th place in the American League.

Harry Byrd threw a five-hit shutout against the Tigers at Briggs Stadium in Detroit on July 29th. It was the first game of a doubleheader, and the A's evened their season record at 45-45.

In the second game, Carl started against Dick Littlefield. Eddie Joost started the game with a home run against Littlefield. The A's added another run on back-to-back doubles by Ferris Fain and Dave Philley.

In the top of the 2nd, Joe Astroth, Carl, and Eddie Joost hit consecutive singles with one out to score a run and chase Littlefield.

Carl retired the first two batters in the bottom of the second, but gave up a home run to Cliff Mapes, halving the deficit.

In the 3rd, the A's added two more runs when Astroth singled them in. Carl followed with another single but was stranded.

Dave Philley was at it again, leading off the 5th with a home run. After two walks and a single, the bases were loaded for Astroth with one out. He hit a sacrifice fly to left, scoring another run, but Sherry Robertson was thrown out trying to advance to third base to end the inning.

Carl took the mound in the bottom of the 4th with a 7 to 1 lead. Pat Mullin greeted him with a solo homer. A Johnny Groth bases-on-balls was sandwiched between two ground outs by Walt Dropo and Cliff Mapes. With two outs, Joe Ginsberg nailed a two-run home run to pull the Tigers within three, at 7 to 4. Carl got Al Federoff to end the inning.

Carl batted to lead off the 5th. He grounded out, but the A's added another run after Eddie Joost tripled and Ferris Fain bunted him home, reaching base safely.

Bob Hooper replaced Carl in the bottom of the 5th, the A's leading 8 to 4. The Tigers erupted for six runs in the inning, and took the lead against Hooper, who walked in two runs, and Sam Zoldak.

The Tigers won the game 10 to 8, Hooper falling to 5-12. It was a no-decision for Carl, who was charged with four earned runs in four innings.

On August 3rd, the A's were in Cleveland for a doubleheader. Bob Feller won the first game 4 to 1, aided by Luke Easter's two-run homer.

Carl started the second game against Steve Gromek. Larry Doby started the scoring in the bottom of the 2nd, nailing a solo home run.

Elmer Valo led off the second with a triple, and scored on Pete Suder's single, tying the game at one apiece.

The score remained 1 to 1 until the bottom of the 5th, when Carl walked two and saw them advance to scoring position on a ground out. Pitcher Gromek hit a sacrifice fly to center, scoring the second run of the game, but Dave Philley tossed the ball to cut-off man Fain, who fired to Suder at third base to nail Merl Combs.

The A's got it right back in the top of the 6th. With one out, Ferris Fain doubled and was later singled home by Elmer Valo.

The A's broke the game open in the 7th, scoring seven runs against three pitchers. Eddie Joost singled in two runs, Dave Philley doubled in two runs, and Gus Zernial hit a two-run homer. Later in the inning, Joe Astroth also had an RBI single. Carl made two of the three outs in the inning.

Carl retired the final nine Indians in order, all of them on balls in play. He also added a single in the top of the 9th, but did not score. The game ended 9 to 2.

Carl improved to 6-3, yielding only three hits in a complete game. Both runs were earned.

The A's improved to 50-48.

In game one of a doubleheader on August 7th at Shibe Park, Harry Byrd defeated the Red Sox to even his record at 9-9. Dizzy Trout fell to 8-9.

In the second game, Carl faced Willard Nixon, who was in the sixth spot in Lou Boudreau's lineup.

Faye Throneberry started the game with a single. Dom DiMaggio followed with a double, putting two in scoring position. Billy Goodman then grounded out, scoring Throneberry, DiMaggio moving to third.

George Kell was next. He hit a shot to third baseman Pete Suder, who fired home to nail DiMaggio at the plate.

Carl then ended the inning, retiring Hoot Evers. He was behind 1 to 0.

In the top of the 2nd, Carl retired the pitcher, Willard Nixon, on a fly to center. He then walked Dick Gernert and gave up a single to Sammy White. Johnny Lipon followed with a bases-on-balls to load them up with one out.

Jimmy Dykes had seen enough, pulling Carl in favor of Johnny Kucab, who retired the next two batters, stranding all three runners.

The Red Sox went on to win the game 8 to 4. Carl was the losing pitcher, falling to 6-4.

By August 12th, at Fenway Park, the A's were back in the pennant race at 54-51, eight games back. Carl was called to face Dizzy Trout.

The Red Sox scored first in the bottom of the 3rd on a foul pop by George Kell, deep enough to plate Faye Throneberry, who tagged up from third.

The A's batted around in the 4th, scoring three runs. Carl added an RBI single. The A's left the bases loaded, but led 3 to 1.

Carl nursed his two run lead into the bottom of the 8th inning. With one out, Faye Throneberry singled. Clyde Vollmer, who had hit 22 homers in 1951, turned on a Scheib pitch and sent it into the stands to tie the game.

The game went into extra innings. Finally, in the top of the 13th, the A's manufactured a run on a Billy Hitchcock single.

Carl then shut down the Sox in the 13th, completing a thirteen inning victory, yielding ten hits and three earned runs. His record improved to 7-4. The A's improved to 55-51, 7½ back in 5th place.

Five days later, on the 17th, Carl was called to start against the Senators at home. He wasn't sharp, giving up five runs, three earned, on six hits and three walks in only three and 2/3 innings. Bobo Newsom replaced him, and did not give up a hit through the 7th inning. The A's erupted for eleven runs in the 7th and 8th to steal the win. Bob Hooper earned the win in relief. The A's improved to 57-56, ten games off the pace.

On August 20th, the Tigers were in town, sending Bill Wight to the mound against Carl.

Ferris Fain started the scoring in the bottom of the 1st with an RBI single.

The Tigers got to Carl in the 3rd, scoring a run on three singles.

The score remained 1 to 1 into the top of the 8th inning. Carl gave up a single to Johnny Groth. Johnny Pesky bunted him to second. After Fred Hatfield flied out, Walt Dropo came to the plate.

Dropo, known as "Moose," had won the American League Rookie of the Year award in 1950, playing for the Boston Red Sox. He had knocked in 144 runs that season, narrowly missing Ted Williams' record of 145 set in 1939. Walt's production slipped considerably in 1951, his home runs falling from 34 to only 11, and his batting average dropping to .239. He had started 1952 with the Red Sox, but was traded with Fred Hatfield, Don Lenhardt, Bill Wight, and Johnny Pesky to the Tigers for Hoot Evers, Johnny Lipon, George Kell, and Dizzy Trout on June 3rd. He would hit 23 home runs the rest of the way for Detroit.

"Moose" did his best to ruin Carl's excellent outing, ripping a pitch into the stands to put Detroit up 3 to 1.

In the bottom of the 8th, with two outs, the A's started a rally. Billy Hitchcock reached on an infield hit. Kite Thomas followed with a grounder to Fred Hatfield at third, who mishandled it, the runners reaching scoring position.

Carl came to the plate next. He ripped a single into right field, scoring Hitchcock and Thomas to tie the game.

Pete Suder then singled to put runners on the corners. Ferris Fain followed with a single, scoring Carl with the go-ahead run.

Bob Hooper saved the game in the 9th, leaving the tying run at third base. The A's won 4 to 3.

Carl was the winning pitcher, improving to 8-4. The A's were now 60-56, eight games back in 5th place.

On Sunday, August 24th, the White Sox were in Philadelphia for a doubleheader. The Sox won the first game to edge the A's out of 4th place.

Carl started the second game against Chuck Stobbs. He put the Sox down in order in the 1st.

The bottom of the inning was a strange one for the A's. Eddie Joost started with a strikeout. Ferris Fain followed with a double. Dave Philley then walked to put two men on base. Philley had been listed as batting 5th on the official lineup card, though he came up third. Gus Zernial followed with a double, apparently scoring two runs, but White Sox manager Paul Richards popped out of the dugout and argued his case. Cass Michaels was supposed to follow Philley. A's manager Jimmy Dykes argued to the contrary with Richards and the four umpires. After deliberating for fifteen minutes, Michaels was declared out, recorded as a putout to the catcher. Zernial's double was disallowed. Fain returned to second and Philley to first. Dykes played the game under protest.

After all of this, Stobbs hit the next batter, Billy Hitchcock, to load the bases. He then walked Joe Astroth to plate a run.

Saul Rogovin was then called to relieve Stobbs, and to face Carl, who ended the inning by grounding into a force at third.

The A's had batted around in the 1st, scoring only one run, sending only seven men "officially" to the plate.

The A's added another run in the 3rd inning on a suicide-squeeze bunt by Billy Hitchcock.

The Sox nicked Carl for a run in the 5th, scoring on a ground out, after two singles and an error.

In the 7th, the A's were bunting in a run again, this time on Dave Philley's attempted suicide-squeeze, on which the runners were all safe. The A's added two more on Cass Michael's single and an error. Carl now had a comfortable 5 to 1 lead. He coasted to a complete game four-hit victory.

Carl improved to 9-4, his ERA dropping to 4.15. The A's tied for 4th place at 63-58, 7½ games out.

The Red Sox came to town on the 29th for a doubleheader. Carl took the mound for the first game against Dick Brodowski.

Allie Clark started the scoring in the bottom of the 1st, plating Eddie Joost and Ferris Fain on a double.

The A's added two more in the 3rd. The Sox got to Carl for a run in the 5th, pulling to within 4 to 1.

In the bottom of the 5th, Ferris Fain hit a two-run homer to increase the lead to 6 to 1.

Carl cruised to another complete-game victory, scattering seven hits, to improve his record to 10-4. His ERA fell to 3.92. Most importantly, after sweeping the Sox in the second game, the A's were only six games out at 66-59.

On September 1st, the A's were in Washington for a doubleheader. The first game was tied at 8 in extra innings, when Carl came to the plate as a pinch hitter in the top of the 10th with men on the corners. Carl ripped a single into left field, scoring the go-ahead run. Ed Wright then pitched a perfect 9th for the save.

In the second game, Carl started on the mound against Julio Moreno. The A's scored first in the 1st, but the Nats scored single runs in the first three innings to build a 3 to 1 lead.

In the 5th inning, Carl led off with a single. He was later doubled home by Dave Philley, making the score 3 to 2.

The Senators added an insurance run in the 7th on a sacrifice fly. It would be all they needed as both pitchers went the distance.

1952
Carl K's
Mickey mantle

Carl fell to 10-5, hurling eight innings, yielding four earned runs on eight hits and four walks. The A's were now 69-61, 7½ games back, but with the sand running out of the hour glass.

On September 6th, the A's were in Boston to face the Red Sox. Carl started against Mel Parnell.

Hoot Evers started the scoring with a three-run home run in the 1st.

The Sox added another run in the 4th on a sacrifice fly by Vern Stephens.

The A's got one back in the top of the 5th, but Carl was nailed for back-to-back home runs by Clyde Vollmer and Vern Stephens. Carl finished the inning but was replaced by Marion Fricano.

The Red Sox won the game 6 to 4. Carl was the losing pitcher, falling to 10-6. He was charged with six earned runs in five innings of work.

After being swept in the second game, the A's fell to 71-66, ten games behind in 6th place.

On Friday September 12th, the A's were in Detroit to face the last-place Tigers. Carl started against Hal Newhouser.

The game was scoreless until the bottom of the 2nd when Carl singled in Billy Hitchcock with two outs.

Cliff Mapes returned the favor in the home 2nd, homering off of Carl.

Carl and Newhouser, the future Hall of Famer, dueled into the 6th inning, tied at 1-1. In the home 6th, the Tigers erupted for four runs, including one on a bases-loaded walk of Hal Newhouser, the pitcher.

The A's came right back in the 7th. Billy Hitchcock led off with a double. After Joe Astroth flied out, Carl plated Hitchcock with an RBI single. Eddie Joost then doubled, and Ferris Fain plated Carl on a ground out. Dave Philley singled to score Joost, pulling the A's to within one at 5 to 4.

Marion Fricano took over on the mound in the 7th and was not scored upon. In the top of the 8th, the A's scored three runs off of two different relief pitchers to go ahead 7 to 5.

The game ended as a 7 to 6 victory for the A's, neither Carl nor Newhouser figuring in the decision. Despite the win, the A's were now 12½ back with 12 to play, eliminated from the pennant race.

On September 16th, the A's were in Chicago for a doubleheader against the White Sox. The A's won the first game 2 to 1, Harry Byrd defeating Billy Pierce.

Carl faced Joe Dobson in the second game. The A's jumped to 1 to 0 lead in the 1st, as Eddie Joost walked and Ferris Fain doubled him home.

The Sox scored two in the third to go up 2 to 1. The score remained the same until the bottom of the 6th, when Eddie Robinson hit a two-run homer, increasing the lead to 4 to 1.

Bob Hooper replaced Carl in the 7th. The Sox went on to win 7 to 1. Carl fell to 10-7. Joe Dobson improved to 13-10.

In the final game of the season, Carl faced the Yankees at Shibe Park on September 28th. The Yanks had locked up another pennant. They sent Ewell Blackwell to the hill.

Rookie shortstop Andy Carey led off the game with a single. Billy Martin followed with a single, putting runners on the corners.

Carl then struck out Mickey Mantle. But Johnny Mize followed with a single, scoring Carey. Yogi Berra then grounded into a double play to end the inning.

In the bottom of the 1st, the A's tied the game on a fly ball by Elmer Valo, and an error.

The Yankees added two in the 2nd, the key hit being a triple by Hank Bauer.

The score remained 3 to 1 until the 6th when Yogi Berra blasted a solo home run off of Carl. It was Yogi's 30th of the season, a new American League record for catchers.

Bill Miller replaced Blackwell for the home 6th. The A's sent eleven men to plate, scoring eight runs, including a two-run triple by Ferris Fain and a three-run homer by Elmer Valo. The A's now led 9 to 4.

Carl coasted the rest of the way, locking in a 9 to 4 victory. His record finished at 11-7 with a 4.39 ERA. At the plate, Carl hit only .220 with no extra base hits in 82 at bats.

The A's finished 79-75 in 4th place.

Gus Zernial's 29 home runs and 100 RBI led the team. Ferris Fain won another batting title with a .327 mark.

On the mound, Bobby Shantz was an amazing 24-7 with a 2.48 ERA. He led the league in wins and was named American League MVP.

On November 22nd, pitcher Harry Byrd was named American League Rookie of the Year.

13.

SORE SHOULDER

On January 15th, 1953, contracts for Carl and Pete Suder were announced on the same day.

On the 27th, the team traded Ferris Fain and Bobby Wilson to the Chicago White Sox for Joe DeMaestri, Ed McGhee and Eddie Robinson.

Two days later, Billy Hitchcock was off to the Detroit Tigers for Don Kolloway.

On February 2nd, the team released Sam Zoldak. Two days later, they released Sherry Robertson.

Spring training kicked off at West Palm Beach, Florida for the Athletics on February 16th. Carl was on hand with the rest of the pitchers to participate in the workouts led by manager Jimmy Dykes.

Carl's first appearance in 1953 was in the bottom of the 9th inning of the 8th game of the season on April 22nd at Griffith Stadium in Washington.

Harry Byrd was leading 7 to 0 going into the inning but was wracked for four runs, including a two-run home run by Jackie Jensen. After walking Pete Runnels with two outs, Carl was summoned from the bullpen. He walked Ken Wood before retiring Wayne Terwilliger on a fly to right to end the game. Carl was credited with a save. The A's were 4-4 in 5th place.

On April 25th, Carl started against the Red Sox at Fenway Park. The A's loaded the bases against Mel Parnell in the 1st, and then scored twice on ground outs.

The Red Sox loaded the bases against Carl in the bottom of the 1st with two outs. Jim Piersall was hit by a pitch, George Kell reached on an error, and Sammy White singled. Gene Stephens then knocked in two unearned runs with a single.

The A's went back on top with a run in the 2nd, Pete Suder scoring on Joe Astroth's single.

The score remained 3 to 2 until the bottom of the 5th. Piersall and Kell ripped back-to-back doubles to tie the game. Dick Gernert then hit a fly to right deep enough for Kell to tag and

192

move to third. After Sammy White grounded out, Carl threw a wild pitch to Gene Stephens, allowing Kell to score. The Red Sox went ahead 4 to 3 and went on to win.

Carl took the loss, falling to 0-1. He gave up two earned runs in eight innings of work. The A's were 6-5.

The A's visited the Browns in St. Louis on May 6th. Carl entered the game in the bottom of the 6th, trailing 3 to 0. He gave up another run on a Johnny Groth RBI single.

Carl loaded the bases in the 7th, and then pitcher Bobo Holoman singled in two. The Browns now led 6 to 0. The A's could not solve Holoman and were shut out.

Carl pitched three innings, yielding three earned runs in the no-decision. The A's dropped to 10-9.

On May 9th, the Washington Senators were in Philadelphia. They built a 5 to 0 lead against Alex Kellner. Walt Masterson was blanking the A's.

Carl entered the game in the top of the 8th and retired the Nats 1-2-3. In the top of the 9th, Mickey Grasso hit one of his two home runs of the season to extend the lead to 6 to 0.

The A's went quietly in the 9th, Masterson notching a three-hit shutout.

Carl had pitched two innings, giving up one run on one hit. The A's dropped to 10-11.

On May 12th, the Browns were in town. Bobby Shantz got into trouble in the 6th inning, falling behind 6 to 2 with two outs. After Johnny Groth singled to put two men on, Carl was summoned from the pen. He ended the inning by retiring Billy Hunter on a grounder.

In the top of the 7th, the Browns added on with Les Moss's RBI single.

The A's got one back in the bottom of the 9th, but the rally faltered. Shantz took the loss, falling to 3-4. Carl pitched 3 1/3 innings of solid relief, giving up only one run. The A's slipped to 10-14.

The Tigers were in Philadelphia on the 15th. Morrie Martin fell behind 5 to 0 by the 5th inning when Carl got the call.

He put up a zero in the 5th, but pitcher Art Houtteman hit a two-run home run off of him in the 6th. One of the runs was unearned.

The A's erupted for five runs in the 6th against Houtteman. Eddie Joost doubled, and Loren Babe singled him home. Eddie Robinson flied out, and Dave Philley walked to put two men on. Kite Thomas, Pete Suder, and Ed McGhee hit consecutive RBI singles. Joe Astroth grounded out to score another run. Carl ended the threat by also grounding out. The A's were now down 7 to 5.

The score remained 7 to 5 into the bottom of the 9th. With one out, Gus Zernial singled. Joe DeMaestri replaced him as a pinch-runner. Eddie Joost then walked, putting the tying runs on base. Next up was third baseman Loren Babe. Babe had been picked up from the Yankees a few weeks earlier. He had been a minor-league star at Syracuse in 1952, and had gotten into twelve games with the Bombers, hitting only .095. Today, though, he got off to a fast start with the Yanks in 1953, blasting two home runs and hitting .333 in his first 18 at bats before New York sold him.

Babe hit a grounder to second. Johnny Pesky flipped the ball to shortstop Harvey Kuenn, covering the bag. Kuenn subsequently threw wildly to first allowing DeMaestri to score, but Babe got caught in a rundown and was tagged out by Pesky to end the game.

Oddly enough, Loren Babe never hit another major league home run, tanking in an A's uniform, batting .224 in 343 at bats. After 1953, he spent the rest of his career in the minors.

The A's lost the game 7 to 6. Carl pitched five innings, giving up no earned runs for a no-decision. The A's fell to 12-15.

On May 17th, Early Wynn and the Indians were at Connie Mack Stadium, facing Bobby Shantz. The Indians led 5 to 1 in the top of the 8th when Carl entered the game in relief. He gave up single runs in each inning, to fall behind 7 to 1. The A's scored two in the 9th to no avail. Early Wynn notched a complete-game victory improving to 4-1. Shantz fell to 3-5. Carl gave up one earned run in two innings. The A's, meanwhile, dropped to 12-17 on the season.

Four days later, on the 21st, Carl again relieved Shantz, but this time due to injury. With two outs in the 4th inning at Fenway Park against the Red Sox, Shantz was pitching to Sammy White when he had to leave the game in the middle of the at bat. The game was scoreless.

Carl entered and walked White, but he got Ted Lepcio to end the inning.

The A's took a 1 to 0 lead in the 6th on a Joe DeMaestri RBI single. They added to the lead in the 7th. After loading the bases with one out, Mickey McDermott faced Carl. Carl stepped into the box and knocked a single to center, scoring two. The A's added three more in the inning to go up 6 to 0. They also added three more in the top of the 9th and led 9 to 0.

Carl cruised through the 9th, yielding only a single to Dick Gernert. The A's won 9 to 0, Carl earning the win with 5 1/3 shutout innings. Carl's ERA dropped to 2.48. The A's improved to 15-18.

The next day, the Red Sox won the first game of a doubleheader 3 to 2. The second game was tied at two going into the bottom of the 12th inning.

Carl was called to pitch. He started the 12th by walking Hoot Evers. After Dick Gernert flied out, George Kell walked. The game then ended on Sammy White's walk-off single, plating Evers.

Carl pitched 1/3 of an inning and was tagged with the loss, falling to 1-2. The Red Sox won again 3 to 2 and improved to 19-13, in 2nd place. The A's fell to 15-20.

After a long train ride, the A's were in Washington on the 23rd for a game against the Senators. With the A's winning 8 to 6 in the 8th inning, Charlie Bishop walked two batters with one out. Carl was called from the pen. He stranded the runners, retiring the next two batters. He also shut down the Nats in the 9th to close out the victory.

Carl earned his 2nd save with 1 2/3 innings of shutout relief. The A's improved to 16-20.

Frank Fanovich started for the A's on May 25th against the Senators. He was incredibly wild, starting the game by walking the bases loaded.

Carl was called before an out was recorded. Despite pitching three of the prior four days, Carl would go the distance in this one. Five runs scored in an ugly 1st, three of them charged to Fanovich. The Nats added another in the 5th to go up 6 to 0. That was the final score. Fanovich took the loss, and Carl gave up three runs in eight innings. His ERA was only 2.77. The A's fell to 16-22.

On May 31st, the A's were at Yankee Stadium. The Yanks jumped out to a 5 to 0 lead against Alex Kellner when Carl was summoned with one out and runners at the corners in the 6th.

1953

Gene Woodling greeted Carl with a two-run double, the runs charged to Kellner. He then retired Mickey Mantle and Hank Bauer to end the inning.

Carl retired the Yanks in order in the 7th before he was replaced by Morrie Martin.

The Yanks won the game 7 to 1. Johnny Sain improved to 5-2. Carl pitched 1 2/3 innings of shutout relief. His ERA dropped to 2.66. The A's slipped to 11 back at 18-24.

Carl started against the Tigers in Detroit on June 4th. The team staked him to a 3 to 0 lead in the 1st against Billy Hoeft.

Carl gave one back in the bottom of the 1st, but Eddie Joost countered in the 2nd with a solo home run.

The Tigers erupted for four runs in the bottom of the 2nd, chasing Carl with two outs. The Bengals ripped six hits in the inning, including two doubles. Carl left trailing 5 to 4.

The A's tied the game in the 8th on a Gus Zernial home run, and ultimately won it in the 10th on a Cass Michaels three-run homer.

Charlie Bishop earned his third win. Billy Hoeft was the loser. Carl thankfully received a no-decision despite giving up five earned runs in 1 2/3 innings. His ERA ballooned to 3.61. The A's improved to 21-24. The Tigers slipped deeper into last place at 10-34.

On June 5th, the A's had moved on to Cleveland to face the Indians. The game was tied at two going into the bottom of the 9th, when Carl relieved Alex Kellner.

Carl sent the game into extra innings, retiring the Indians quickly.

The A's were unable to score in the top of the 10th. In the bottom of the inning, Carl walked Larry Doby and gave up a single to Al Rosen, putting men on the corners. Carl then pitched carefully to Harry Simpson, loading the bases with no one out.

Morrie Martin was then called to face Hank Majeski. He lifted a fly ball to right field deep enough for Doby to tag and score. The game ended 3 to 2. Carl was charged with the loss, his record now 1-3.

Two days later, still in Cleveland, Carl was called in the bottom of the 4th with one out after Morrie Martin had given up a two-run home run to tie the game at four. After retiring George Strickland, Joe Tipton blasted a home run to give the Indians and

Bob Feller the lead, 5 to 4, Carl ending the inning by retiring Feller on a fly out.

In the bottom of the 5th, the Indians increased their lead when Larry Doby blasted a two run homer.

In the bottom of the 6th, Carl gave up another run on Bob Feller's RBI single. The Indians led 8 to 4.

Bob Feller then cruised to victory, notching his second win against three loses. Carl fell to 1-4. He gave up four earned runs in 2 2/3 innings. His ERA rose to 4.30. The A's dropped to 21-28 after being swept in the subsequent second game of the doubleheader.

On June 9th, in Chicago, Billy Pierce was beating the A's 5 to 1 when Carl mopped up in the 9th in relief of Frank Fanovich. He put the Sox down in order. The A's were unable to mount a rally, and lost 5 to 1.

The Browns were in Philadelphia on the 14th for a doubleheader. Harry Byrd won the first game 4 to 1, improving his record to 6-6, beating Don Larsen.

Carl was called to start the second game against Harry Breechen.

The A's got out to a 1 to 0 lead in the 2nd when Ed McGhee doubled in a run. They added another run in the 6th on Cass Michaels' home run. Cass Michaels drove in another run in the 8th against Satchel Paige when he grounded out.

The Browns finally got to Carl in the 8th, when, with two outs, Roy Sievers singled and Vic Wertz doubled him home.

In the top of the 9th, Carl batted against Satchel Paige and reached on a single, but Paige escaped any further trouble.

The final score was 3 to 1, Philadelphia. Carl was the winner, improving to 2-3. He gave up only one run on six hits in nine innings pitched. Harry Breechen took the loss, falling to 1-8. The A's improved to 27-29, while the Browns slipped to 19-38.

June 18th, the Indians were in Philadelphia. Bob Lemon took the mound against Carl.

The A's jumped out to a 1 to 0 lead in the 1st on Gus Zernial's RBI single.

Carl held the Indians scoreless until the 4th. Al Rosen led off with a double. After retiring Larry Doby, and walking Harry Simpson, Carl got George Strickland to foul out to first base. However, Joe Ginsberg lashed a two-out single scoring Rosen. Bob

Lemon followed with another two-out single, scoring Simpson. Carl walked the next batter before retiring Bobby Avila with the bases loaded.

The A's took the lead against Lemon in the bottom of the 5th. Dave Philley drove in a run with a single. Eddie Robinson then followed with a sacrifice fly. Robinson had been traded by the White Sox to the A's along with Joe DeMaestri and Ed McGhee for Ferris Fain and Bobby Wilson in the off-season.

The Indians tied the game at three in the 8th on Al Rosen's solo home run. They took the lead in the top of the 9th on Bob Lemon's RBI single with one out.

Morrie Martin relieved Carl and retired the next two batters to end the threat.

In the bottom of the 9th with one out, Joe Astroth ripped a Lemon pitch into the seats to tie the game at four.

The Indians went on to win 6 to 4 in extra innings, Bob Lemon improving to 8-6. Morrie Martin was tagged with the loss. Carl received a no-decision, pitching 8 1/3 innings, yielding four earned runs.

Only three days later, Carl was called again to start the second game of a doubleheader against the White Sox in Philadelphia. The A's had won the first game 5 to 0 behind Harry Byrd.

The A's jumped to a 1 to 0 lead in the 1st on a Gus Zernial single against Bob Keegan.

Fred Marsh tied the game in the 2nd with a solo home run off of Carl.

Carl helped himself in the bottom of the 2nd, singling in Ed McGhee, who had tripled. The A's led 2 to 1.

In the top of the 3rd, pitcher Keegan and Nellie Fox singled. Former Athletic Ferris Fain stepped to the plate. He blasted a Scheib pitch into the stands for a three-run home run.

After Minnie Minoso singled, Frank Fanovich was called to replace Carl. Fanovich gave up a triple to Sam Mele, chasing in Minoso, ending Carl's line for the day.

The White Sox went on to win 9 to 4. Carl was charged with the loss, falling to 2-5. He had given up five earned runs in only two innings of work.

The next day, June 22nd, Carl was called to mop up the last three innings of a 5 to 0 loss to the Tigers at Connie Mack Stadium. Carl pinch-hit for Marion Fricano in the 6th, and took the mound in the 7th. He held Detroit scoreless for the final three innings, receiving a no-decision.

On June 28th, the Browns were in Philadelphia for a doubleheader. Don Larsen had won the first game for St. Louis, 4 to 1.

Carl took the mound for the A's in the second game against Mike Blyzka.

Both teams were scoreless until the top of the 7th, when the Browns scored on a suicide-squeeze bunt by Jim Dyck.

The A's tied the game in the bottom of the 8th on a sacrifice fly by Eddie Robinson.

Carl then retired the Browns in order in the 9th, getting Dick Kokos, Roy Sievers and Vic Wertz on fly balls.

In the bottom of the 9th, rookie Blyzka retired the first two batters, but gave up a triple to Joe Astroth.

Satchel Paige was then summoned from the pen with two outs and a runner on third. Carl stepped to the plate. He nailed a single to center to score Astroth with the walk-off run.

Carl improved his record to 3-5 and dropped his ERA to 3.79.

July 5th was not a good day for Carl. The Red Sox were in town. He was slated to start against Mel Parnell. Carl did not get out of the 1st inning.

Billy Goodman led off with a double. After Hoot Evers struck out, Dick Gernert doubled to drive in Goodman. George Kell then doubled on a pop fly, Gernert making it to third. Tom Umphlett then singled in a run. Carl intentionally walked Jim Piersall to load the bases. He followed by walking in a run.

Marion Fricano got the call to replace Carl with only one out in the 1st and the bases loaded. The Red Sox were leading 3 to 0.

Fricano allowed all of the inherited runners to score, and two more, before handing the ball to Joe Coleman to finish the inning.

The A's used three pitchers in the 1st inning, and were behind 8 to 0.

The Red Sox went on to win easily 10 to 2. Mel Parnell improved to 11-4. Carl dropped to 3-6. He had given up six earned runs in only 1/3 of an inning. The A's had lost their sixth in a row, dropping to 32-44.

The next day, July 6th, the Yankees were at Connie Mack Stadium. In the top of the 4th, Billy Martin ripped a two-run double with one out to chase Charlie Bishop. Carl got the call to replace him with the score 4 to 0 in favor of New York. Carl followed by retiring Phil Rizzuto and Vic Raschi to end the inning.

The A's got one back in the bottom of the 4th, but Carl loaded the bases in the 5th and then hit Gil McDougald with a pitch, forcing in a run.

In the bottom of the 5th, Carl started the inning with a single off of Raschi. He moved to second on Dave Philley's walk. With two outs, Gus Zernial doubled to score Carl.

The score was 5 to 2. The Yankees went on to win 5 to 3. Carl pitched 4 2/3 innings of one run ball for a no-decision.

The teams were going in opposite directions, the Yanks improving to 52-24, in first place. The A's fell to 32-46, in 6th place.

The A's were at Fenway Park on July 11th. The game was tied at three apiece in the bottom of the 9th when Frank Fanovich game up a single to Tom Umphlett. Carl was summoned from the pen to stop the rally.

Jim Piersall tapped what was supposed to be a sacrifice bunt back to Carl, who wheeled to catch the lead runner, but could not get anyone out on the play.

Milt Bolling then followed with another attempted sacrifice bunt. Carl fielded it and threw wildly to first, allowing the winning run to score.

Carl's line was zero innings pitched and no runs allowed. But his defense certainly handed the loss to Fanovich, who fell to 0-2.

The next day, the A's continued their series at Boston. Trailing 5 to 1 in the bottom of the 4th, Jimmy Dykes replaced Morrie Martin with Carl.

He put down the Sox in order in the 4th. In the bottom of the 5th, Billy Goodman led off with a triple, and scored on Dick Gernert's single. This score held until the bottom of the 7th.

Hoot Evers and George Kell singled in the inning. With one out, Del Wilber swatted a three-run home run to put the Sox up 9 to 1. Carl completed the inning without further harm, and turned the ball over to Joe Coleman.

The A's scored four in the 8th to no avail.

The final score was 9 to 5. Carl gave up four earned runs in four innings of work. The A's fell to 33-51.

On July 28th, the Browns were at Connie Mack Stadium. With the bases loaded and one out, and the A's trailing 4 to 2, Carl was summoned to bail out Harry Byrd.

He retired Billy Hunter on a fouled bunt. He then put down Bob Cain on a fly to left.

The A's got one back in the 3rd, scoring a run on Eddie Robinson's double play.

Carl mowed down the Browns in the 4th. In the bottom of the inning, the A's scored four runs, including Carl, who had walked.

Carl gave two back in the top of the 5th, making the score 7 to 6. Morrie Martin then replaced Carl in the 7th.

The A's went on to win 9 to 7, Morrie Martin earning the win, while Don Larsen took the loss. Carl, once again, got a no-decision. He threw 3 2/3 innings, giving up two runs.

On August 2nd, the team announced that Carl had been put on the disabled list with a sore shoulder. He would not pitch again until September.

"I had torn tendons in my shoulder," explained Carl. "My shoulder hurt really bad. I tried ice and then heat, but nothing helped."

On September 3rd. Carl was back with the team and asked to start against the Indians in Cleveland. He and Dave Hoskins exchanged zeros until the bottom of the 4th.

In the inning, Carl gave up an RBI single to Wally Westlake, and a bases-loaded double to Jim Hegan that cleared the bases.

Carl finished the 4th inning, trailing 4 to 0, and returned the dugout.

"What's the matter?" asked Jimmy Dykes, "You're not throwing well. Do you have a sore arm? I'm taking you out!"

Carl cursed at him as he headed down the steps to the clubhouse. He was pulled for a pinch hitter in the 5th.

The Indians went on to win 9-4, Carl taking the loss, dropping to 3-7. The team fell to 52-82.

Carl's last appearance of the season was on September 7th against the Senators at home. He pitched the 6th inning, relieving Charlie Bishop with the team behind 4 to 2. Carl gave up a two-run home run to Eddie Yost to increase the deficit to 6 to 2. The A's lost 6 to 3. Carl gave up two runs in one inning. His ERA for season finished at 4.88. He was 3-7 and sore-armed.

4.88

The A's dropped to 52-86 and had sixteen more to play. They ended the season at 59-95, in 7th place.

*1954
Eddie Joost
new mgr.*

Gus Zernial led the team with 42 home runs and 108 RBI. Eddie Robinson hit 22 homers and knocked in 102. Dave Philley hit .303 to lead in batting average.

On the mound, Alex Kellner (11-12) and Harry Byrd (11-20) led the team in wins.

After the season, it was announced that Eddie Joost would take over as manager, replacing Jimmy Dykes.

Bobo Newsom was released on November 19th. Cass Michaels was purchased by the White Sox the next month.

On December 17th, the Baltimore Orioles traded Bob Cain to the Athletics for Joe Coleman and Frank Fanovich.

14.

HEADING WEST

Carl went to spring training in 1954, but he couldn't get the soreness out of his shoulder. Trying to pitch another season without the zip on his fastball, the right-hander was in trouble.

Carl made one appearance for the A's in 1954. On May 3rd, the first-place White Sox were at Connie Mack Stadium to take on the 8-6 A's. Carl started for Philadelphia against Cuban Sandy Consuegra, who was starting what would be his only All-Star season.

The first batter of the game was All-Star shortstop Chico Carrasquel. He lined a ball to center field, out of the reach of Vic Power, and easily reached second.

All-Star second baseman and future Hall of Famer, Nellie Fox, was next up. He punched a ball just past second baseman Spook Jacobs, who could not nab it before Carrasquel scored.

All-Star right fielder Minnie Minoso stepped in. Carl must've felt he was pitching in the All-Star Game, given the lineup he was facing! Minoso had hit .313 in 1953 and led the American League in stolen bases. Minoso hit a shot toward shortstop Joe DeMaestri, who flipped to Spook Jacobs to force Fox, who threw to first to nail Minoso. Now it seemed Carl could see his way out of the inning.

Ferris Fain, another All-Star, was a former batting champion and former teammate, having hit .344 in 1951, and .327 in 1952 while with the Athletics. Though the 1953 campaign had yielded only a .256 pace for the first baseman, he had landed Joe DeMaestri, Ed McGhee, and Eddie Robinson for the A's. Fain would hit .302 in this injury-shortened season, the last time he would hit over .300. Perhaps Carl knew a little more about the tendencies of his former teammate. He struck Ferris out looking.

The Athletics went down in order in the 1st. Carl returned to the hill for the top of the 2nd. Veteran left fielder Willard Marshall was a former All-Star for the New York Giants. He was getting a rare start for the Sox, where he was a pinch hitter and defensive replacement. Marshall hit a ball to center that Vic Power was able to pull in for the first out.

5/7/54
Carl sold
to St Louis

Next up was Grady Hatton, the third baseman who had been an All-Star with the Cincinnati Reds in 1952. In a few weeks, he would be traded to the Boston Red Sox for future Hall of Famer George Kell. He worked a walk and took first.

Catcher Sherm Lollar had been an All-Star for the St. Louis Browns in 1950. He was at the beginning of a stretch in which he would appear in six of the next seven mid-summer classics. Lollar would also win gold gloves for three consecutive seasons from 1957 to 1959. He grounded a ball to third baseman Jim Finigan, who threw to Jacobs at second to try and putout Hatton, but Hatton was called safe. However, Spook's throw to first was in time to nail the slow-footed catcher for the second out.

With Hatton on second, center fielder Johnny Groth stepped to the plate. He was the first non-All-Star to do so for the White Sox. Johnny lifted a ball to left which was caught by Gus Zernial for the final out.

Again, the A's failed to score, the game remaining 1-0 in favor of the Sox.

As the top of the 3rd began, it became quickly apparent that something was not right with Carl. Pitcher Sandy Consuegra, was a typical light-hitter. He knocked a ball up the middle and into center field for a single.

Chico Carrasquel then followed with a single to left, putting men on first and second and nobody out.

Nellie Fox then went the other way, singling to right field, and loading the bases.

Next up was Minnie Minoso. He had led the American League in being hit by a pitch the last three seasons, and would do so again in 1954. In fact, at this writing, he is still ranked ninth all-time in this category. Suffice to say, Minnie liked to crowd the plate.

In a very strange end to an otherwise respectable Philadelphia career, the last pitch thrown by Carl as a member of the A's plunked Minnie Minoso, sending him down to first and forcing in a run, Consuegra crossing the plate.

Recalling the incident in 2014, Carl said, "I hit Minoso by accident. He always stood on top of the plate. The pitch hit him on the head, knocking him down. He laid in the dirt for a while, but as I walked up to him to see if he was alright, he jumped up and went to first."

Manager Eddie Joost had seen enough. He came to the mound, summoning Art Ditmar from the bullpen. The score was now 2-0, but the bases were loaded, and no one was out.

The dangerous Ferris Fain strode to the plate to face Ditmar. All three runners on base belonged to Carl. One of Art's pitches crossed-up catcher Joe Astroth, the ball rolling to the backstop. An alert Chico Carrasquel scored and the other runners moved up.

Fain then singled to center, scoring Fox and Minoso. All three runs were charged to Carl. Rookie Ditmar, in only his second game, gave up four more runs, making it an eight run 3rd for the Sox. They would go on to win 14 to 3.

Four days later, on May 7th, Carl was sold to the National League's St. Louis Cardinals on a conditional deal. Meanwhile, Georgene was expecting their fourth child. Son Kenneth Paul Scheib was born soon after.

Now a teammate of Stan Musial and Red Schoendienst, Carl was named the starting pitcher by the Redbirds manager, Eddie Stanky, for their game in Philadelphia on May 16th.

The Phillies were 15-11 and in first place. They shared Connie Mack Stadium with the A's, but this was Carl's first experience in the visitor's clubhouse and dugout. He had been on the other side since 1943. Now in his eleventh season, he was seeing things very differently.

His teammates were kind enough to spot him a one-run lead in the top of the 1st as Stan Musial drove in Solly Hemus, while hitting into a force play.

Carl's first batter in the National League was the lead-off man for the Phillies, third baseman Willie "Puddin' Head" Jones. Jones had been an All-Star and key member of the 1950 Whiz Kids. Carl outmatched him, striking him out.

Next up was the catalyst of the Phillies, Richie Ashburn. "Whitey," as he was known, was a career .300 hitter and would win the batting title the next season in 1955. The future Hall of Famer was a tough out, and rarely struck out. Carl K'd him too!

Things were really looking up for Carl. Maybe the Cardinals had made a great deal. Maybe Carl just needed a change of scenery.

First baseman Johnny Wyrostek stepped in. He had been an All-Star for the Cincinnati Reds in 1950. Wyrostek drew a walk and trotted to first.

Batting clean-up was the dangerous Del Ennis, who had driven in 125 runs the prior season. Ennis was a right-handed power-hitter. He ripped one of Carl's offerings to the gap in center, moving Wyrostek to third as he cruised into second.

Next up was second baseman Granny Hamner. Stanky, seeing rookie Danny Schell in the on-deck circle, signaled to catcher Del Rice to put him on. Carl then intentionally walked Hamner to load the bases.

Right fielder Schell was hitting .143 in only seven major league at bats. If Carl could retire the rookie, he'd escape the trouble, but it was not to be. The light-hitting Schell lined a ball to center for a double, plating Wyrostek and Ennis and moving Hamner to third. The Phillies now led 2 to 1.

Catcher Smoky Burgess was next up. He was in the midst of his best season as a hitter. He would end up with a .368 average and his first All-Star appearance. Carl was able to get him on a dribbler to second. Schoendienst and first baseman Alston both charged the ball. Red picked it up and tossed to Carl covering to end the inning, stranding Hamner and Schell.

In the top of the 2nd, the Cards tied it up, scoring Alston on Del Rice's sacrifice fly. Carl had followed Rice at the plate but made the second out, popping out to Hamner at second. The inning ended with the score locked at 2-2.

The bottom of the 2nd was a breeze for Carl. Batting 8th was shortstop Bobby Morgan. Morgan had been a backup for Brooklyn, spelling Billy Cox and Peewee Reese. The Phils traded for him in the off-season and made him the everyday shortstop. He popped out to first baseman Tom Alston.

Pitcher Paul Penson was making his first big league start for the Phils this day, and stepped in for his first major league at bat. Penson rolled a ball to Alston who stepped on the bag for the second out.

Puddin' Head then took his turn but fared no better, grounding out to shortstop Solly Hemus.

In the top of the 3rd, the Cardinals could not make anything of Schoendienst's single. Musial flied out to center. Jablonski grounded out.

Still knotted 2-2, Carl took the mound for the bottom of the 3rd. First up was Whitey Ashburn. The Whiz Kid slapped a single to left.

Johnny Wyrostek then followed with a blast into the seats, driving in two and giving the Phils a two-run lead.

Del Ennis was next. He had doubled in the 1st inning. This time, he improved upon that with a home run, hitting one back-to-back. Carl was clearly shaken.

Granny Hamner stepped to the plate as the bullpen was busy. Carl walked Hamner and was removed from the game by Eddie

Stanky. He strode back to the dugout in front of 24,495 Philadelphia fans, trailing 5 to 2.

The Phillies would win the game 8 to 4, tagging Carl with the loss, his last decision in the major leagues.

Six days later, on May 22nd, Carl was back in St. Louis, in the bullpen at Busch Stadium. His first-place Cardinals were playing the Cincinnati Reds.

Rookie Art Fowler had started for Cincinnati, and had handcuffed the Cards all day, scattering eight hits. Only Stan Musial had managed two hits against him, yielding no RBI. With the Cards behind 4 to 2, Carl took the hill in the 8th. It would be one of his more dominant relief appearances, retiring all six men in order, including strikeouts of Jim Greengrass, Ed Bailey, and Fowler.

Unfortunately for the Cards, Fowler had their number that day. Art struck out Musial in the 8th, and closed them out easily in the 9th, securing the 4 to 2 win.

Two days later, on Monday May 24th, the Cubs were in town, the Cards had lost two games, slipping to 3rd place in the tight National League race.

Vic Raschi, who had been purchased from the Yankees in the off-season, was expected to be an ace for the Cards. He experienced some arm problems after the 1st, and left the game. Stu Miller was summoned to be the long man and struggled, giving up four runs on six hits and two walks in less than four innings.

Carl received the call in the top of the 5th with two outs and men on first and third.

Third baseman Randy Jackson drew a walk, moving Ralph Kiner to second. Dee Fondy was on third.

Rookie shortstop Ernie Banks then walked to the plate. The bases were loaded. The future Hall of Famer had a great opportunity to break the game open. Carl looked in, wound up, and uncorked a wild pitch, scoring Fondy. The Cards now trailed by 4.

Ernie put a charge into a subsequent pitch, sailing a ball into right where Stan Musial made the catch for the final out.

The bottom of the 5th looked promising. Jablonski, Alston, Repulski, and Rice hit four consecutive singles off starter Jim Davis, plating one and leaving the bases loaded for Carl.

Eddie Stanky could have called for a pinch hitter, but Carl had a reputation with the stick, and had a major league grand slam on his resume.

1954 MLB career ends at age 27!

In his last at bat in the major leagues, Carl stepped to the plate against Jim Davis, a 29-year-old rookie. Davis had just yielded four straight hits, and the hometown fans were hoping for more.

Unfortunately for Carl and the Cardinals, he tapped a ball back to the mound. Davis grabbed it and threw home to Joe Garagiola for the force. Carl took the base at first, and the others moved up.

The following account from the *Medford Mail Tribune* on May 25th, 1954 details what happened next:

> Eddie Stanky, a man who has had his share of rhubarbs with umpires, today had a fine chance to win a delayed argument—the protest of his St. Louis Cardinals 0-2 defeat by the Chicago Cubs Monday night. The peppery pilot held up the game for 15 minutes as he alternately ranted, pleaded and reasoned against the weird conflict of decision that choked off a promising 5th inning rally. The Cardinals were trailing 4-0 when the disputed play occurred. Rookie pitcher Jim Davis, making his first major league start, had held the Cards to one single for the first four innings. But in the 5th, they began getting to the 28-year-old southpaw. Ray Jablonski, first up, singled. So did Tom Alston, Rip Repulski, and Del Rice to chase one run across. After Carl Scheib forced Alston at home plate for the first out, the ruckus started. Wally Moon hit a low flying drive to Ralph Kiner and the left fielder apparently made a diving catch. But third base umpire Hal Dixon gave the safe sign, sending Rice galloping toward third and Repulski on his way home. Second base umpire Tom Gorman simultaneously called Moon out, ruling Kiner's dive a fair catch. After Kiner's throw to the vacated second base spot was ruled the tail end of a double play, Stanky and his men stormed on the field. When the uproar ended and the players returned to their positions, Chief Umpire Larry Goetz informed the press box that Repulski had scored before the put-out at second base and his run counted. After the game, Goetz went a great deal further. It was, he said, "lousy umpiring."

Thus, the inning ended with Carl being forced out at second base in all of the confusion.

Back on the mound, first up was catcher Joe Garagiola. The future broadcaster and panelist on *The Today Show* was in his last season in the big leagues at the tender age of twenty-eight. He turned his left-handed bat on a Carl offering and launched it into the stands for a home run. It would be the last one Carl allowed in his major league career.

Center fielder Bob Talbot was next up. He was a light-hitting rookie known for his defense. He tapped a ball back to the mound. Carl fielded it and threw it first. It would be the last out Carl recorded.

The last batter Carl faced in the major leagues was pitcher Jim Davis. Davis was on his way to throwing a solid complete-game victory. Carl was unable to keep the ball near the plate, walking Jim.

Eddie Stanky had seen enough. Walking the pitcher was usually the last thing a manager wanted to see from his pitcher. Carl handed the ball over to Stanky, and exited the field. At twenty-seven, unbeknownst to him at that time, his major-league career was over.

"I didn't like playing for the Cardinals," said Carl. "Manager Eddie Stanky fined me for missing a sign on the bench. If a player failed to get a sacrifice fly, he was fined. If he failed to bunt, he was fined. Stan Musial told Stanky to 'shove his fines.' The team was not very friendly to him and never shared the best places to eat. Fortunately, I was only there a month or two."

The next week, on Tuesday June 1ˢᵗ, the St. Louis Cardinals returned Carl to the Philadelphia Athletics, who subsequently released him.

On Friday, June 4ᵗʰ, Carl signed a contract with the Portland Beavers of the Pacific Coast League. The Beavers, affiliated with the Baltimore Orioles, were mired in last place in the PCL, 15½ games back of league-leading Hollywood. According to a news report, Carl said 'he would leave by plane today to join the team in San Francisco.'

Carl's troubles followed him to Portland. His first game in the Pacific Coast League was on June 10ᵗʰ at home against Seattle. The Beavers raced to a 6-0 lead, but Carl couldn't hold it, lasting only four innings.

On July 23rd, Carl pinch-hit in the 8th inning against Sacramento and hit a game-tying two-run home run to left field off of Bud Daley. Daley would win sixteen games in back-to-back seasons for the Kansas City A's in future seasons.

Four days later, on July 27th, Carl struggled in relief against the San Diego Padres., facing eleven batters in a seven-run 6th.

On Friday, July 20th, Carl entered a game against Los Angeles. He had relieved in the 5th inning and then came to bat in the 7th. Carl clouted a game-winning three-run homer against Bob Spicer, who would later get a few major league starts for Kansas City. Carl was also the winning pitcher.

August 18th, Carl was again a hero with the bat and with his arm, in an extra-inning game against the Oakland Acorns. He entered the game in the 8th as a reliever with the Beavers behind 2 to 1. In the bottom of the 9th, Carl came to bat and singled to center. He went to third on Austin's single, and scored when Eddie Basinski blooped a single over second. The game continued for thirteen innings at 2-2, until it was suspended due to a downpour. It ended as a tie, but Carl threw six scoreless innings.

In the second game of the doubleheader against Seattle on Sunday, August 22nd, Carl did it again. He started a rally with a single, and then scored one of the two tying runs driven-in by Wally Judnich, forcing extra innings. Carl earned his second win by blanking the Rainiers for the final 4 1/3.

Labor Day, September 6th, Carl started the second game of a double-dip and scattered six hits while beating San Francisco 2 to 1. It was his third and final win of the season.

While Carl had struggled on the mound earlier in his days with the Beavers, he finished 3-3 with a 5.31 ERA. With the bat, though, he hit .361 knocking 13 hits in 36 at bats, including two home runs. Still only 27, Carl contemplated switching to the outfield again, a position he played for three innings for the Beavers in 1954.

15.
BEAVER WITH A BAT

When the Beavers opened training camp in Glendale California on March 1st, 1955, Carl had not yet signed his contract, holding out for a better deal. He and the team came to terms on the 3rd.

On March 15th, the Beavers played the UCLA Bruins in a spring training game. Carl was the first of three pitchers who scattered only four hits among them while winning 3 – 0.

Five days later, Carl and Dick Waibel combined to defeat the Hollywood Stars 8 to 1.

Following is an article in the March 22nd edition of the *La Grande Observer* from La Grande, Oregon, regarding the prospects for the Portland Beavers in 1955:

Portland Beavers Are Expected to Be Tough
By SCOTT BAILLIE United Press Sports Writer

The Portland Beavers, bolstered by six player deals in the past three months, served notice today that they will be a lot tougher in the Pacific Coast League race than last year's eighth-placers which were left at the post. Manager Clay Hopper, who had never finished lower than sixth in 21 campaigns until 1954, is certain the Beavers will cause a lot of woe around the circuit. "The club will have a lot more power at first base in Ed Mickelson, whom we drafted from Shreveport of the Texas League," Hopper said. "And we'll be a lot faster with Artie Wilson, whom we got from Seattle for Rocky Krsnich and Jehosie Heard. Sam Calderone is down from the Milwaukee Braves to catch and will do most of it." Those three players were obtained after General Manager Joe Ziegler took office in mid-December as Portland residents bought the club from Vancouver brewer George Norgan and turned the Bevos into a home-owned team. Ziegler also purchased outfielder Dick Whitman and pitcher Wally Hood from Montreal along with outfielder Rusu Sullivan who hit .333 and clubbed 17 home runs with Little Rock of the Southern Association in 1954. Mickelson batted .335 at Shreveport, also hit 17 home runs and drove in 104 tallies. He is taking over the vacancy created when Hank Arft, a .261 hitter with Portland last year, decided to hold out. Arft wound up with his outright release. "Mickelson will help us at first even if he has his worst year," Hopper said. Good, grey Clay also warned Wilson, who hit .336 last year at Seattle and led the PCL in three-base hits with 10, may run Eddie Basinski right off second. Basinski has been custodian of the middle sack at Portland for 7½ seasons without too much competition, but he has it now. Hopper said the gentle violinist may be better on double plays than swift Artie but is strictly a .250 hitter and that's bad with the new regime going for harder hitting. Frankie Austin has nothing to fear at shortstop though, Hopper said he is slated for his seventh year there as a Beaver and is the best short-fielder in the league as far as Hopper is concerned. When Krsnich went to Seattle in the Wilson deal, third base apparently was left in full possession of Don Eggert. Hopper also is delighted with the work of rookie Ron Jackson, who can play any infield spot and may become a top utility man. Jackson hit .316 at Victoria of the Class A Western International League last year. The pitching is better with the arrival of Wally Hood but Hopper said the former major leaguer still must win a spot on the mound. The biggest man there seems to be Lefty Royce Lint, who had a 22-10 mark at Portland in 1953 and then was 2-3 with the St. Louis Cardinals last year. Lint has rejoined southpaw Glenn Elliott (12-15) on a starting staff to be rounded out by righties Dick Fiedler (11-12) and Dick Waibel (11-10) with Lee Anthony, ancient Red Adams, Carl Scheib, and Larry Ward around for relief. The outfield is loaded with names but there isn't a center fielder in the bunch. Dino Restelli, Fletcher Robbe and Wally Judnich are back but being pushed by slugging rookie Bob Caselli, an erstwhile pitcher. "When we land a fast center fielder everything will be fine," Hopper declared. Don Lundberg and Ron Bottler figure to give Calderone a rest when he needs one behind the plate.

On Saturday April 9th, Carl relieved Red Adams in the 8th inning of a tie game with the Los Angeles Angels. Adams had thrown a dozen big league innings for the Cubs back in 1946. He spent 16 of his 19 seasons in the Pacific Coast League, most of them for Portland. He won 193 games in his minor league career. This evening, he handed Carl a 2-2 tie in the 8th. Carl held the Angels at bay until the bottom of the 10th, when catcher John Pramesa blasted the game-winning homer. Pramesa had hit 13 home runs over four seasons in the National League with the Reds and Cubs from from 1949 to 1952.

Six days later, on Friday April 15th, Carl was the victim of another homer which widened a 3 to 1 lead, easing San Francisco's victory over the Beavers. Chuck Stevens hit the three-run shot off of Carl. Thirty-six-year-old Stevens had played three seasons for the Browns in the 40s.

On April 24th, San Diego and Portland played a twenty inning game, as the second of a doubleheader. Carl lucked into a win, pitching the 20th, after which the Beavers scored a run.

Six days later, he was the beneficiary of another extra-inning win, pitching the 10th in a ten-inning affair against Sacramento.

On May 17th, Carl wasn't so lucky as he allowed the winning run in relief against Seattle on a bad hop hit past the third baseman, evening his record at 2-2.

Carl was back to winning in extra innings on May 30th against the Hollywood Stars. He had provided a key sacrifice bunt in the 9th and pitched two innings for the win.

On June 18th, Carl entered the game at Hollywood in the 9th inning with a 4 to 1 lead. He got the final out on a deep fly to center with two on.

On July 3rd, Carl was credited with a win in a wild 8 to 6 affair against Los Angeles. He pitched the final four innings of the second game of a double-dip.

Twenty days later, on the 23rd, Carl preserved a 7 to 3 win over Sacramento and added an RBI on a hit of his own.

On July 31st, Carl notched his 7th win of the season, beating Sacramento with solid relief pitching.

Carl had the lumber out on August 12th against San Francisco. He had relieved in a back and forth affair, tallying two hits in three at bats. Unfortunately, on the mound, he was on the down side of a 6 to 5 loss.

In another Beaver loss on August 15th, Carl scored a run after a hit and provided three innings of solid relief.

On August 20th, Carl knocked another hit and scored on a sacrifice fly to give the Beavers the lead over Seattle. The Beavers couldn't hold the lead however, despite his solid effort.

Six days later, on the 26th, against Oakland, Carl got the final three outs for a save in a 5 to 4 win.

In his last action of the season, on September 2nd, Carl started against Seattle, scattering nine hits in a 3 to 0 loss. He finished the season 7-4 with a 3.45 ERA. At the plate, he hit .353 with 12 hits in 34 at bats.

"I remember running into Dick Powell who was directing *The Conqueror* in Hollywood," said Carl, recalling his Pacific Coast League trips to California. "I met John Wayne at that time. He was starring in the movie.
"At other times, I ran into John Carradine and Chuck Connors would come out and hit batting practice."

The call to the majors did not come in 1955, and Carl was sold SOLD to San Antonio of the Texas League on December 1st during the annual minor leagues winter meetings.

16.

TEXAS LEAGUE ALL-STAR

The article in the April 3rd, 1956, edition of the *The Odessa American*, from Odessa, Texas, did not look kindly on the upcoming season for the San Antonio Missions or their veteran hurler from Gratz:

Padres Face Long Summer In TL Play

It's apt to be a "long summer" for San Antonio baseball fans unless Manager Joe Schultz manages to work some miracles with the material the parent Orioles have given him.

The club seems to be fairly well set at its Dunedin, Fla., base and going on the records there isn't enough mound and bat power on the club to make it a serious first division contender.

Schultz has just about all the help he can expect from Baltimore since that club already has pared its roster nearly to the bone prior to leaving Arizona for the swing home.

The pitching situation is the saddest of the lot and the brightest spot seems to be third base where a flashy teenager, Brooks Robinson has been cavorting in fine fashion. The 18-year-old Robinson hit .331 at York, Pa. last year and has shown excellent possibilities in camp this spring.

If Schultz had to pick his four starters today, they probably would be Bill Diemer, a portly right-hander who had a 13-13 record in relief roles here last season: Bob Schmitt, who wasn't too impressive in a brief post-service team fling with the Missions last summer when he had a 2-2 mark: Carl Scheib, the veteran ex-Philadelphia Athletics moundsman with a record of three years of sore arms; and southpaw Hal Hudson, a good performer here in 1950 who couldn't make the club a year ago.

Willie Powell, a cagey veteran picked up from Havana of the International League, might make the grade, as might Alton Brown, a 29-year-old graduate of York. Some of the livelier looking kids on the staff include Kelly Searcy, Dick Luebke, and Marvin Wifniewski.

Dave Roberts, the fleet Negro first baseman who burned up the league early last year only to wind up with a .232 average, has been sent back and probably will beat out another negro, 6 foot 5 inch George Thompson, just out of service.

Bob Caffrey, who hit .266 last season, has also been returned and will be at second base, while Robinson will be at third.

Marlyn Holtrapple, a .292 hitter at York, probably will win out at short over Mary Breeding, a Class D rookie.

Stan Hollmig, the former Texas Aggie who hit .285 and powered 21 home runs last season, will be back at left field, while Willie Tasby, a .279 hitter in 45 games here, and Carl Powis, who hit .268 at Seattle, will round out the outfield. Don Moitzoa, up from Stockton, Calif., where he hit .336 might break into this group.

The catching duo of Marty Tabacheck and Mike Gaspar hasn't been too impressive, but it appears they'll have to do.

On April 23rd, the Missions were in Houston to face the buffs. San Antonio got out to a 6 to 1 lead, but starter Dick Luebke had a difficult 4th, narrowing the lead to three. It would be six more years until Luebke would pitch for the Orioles for ten games in 1962. Today, young Dick was off to the showers as Carl was summoned to nail down the win. He went the rest of the way to earn the 11 to 5 victory.

Monday night, May 6th, Carl literally took control of the game against the Tulsa Oilers at San Antonio. Following is the account from the *Lubbock Morning Avalanche* the following day:

Pinch Hit Brings Padres 4-3 Win

San Antonio's acting manager, Carl Scheib, inserted himself as a pinch hitter with the bases loaded in the 8th inning Monday night and rapped out a two-run single that beat the Tulsa Oilers 4 to 3 in a Texas League game. The victory gave the Padres a tie with Fort Worth for the league lead. Scheib's blow off relief pitcher Bill Tremel came on the first pitch. It broke up a pitching duel between lefty Jehosie Heard and the Missions' Bill Bethel. Heard was charged with the loss, his first of the season against two wins. Bethel gained his second victory against one loss. The Missions pulled four double plays, including one to end the game. Scheib, a pitcher, took over the managerial reins after Manager Joe Schutz was chased by umpire Tex Parker in the 6th inning.

The win pulled the Missions into a tie with Fort Worth for the first place in the Texas League.

Two nights later, on May 9th, Carl was the goat. He was called upon in the 9th to preserve a tight 4 to 3 lead against the Tulsa Drillers. The bases were loaded and two out when Lloyd "Frank" Jenney pinch-hit for Tulsa. He hit a grand slam, flipping the win to Tulsa, 7 to 4. The Missions slipped to 2nd place.

On the 11th, Carl was back on the hill, pitching the last four innings of a wild 11 to 8 win over the Oklahoma City Indians. He was the 4th pitcher into the game, earning the win as the Missions took the lead, and tied for first place.

Sunday May 13th, the Missions took both games of a doubleheader against Oklahoma City. It was Carl's pinch-hit home run that won the first game. The shot came in the 8th inning against Ernie Groth, who had pitched briefly for the Indians and White Sox in the late 40s. Carl then went to the mound, and was also the winning pitcher.

Two days later, on the 15th, Carl started against the Dallas Eagles. The Missions won 7 to 2, increasing their lead.

May 29th, Carl took his first loss of the year as the Missions fell 11 to 6 to Tulsa. Al Lary was the winner for the Drillers. He would win over 100 games in the minors, but only saw two brief stints with the Cubs in 1954 and 1962. The Missions had faded to 7th place.

On June 20th, with the Missions up 9 to 8 in the 9th, Carl was called to save the victory for Bill Diemer. Carl throttled the rally, and the Missions eeked out a win.

Ten days later, on June 30th, Carl was the starting pitcher against the Dallas Eagles at Dallas. Through the 8th, it was a 1-1

1956
San Antonio

pitchers' duel against Freddy Rodriguez. The Cuban hurler, now 32, had a long career in the minor leagues, earning 146 wins. He would have two brief tenures with the Cubs and Phillies in 1958 and 1959. This day, he was matching the former Mackman pitch by pitch, until the top of the 9th, when the Missions exploded for five runs. Carl, who had yielded a run in the 8th, gave up another in the 9th, and won 6 to 2, it what was a four-hit complete game.

In Dick Peebles' column in the *San Antonio Express* on Friday July 13th, he surmised Carl and Bob Caffrey were likely to represent the Missions at the Texas League All-Star game in Dallas the next Thursday night. He said, "Writers around the league lean towards Carl because of his pitching and batting prowess."

That night, at Oklahoma City, against the Indians, Carl entered the game in the 7th as a relief pitcher. The teams went into extra-innings. In the top of the 12th, Carl scored the go-ahead run on Vern Grace's double. He pitched the final six innings to get the win.

The next day, Carl was named to the Texas League All-Star team to face the league-leading Dallas Eagles at Dallas.

The game that Thursday night was not a good one for the Texas League stars. They fell in a lopsided loss to Dallas, 7 to 1. Carl pitched a scoreless bottom of the 8th.

On July 28th, Carl was a hero on the mound and with the bat. At home against Austin, his clutch single in the bottom of the 9th held the Missions to a 5 to 4 win. Carl was also the winning pitcher, improving his record to 7-3.

Four days later, on August 1st, Carl pitched, perhaps, the longest outing of his professional career, going all twelve innings of a 5 to 5 deadlock with Shreveport. In the top of the 13th inning, with one out and two on, the Sports' manager, Mel McGaha, pinch-hit against Carl. Mel ripped a pitch over the fence for a three-run homer. Carl was pulled after 12 1/3 innings, and was tagged with the loss despite all of the work. McGaha never played in the major leagues, but he did manage the Cleveland Indians in 1962 to an 80-82 record, and later the Kansas City Athletics to 100+ loss seasons in 1964 and 1965.

August 16th, Carl started against the league-leading Dallas Eagles. He scattered four hits, two of them homers, in collecting the complete-game victory. The loss ended an eight-game winning streak for Dallas.

Later that month, on the 29th, the Missions were holding onto the fourth and final play-off spot in the Texas League after a seven-game winning streak. In the 9th inning of a loss to Oklahoma City, Carl hit his final home run in professional ball.

By the end of the season, the Missions had slipped back to 76-78, out of contention. Carl was the leading hitter on the team with at least 100 AB, hitting .333 in 111 attempts, including 2 home runs and 19 RBI. He was 43 at bats short of appearing third on the leader board for the entire Texas League. On the mound, Carl was 10-5 with a 4.56 ERA. His 150 innings were his most at any level since 1952, not bad for a "sore-armed" pitcher. In the end, it would be teen phenom, and future Hall of Famer, Brooks Robinson, who would be called up to the Baltimore Orioles in September. Brooks, who had been summoned the prior season after a stellar first professional season at York, was now nineteen years of age, ten years Carl's junior.

17.

MISSIONS ALMOST ACCOMPLISHED

Now thirty years old, Carl was back with San Antonio for the 1957 season. On Wednesday April 24th, he pinch-hit in the 9th against the Houston Buffs, but struck out as the Missions lost.

On April 30th, he was called to pitch in relief against the Buffs, also in a losing cause.

Four days later, on May 4th, Carl started against Austin, and contributed two hits and an RBI. The team won 7 to 5, but Carl was not around to earn the win.

Tuesday May 14th, Carl was on the downside of a tough 2 to 0 loss to the Dallas Eagles, bested by Murray Wall, whose 16-7, 1.79 ERA, performance in 1957 would be noticed by the Red Sox. Wall, who had pitched one game for the Brooklyn Dodgers in 1950, was called up at age 30 by the Red Sox.

June 11th, Carl started against Shreveport and was knocked out in the 3rd after giving up five runs. The Missions came back to win the game, sparing Carl the loss.

On Tuesday July 23rd, Carl took the mound in the first game of a doubleheader at Oklahoma City. He fired a four-hit shutout, winning 8 to 0. This ended a three game losing streak for the Missions, who then dropped the nightcap 9 to 3.

A couple weeks later, on August 5th, Carl got the call to face the Dallas Eagles in Dallas. He scattered nine hits en route to a 3 to 1 win.

Thursday, August 15th, Carl pitched in relief against Fort Worth in a tight 3 to 3 contest. With two outs in the 9th, Carl singled in the winning run for the Missions also garnering the win on the mound.

By late August, the Missions were creeping into play-off contention. Carl helped hold a lead August 22nd against Oklahoma City.

On Labor Day, September 2nd, Carl was the winner in a 6 to 3 decision against Houston.

September 7th, he went the distance for the victory in a stellar four-hit performance, winning 4 to 1. The win helped lock up a play-off berth for the Missions.

Carl was called upon to start the second game of the play-off series with Houston on September 11th. With the Missions up one game to none, Carl was brilliant, hurling seven shutout innings when it counted most. He had added two hits to the cause at the plate. Unfortunately, in the 8th, Carl ran out of gas and was replaced by Luebke. The Missions' relief corps could not hold off Houston, and the Missions went down 4 to 3, knotting the series at a game apiece.

San Antonio and Houston fought on. With the Buffaloes up 3 games to 2, the Missions rallied for a 5 to 3 victory on September 15th. This tied the series and forced a deciding 7th game. Carl picked up the win. It would be his last as a professional.

Fate was on the side of the Buffaloes, however, as they went on to win the series and then best Dallas for the Texas League crown.

Carl finished 1957 with a 6-2 record and 3.79 ERA. At the plate, he had tailed off considerably, hitting .177. He had hit well over .300 his prior three minor-league seasons, but this dud dropped his career average to .292 to go with a respectable major league average of .250.

18.
AFTER BASEBALL

It was quietly announced in the April 14th, 1958 issue of the *Shamokin News-Dispatch* that Carl had decided to retire from baseball. The article mentioned he planned to enter into private business in San Antonio, Texas where he had played for two seasons on the Missions.

A few years later, the *San Antonio Express and News* posted a humorous item in a column on July 29th, 1962 about Carl at the ballpark:

Too Hot

Carl Scheib, greatest schoolboy pitcher ever to come out of Philadelphia (He was a regular starter for the Philadelphia and Kansas City A's, later played for the local Missions, now runs a car wash on upper San Pedro); went to Houston last Sunday to watch the Colt 45s in an afternoon game. [Quote] "The park has no roof. They had to carry out three fans. It was so hot and my shirt so wet after the 2nd inning, I left."

Said Carl in an interview in 2006, "I had no education, and I didn't have a lot of choices. I worked in a store for a month. Then I leased my own business in San Antonio, a service station with an automatic car wash. I ran that business for twelve years. Later, I sold and installed equipment for the fellow who handled that car wash business. When I reached sixty-two, I just retired."

During the mid-1990s, the Philadelphia Athletics Historical Society organized several annual reunions. Carl was always happy to attend and enjoyed the camaraderie with his former teammates and longtime fans.

June 18th, 2005, was a very special day for Carl. His hometown of Gratz, Pennsylvania declared the day "Carl Scheib Day." They honored the former hurler with a series of events, including unveiling a plaque in his honor at the local ballpark.

"When I got there," Carl said, "I was really surprised. I was overwhelmed. They put a nice, big monument up of me. People who lived there 30 or 40 years knew all about it. I've never had so many people come up to me for autographs. It was really a great day!"

Reflecting about his career in 2006, Carl called it a privilege to be a major leaguer. He said he wouldn't trade his experiences for anything.

Carl continued, "The way I got to the big leagues, the opportunity I had, coming from a small town, getting a tryout from Connie Mack, I consider myself very, very lucky. I got the opportunity to learn and stay in the major leagues. I always respected my elders, but I tried to learn and do my best. Earle Brucker, our bullpen coach, helped me a lot. He would talk to me about baseball fundamentals. Those were the days when most guys wouldn't help you, so I was lucky to enjoy such a good, long career.

"Looking back on my life, baseball has been good to me, pension-wise, every way. In those years we loved to play the game. I thank the people who helped me, and the Philadelphia ball club for the opportunity to play in the major leagues, and the Good Lord for giving me the talent. I will always remember it as a time when guys loved to play the game.

"The main thing I regret was not being able to meet and thank the salesman who wrote the letter and gave me my chance."

EPILOGUE

. . . Carl snatched the two tickets from the ticket window and headed for the gate, wife in tow.

They entered the park and handed the tickets to the doorman.

"Just where are these seats?" asked Carl.

"384–left field–upper deck," he replied. "There's an escalator down the third base side, to your left."

Carl and Sandy trekked across the park to the upper reaches of Camden Yards.

"Nosebleed seats," grumbled Carl.

"But at least we got two!" said Sandy.

The couple watched the entire game from on high, but as it was ending, still fuming over the incident, Carl declared he 'would never watch another game in Baltimore.'

END NOTES

Interviews with Carl Scheib at his home, San Antonio, Texas, April 27-30, 2014 and numerous phone calls from 2014-2016.

Interview with Paul Scheib, Millersburg, Pennsylvania, Saturday May 31, 2014.

Interview with Charles Schoffstall, Gratz, Pennsylvania, Saturday May 31, 2014.

All major league baseball game play-by-play and major and minor league statistics are courtesy of the online Baseball Reference at www.baseball-reference.com.

Many game anecdotes and other commentary were gleaned from dozens of period newspapers accessed at www.newspapers.com.

Other happenings in baseball were gleaned from various annual baseball web pages access at www.wikipedia.com, for instance "1948 in baseball."

Genealogical information was accessed at www.ancestry.com.

Local game results were from articles in the *Sunbury Daily Item,* preserved on microfilm at the Degenstein Library in Sunbury, PA.

Carl's World War II baseball experiences and earlier interview quotes were taken from Jim Sargent's biographical article at the Society for American Baseball Research at http://sabr.org/bioproj/person/93562fe6.

The story of Carl's discovery by the traveling salesman Al Grossman was based on Clifford Kachline's article in *The Sporting News* on June 30, 1948. It should be noted this account was not completely accurate, and has been corrected based on other accounts and interviews, including the subject.

BIBLIOGRAPHY

Berkow, Ira. *The Corporal Was a Pitcher: The Courage of Lou Brissie*. Chicago: Triumph Books, 2009.

Gratz Historical Society, The. *A Comprehensive History of the Town of Gratz, Pennsylvania*. Gratz, PA: The Gratz Historical Society, 1997.

Gratz Historical Society, The. *Memories Volume 2*. Gratz, PA: The Gratz Historical Society, 1987.

Gratz Historical Society, The. *Memories Volume 3*. Gratz, PA: The Gratz Historical Society, 1988.

Gratz Historical Society, The. *Memories Volume 4*. Gratz, PA: The Gratz Historical Society, 1990.

Gratz Historical Society, The. *Memories Volume 5*. Gratz, PA: The Gratz Historical Society, 2005.

Gratz Historical Society, The. *Memories Volume 6*. Gratz, PA: The Gratz Historical Society, 2013.

Jordan, David M. *The Athletics of Philadelphia: Connie Mack's White Elephants, 1901-1954*. Jefferson, NC: McFarland & Co., 1999.

Kashatus, William C. *The Philadelphia Athletics*. Charleston, SC: Arcadia Publishing, 2002.

King, David & Tom Kayser. *The Texas League Baseball Almanac*. Charleston, SC: The History Press, 2014.

Klima, John. *The Game Must Go On: Hank Greenberg, Pete Gray, and the Great Days of Baseball on the Home Front in WWII*. New York: St. Martin's Press, 2015.

Kulick, Bruce. *To Everything a Season: Shibe Park and Urban Philadelphia, 1909-1976*. Princeton, NJ: Princeton University Press, 1991.

Macht, Normal L. *The Grand Old Man of Baseball: Connie Mack in His Final Years, 1932-1956*. Lincoln, NE: University of Nebraska Press, 2015.

Mack, Connie. *My 66 Years in the Big Leagues*. Mineola, NY: Dover Publications, 2009.

McGuire, Mark & Michael Sean Gormley. *Moments in the Sun: Baseball's Briefly Famous*. Jefferson, NC: McFarland & Co., 1999.

Purdy, Dennis. *The Team by Team Encyclopedia of Major League Baseball*. New York: Workman Publishing, 2006.

Taylor, Ted. *The Ultimate Philadelphia Athletics Reference Book, 1901-1954*. Xlibris Corporation, 2010.

Threston, Christopher. *The Integration of Baseball in Philadelphia*. Jefferson, NC: McFarland & Co., 2003.

Westcott, Rich. *Shibe Park – Connie Mack Stadium*. Charleston, SC: Arcadia Publishing, 2012.

INDEX

Marchildon, Phil, 20, 29, 43, 46, 59, 66, 72, 74, 81, 86, 142
Marion, Marty, 178
Marsh, Fred, 198
Marshall, Willard, 203
Martin, Billy, 160, 172, 191, 199
Martin, Hersh, 35
Martin, Morrie, 157, 161, 165-167, 171, 173, 174, 193, 196, 198, 200, 201
Masterson, Walt, 95, 152, 193
Maxwell, Charlie, 167, 171
Mayo, Eddie, 20, 26, 28, 29, 48
Mays, Willie, 71
McCahan, Bill, 45, 66, 68, 72, 87, 91
McCarthy, Charlie, 10-11
McCarthy, Joe, 21
McCosky, Barney, 32, 48, 50-53, 59, 69, 72, 76, 77, 79-82, 145, 157, 159, 173, 180, 183
McDermott, Mickey, 195
McDougald, Gil ,160, 171-173, 176, 179, 182, 200
McGaha, Mel, 218
McGhee, Ed, 192, 194, 197, 198, 203
McGowan, Bill, 157
McGuire, Jack, 169
McNair, Eric, 20
McQuinn, George, 27, 50, 51, 53, 55, 63, 68, 69, 74
Mele, Sam, 43, 44, 84, 167, 184, 198
Metkovich, George, 47, 58
Metheny, Bud, 26, 27
Michaels, Cass, 46, 54, 97, 98, 178, 188, 196, 197, 202
Mickelson, Ed, 211, 212
Middleburg, 18
Miller, Guy, 13
Miller, Johnny, 15
Miller, Stu, 207
Millersburg, 11, 12, 15, 225
Minoso, Minnie, 157, 159, 173, 184, 198, 203-205
Mitchell, Dale, 47, 79, 92, 137-139, 143-145, 148, 149, 170, 173, 174, 179, 180
Mix, Tom, 11
Mize, Johnny, 146, 152, 173, 191
Moitzoa, Don, 216

Moon, Wally, 208
Moore, Gene, 24
Moreno, Julio, 154, 178, 189
Morgan, Bobby, 206
Morgan, Joe, 138
Morgan, Tom, 182
Morrow, Art, 34
Moses, Wally, 45, 52, 79, 83, 88, 95, 98, 100, 136, 141, 148, 149, 157, 163, 164, 169, 170
Moss, Les, 57, 65, 91, 96, 97, 167, 193
Mullin, Pat, 48, 57, 76, 147, 158, 165, 166, 170, 185
Muncrief, Bob, 27, 33
Murray, Joe, 152-154
Murray, Ray, 157, 184
Musial, Stan, 205-207, 209

N
New Berlin, 16, 18
New Cumberland Army Base, 50
Newhouser, Hal 35, 56, 57, 85, 147, 177, 180, 190
Newsom, Louis "Bobo," 30, 31, 35, 37, 38, 39, 187, 202
Niarhos, Gus, 73, 74, 159
Nixon, Willard, 167
Noren, Irv, 135, 167, 168, 175, 179
Norgan, George, 211
Nuremberg, 41
Nuremberg Trials, 41
Nuxhall, Joe, 18, 33

O
O'Brien, Tommy, 94
Ostrowski, Joe, 91, 101, 146
Overmire, Stubby, 95, 159, 164, 172

P
Page, Joe, 81, 99, 142
Paige, Satchel, 72, 89, 169, 178, 184, 197, 199
Papish, Frank, 46, 54, 61, 70, 72
Parker, Tex, 217
Parnell, Mel, 44, 87, 88, 153, 157, 190, 192, 199
Peck, Hal, 47
Peebles, Dick, 218
Penson, Paul, 206

Pesky, Johnny, 43-45, 52, 57, 68, 70, 75, 78, 83, 84, 88, 94, 95, 103, 136, 152, 167, 168, 187, 188, 194

Philley, Dave, 46, 76, 137, 157, 159, 163, 164, 167-171, 177, 178, 181, 185, 186, 188-190, 194, 198, 200, 202

Pierce, Billy, 184, 191, 197

Pieretti, Marino, 71

Piersall, Jim, 192, 199, 200

Pillette, Duane, 100, 184

Platt, Whitey, 90

Pofahl, Jimmy, 20

Porterfield, Bob, 99, 179

Potter, Nels, 32, 35, 64, 65

Powell, Dick, 214

Powell, Willie, 215

Power, Vic, 203

Powis, Carl, 216

Pramesa, John, 213

Priddy, Jerry, 24, 25, 91, 140, 147, 158, 165

R

Radcliff, Rip, 30

Railroad Transportation Division, 41

Raschi, Vic, 56, 62, 80, 81, 99, 102, 141, 163, 173, 176, 200, 207

Reese, Peewee, 206

Restelli, Dino, 212

Reynolds, Allie, 33, 68, 69, 74, 151, 152

Rhawn, Bobby, 92

Rice, Del, 206-208

Richards, Paul, 188

Riegle, Lee, 14

Ripple, Jimmy, 23

Rivera, Jim, 178

Rizzuto, Phil "Scooter," 50, 51, 53, 54, 56, 63, 73, 74, 81, 99, 102, 141, 146, 152, 160, 161, 163, 176, 200

Robbe, Fletcher, 212

Roberts, Dave, 216

Robertson, Sherry, 25, 77, 85, 94, 185, 192

Robinson, Aaron, 50, 51, 53, 55, 63, 70, 90, 147

Robinson, Brooks, 2, 215, 216, 219

Robinson, Eddie, 47, 83-85, 93, 94, 135, 150, 159, 184, 191, 192, 194, 198, 199, 201-203

Robinson, Jackie, 43, 80

Rocco, Mickey, 28, 29

Rodriguez, Freddie, 217

Rogovin, Saul, 184, 189

Rosar, Warren "Buddy," 29, 44, 48, 49, 51, 60, 69, 70, 74, 76-79, 104, 171

Rosen, Al, 137, 138, 143, 144, 149, 162, 165, 169, 170, 173, 180, 183, 196-198

Rothermel, Robert "Gummy," 13, 17

Ruffing, Red, 67

Rullo, Joe, 28

Runnels, Pete, 178, 192

Russell, Rip, 44, 45

Russo, Marius, 23

Ruth, Babe, 35, 44, 52, 65, 75

S

Sain, Johnny, 174, 176, 177, 196

Sanford, Fred, 57, 58, 141, 142

Savage, Bob, 47, 52, 55, 62-64, 70, 75

Scarborough, Ray, 81, 92-94, 135, 150, 151, 156, 157, 167

Scheib, Alfreida (sister), 3, 9

Scheib, Barbara Ann (daughter), 82

Scheib, Carl Alvin Jr. (son), 176

Scheib, Edna (sister), 3, 9

Scheib, Elizabeth Louise, 3

Scheib, Emma Jane, 17

Scheib, Georgene (wife), 60, 67, 82, 119, 156, 176, 205

Scheib, Joshua, 17

Scheib, Kenneth Paul (son), 205

Scheib, Oliver D. (father), 3, 9, 12, 16-17, 20-22, 105

Scheib, Paul (brother), 3, 4, 11-14, 67, 116, 117, 225

Scheib, Pauline G. (mother), 3, 4, 9, 11, 16, 17, 105

Scheib, Sandra Lee (daughter), 156

Scheib, Sandy (wife), 1, 2, 224

Scheib, William, 3

Schell, Danny, 206

Schmees, George, 181

Schmidt, Mike, 71

Schmitt, Bob, 215
Schoendienst, Red, 205, 206
Schoffstall, Blair, 7
Schoffstall, Charles, 4-9, 225
Schultz, John, 215
Searcy, Kelly, 216
Seerey, Pat, 70, 71
Selinsgrove, 11, 16
Seventh Battalion, 39
Shade, Allen "Spirty," 10
Shade, Cyril "Shadee" or "Zero," 13-14
Shadow Ball, 10, 108
Shamokin, 11
Shantz, Billy, 60
Shantz, Bobby, 60, 85, 86, 89, 90,
  94-96, 101, 125, 135, 139, 143,
  150-152, 154, 171, 175, 176, 182,
  191, 193, 194
Shea, Spec, 74, 172
Siebert, Dick, 21, 22, 23, 27, 34, 37
Sievers, Roy, 90, 91, 96, 161, 197, 199
Silvera, Charlie, 99, 102
Simmons, Al, 31, 35
Simpson, Harry, 162, 169, 173, 174,
  180, 182, 183, 196-198
Sisler, George, 35
Sitlinger, Jacob, 14
Skaff, Frank, 24, 28
Smeltz's Grocery, 17, 111
Smith, Al, 32
Southworth, Bill, 21
Speaker, Tris, 35
Spence, Stan, 24, 70, 75, 77, 90, 91
Spicer, Bob, 210
Staller, George, 27, 29
Stank, Eddie, 205-209
Stengel, Casey, 100, 146, 162, 164
Stephens, Bryan, 65
Stephens, Gene, 192, 193
Stephens, Vern, 35, 36, 70, 75, 78,
  83, 84, 94, 103, 152, 156, 167,
  171, 174, 181, 190
Stevens, Chuck, 213
Stewart, Bud, 93, 94, 135
Stirnweiss, Snuffy, 50, 51, 53, 54,
  56, 73, 74, 81
Stobbs, Chuck, 102, 136, 145, 180,
  188, 189
Strickland, George, 196, 197
Stroup, Sam, 14

Stuart, Marlin, 86, 87
Suder, Pete, 24, 25, 28, 29, 44, 48,
  51, 57, 60-65, 69, 70, 72-74, 76-
  79, 84, 85, 87, 96, 98, 99, 100,
  129, 136-138, 140, 145, 147, 148,
  158, 172, 173, 175, 176, 181, 184,
  186, 188, 192, 194
Sullivan, John, 24, 25, 72, 90
Sullivan, Rusu, 211
Swift, Bob, 23, 24, 26, 27, 30, 48,
  62, 147

T
Tabacheck, Marty, 216
Talbot, Bob, 209
Tasby, Willie, 216
Tebbetts, Birdie, 45, 69, 75, 77, 78,
  84, 173, 179
Terwiliger, Wayne, 192
Thomas, Kite, 175, 182, 184, 188,
  194
Thompson, Forrest, 77, 78
Thompson, George, 216
Throneberry, Faye, 181, 186, 187,
Throneberry, Marv, 181
Tipton, Joe, 104, 147, 149, 151, 157,
  160, 161, 182, 196
Tower City, 12
Tremel, Bill, 216
Tresh, Mike, 46
Trosky, Hal, 36
Trout, Paul "Dizzy," 27, 35, 36, 48,
  64, 65, 86, 87, 158, 159, 164, 170,
  177, 186-188
Trucks, Virgil, 54-56, 75, 76, 90, 91,
  139
Truman, President Harry, 135
Tucker, Thurman, 46, 102, 137, 143
Twin County League, 14-15

U
Umholtz, Georgene (wife), 60, 67, 82,
  119, 156, 176, 205
Umphlett, Tom, 199, 200
Upper Dauphin County Scholastic
  League, 15
Upton, Tom, 142, 161

V
Valley View, 14

Valo, Elmer, 46, 48, 50, 51, 58, 62,
63, 69, 72, 77-79, 81, 84, 85, 87,
92-94, 97, 99, 100, 103, 143, 146,
151, 157, 160, 166, 170, 177, 179,
182, 183, 186, 191
Verble, Gene, 157
Vernon, Mickey, 60, 77, 84, 85, 87,
89, 167, 168, 175, 178
Vollmer, Clyde, 85, 93, 94, 152, 171,
172, 174, 187, 190

W

Wagner, Hal, 27, 28
Wagner, Honus, 35
Wahl, Kermit, 143, 149, 150, 156-
158, 162, 164
Waibel, Dick, 211, 212
Wakefield, Dick, 36, 64, 65
Wall, Murray, 220
Ward, Larry, 212
Wayne, John, 214
Weafer, Hal, 23
Weatherly, Roy, 25-27
Webb, Skeeter, 64, 76
Weigel, Ralph, 83
Weik, Dick, 77, 78, 81, 85, 98
Welaj, Johnny, 20, 22, 24, 28, 29
Welteroth, Dick, 93
Wertz, Vic, 48, 57, 86, 88, 90, 91,
139, 140, 150, 158, 165, 166, 168,
170, 177, 197, 199
West Branch League, 16-17
Westlake, Wally, 201
Wheaton, Woody, 28, 33, 35
White, Don, 64, 72, 100
White, Hal, 47
White, Jo Jo, 20, 26, 27, 33
White, Sammy, 181, 187, 192-195
Whitman, Dick, 211
Widmar, Al, 140, 153, 159
Wifniewski, Marvin, 216
Wight, Bill, 63, 64, 187, 188
Wilber, Del, 200
Williams, Hal, 15
Williams, Ted, 32, 43-45, 52, 54, 57,
73, 75, 78, 83, 84, 88, 94, 103,
136, 145, 156, 157, 167, 171, 172,
174, 188
Williamstown, 12
Wilson, Artie, 211, 212

Wilson, Bobby, 191, 198
Wilson, Jim, 85
Witmer, Elwood "Dix" or "Witty," 13-14
Wolff, Roger, 22, 29, 30, 39
Wood, Ken, 154, 174
Woodling, Gene, 99, 100, 101, 141,
146, 151, 160, 179, 182, 196
Woods, Pinky, 33
Wright, Ed, 184, 189
Wright, Taffy, 55, 61, 76, 83, 84, 92-
94, 156,
Wright, Tom, 184
Wynn, Early, 31, 61, 72, 84, 85, 87,
138, 143, 170, 174, 194
Wyrostek, Johnny, 205, 206
Wyse, Hank, 136, 137, 138, 139,
140, 142, 146, 148, 150, 153, 158,
159

Y

Young, Bobby, 169, 178
York, Rudy, 21, 28, 36, 44, 45, 49
Yost, Eddie, 61, 83, 135, 157, 168,
179, 201

Z

Zarilla, Al, 35, 57, 136, 152
Zernial, Gus, 157, 166, 167, 175,
177, 178, 180, 182, 183, 186, 188,
191, 194, 196-198, 200, 202, 204
Ziegler, Joe, 211
Zoldak, Sam, 31, 158, 169, 170, 175,
179, 182, 185, 192
Zuber, Bill, 22

CPSIA information can be obtained at www.ICGtesting.com
Printed in the USA
BVOW08*1837120716

455294BV00003B/9/P